MOTHERS, BABIES AND THEIR BODY LANGUAGE

MOTHERS, BABIES AND THEIR BODY LANGUAGE

Antonella Sansone

KARNAC

LONDON   NEW YORK

First published in 2004 by
H. Karnac (Books) Ltd.
6 Pembroke Buildings, London NW10 6RE

British Library Cataloguing in Publication Data

A C.I.P. for this book is available from the British Library

ISBN 1 85575 355 3

Designed and produced by The Studio Publishing Services Ltd, Exeter EX4 8JN

Printed in Great Britain

10 9 8 7 6 5 4 3 2 1

www.karnacbooks.com

CONTENTS

For my father,
who is in many ways co-author of this book

And for my mother
who grew me in her womb

ACKNOWLEDGEMENTS

Many people have helped me in the writing of this book. I am espe-cially grateful to the parents and babies at the Birth Unit of the St John and St Elizabeth Hospital in London, who gave me this unique learning opportunity. They have been my best teachers. Using English, my second language, often meant that I called on my body language, a more child-like language, which facilitated the com-munication with infants.

I should like to thank the parents who told their birth stories and who wrote about their experience in great depth for their will-ingness to share their feelings. The list of thanks follows in chrono-logical order.

I thank my parents, whose internal presence and emotional and practical support strengthened my confidence in this book and in my work experience in London. While writing this book, I have undergone a kind of rebirth and overcome many conflicts with them. Thanks also to my elder brothers for their important part in my primary stage of life, which has been the driving force behind this book.

I am very grateful to Vezio Ruggieri, Professor of Psycho-Physiology at the Department of Psychology at Rome University

"La Sapienza", for his invaluable integrated model, to which this book refers extensively. I have adopted his integrative view of psychological phenomena, from which I have benefited enormously in developing a research project on the female body image and its effects on pregnancy, birth, and early interactions with the baby, and as the beneficiary of the Leonardo da Vinci Fellowship.

My thanks also go to Yehudi Gordon, consultant obstetrician at the Birth Unit and the pioneer of water birth in the UK, who was consistently available when feedback was needed, despite his full-time commitment to his own work. He almost invariably demonstrated a lively interest in my observations. At a very early stage of my work in London, I benefited from Yehudi's constructive criticism of my writing and from his expertise in obstetrics and water birth, as well as in psychological issues.

I thank the Birth Unit of St John and St Elizabeth Hospital for providing unique observational settings through pre- and post-natal classes, and to its midwives for their contributions to my research. I am particularly indebted to the midwife and homeopath, Catherine Lillis, for the enormous amount of support, encouragement, and practical help that she provided during the writing of this book.

I am especially grateful to Peter Walker, the pioneer of baby massage in the UK, for providing unique settings for observing the primary mother–infant interactions. In particular, his baby massage classes offered me a context for observing the ways in which both parent and infant may adapt to each other as the relationship develops, and they were a major source of inspiration for this book. While observing Peter Walker's classes, I made a life-changing discovery. In terms of academic knowledge, I greatly valued his extensive practical experience with parents and infants and my experiential study in his classes, as well as in other pre-natal and post-natal classes at the Birth Unit. Peter Walker gave me the confidence to keep working on my manuscript.

Many thanks to Janet Balaskas and the Active Birth Centre, for providing, through her pre-natal yoga classes, an interesting context for observation and follow-up.

The Tavistock Clinic in London should also be acknowledged, especially for its infant observation seminar, a fundamental component of the MA in Psychoanalytical Observational Studies.

Special thanks also to Dr Ludwig Janus, President of the International Society of Prenatal Psychology and Medicine (ISPPM), of which I am honoured to be a member. Over the past few months, we have seen rapidly growing public interest in topics from the field of pre-natal and perinatal psychology and medicine. This is no doubt partly due to the conferences in Sardinia, Nijmegen, and Budapest that were organized by the Society.

Heartfelt thanks to my partner, David Southwood, who helped me with photography and printing, but more importantly, with his warm support.

Other people have helped in practical ways and enabled me to keep writing and typing with their practical and emotional support. There are others whom I have not mentioned but would like to thank for having encouraged my work and given me material on which to base observations and reflections.

Antonella Sansone is a research/clinical psychologist particularly interested in pre- and post-natal life. She is a yoga practitioner and this reflects her belief in the importance of the mind and body unity and balance as foundation of health. As a baby massage teacher, she believes that mindful massage for infants has the potential to regulate the mother–baby psychobiological rhythms and thus be a vital part of the bonding process and a reassuring extension of the womb environment.

FOREWORD

I have known Antonella Sansone since she worked on the Birth Unit at St John & St Elizabeth Hospital, and I am very pleased to write the Foreword for her book. Antonella is passionate about the value of touch and communication between babies and parents. We share a similar philosophy.

Mothers, Babies and Their Body Language emphasizes the importance of communication and early attachment for babies. In these early years a secure and loving space for growth, where there is loving communication and a feeling of being held, heard, and understood, supports a baby's confidence and ability to trust, and is the foundation for emotional and physical well being. The effects of the early years continue throughout life.

This book acknowledges the value of both mother and father "being there" for their baby during pregnancy and after birth, with "quality time" to acknowledge, respect, and enjoy the presence of their baby. It acknowledges that new parents are also affected by previous events in their lives, which create patterns of behaviour that are subsequently played out in their partnership and, more importantly, in the relationship with the new baby. Many parents face confronting emotional issues during pregnancy and beyond.

The body language of parents expresses many things, including their emotional and spiritual life, their physical way of being in the world, and their ability to accept and interact with their new baby. Body language is also a manifestation of different cultural patterns and the way emotions are expressed and shared in relationships. In some cultures it is normal for a baby to be lovingly touched twenty-four hours a day during the first two years of life, whereas in others, particularly in the industrialized West, touch is much less common.

A baby's body language is extremely expressive, and every baby's brain is amazingly developed before birth. Inside the brain "hard wiring" ensures that all human beings are geared to communicate with their caregivers from their earliest days, and to attract their parents (and other adults and children) into conversation. Human babies are dependent for longer on their caregivers than any other mammal on earth and this longer period allows development of complex communication and strong emotional bonding. The attachment between a baby and his or her early caregiver is profound, and its importance in the baby's future development and well being has been recognized for thousands of years. There has been a particular focus on this in psychological literature during the past fifty years.

Antonella uses a model of baby massage and baby gymnastics to illustrate the value of touch and communication in a baby's feelings of security. Babies appreciate being fed and nourished physically as well as emotionally by eye contact, smell, touch, taste, and above all, by quality time with their parent. All parents and babies are naturally inclined to communicate with one another. Adults instinctively speak in a special tone called "Motherese", a melodic tone that is universal and perfectly suited to babies. Babies may not understand exactly what is being said, but they certainly respond to the tone and to the warmth and the feelings behind the tone. Every parent's communication with their baby includes body language, eye contact, and vocal sounds and touch. If we, as parents, are tuned in to our babies, and acknowledge and respond to the variety of subtle signals that are the basis of loving communication, we will boost our children's self-esteem and confidence to thrive and fulfil their potential.

Antonella has had many influences in her work. These include her training in Italy under Dr Ruggeri; her time spent on the Birth

Unit in London; her involvement in massage and baby yoga through Peter Walker; and her time spent in the psychoanalytically-orientated Tavistock Institute in London. This book amalgamates these influences with psychoanalytic concepts of parenting and psychological and physical theories about communication and bonding.

Mothers, Babies and Their Body Language is an interesting and inspiring book that aims to bring the wisdom of traditional societies into the modern-day setting. I recommend it highly.

Yehudi Gordon
Consultant Active Birth Obstetrician and Founder of the Birth Unit
April 2004

Introduction

Why I wrote this book

I n this book I shall describe, through an eighteen-month research and observational study from pregnancy to the earliest months of life, the complex interactions between mother and baby. My oil paintings and photographs help me to portray different aspects of the parent–baby relationship and explore what may lie behind its surface phenomena. I have found a lot of similarities between painting and observing. Painting is about fixing a process and capturing a dynamic state. Usually I paint images of diverse beliefs and interpretations, the detail of the colours, outlines, and silhouettes of lowlands and hills after a journey. The ruthlessness of mountains and wider space of sea convey ideas about the process of change.

In observing the rich body language of mothers and babies, a similar albeit more complex process occurs. Observation is the essence of therapy and painting can be the healthy effect. I shall be attempting to convey in words the moment-by-moment changes during mother–baby interactions, as well as to portray the vital interrelationship between the baby's physical and its psychological development, which are closely interrelated. Language cannot do full justice to the richness of the complex landscape of primary relationships.

Children struggle to assert themselves in an adult world that is often entirely deaf to their voices. In a world in which everyone rushes around and there is no time to stand back and observe, I have tried to express in words what the tiny baby is capable of communicating with her extraordinary abilities. It is the power to enter life itself.

I attempt to remove my adult mask in order to get in touch with my inner child and to be able to understand the baby's language better. "Childhood" is often an adult construction of projections that are difficult to dismantle. For example, immense pressure is imposed on young children from the moment they are born to become independent. The effect is more often than not the opposite of this. Independence and self-confidence are nurtured by an experience of attuned communication provided by the earliest caregivers, and this forms the basis for a fulfilling attachment.

A baby needs to be observed for what she is. Only by rediscovering their own inner child through primary body language—eye contact, touch, smell, facial expressions, movements, and gestures—can parents get closer to their baby's feelings and needs and to the basic anxieties that infants and young children inevitably encounter as a condition of life.

By removing our adult resistances and intellectual attitudes when dealing with infants, we can support children in helping themselves to grow up self-confident and strengthened by their own experiences and explorations of their surrounding environment. By becoming self-confident individuals, they will be more likely to contribute to building a well-functioning society.

As a psychologist, I have found that learning to interpret babies' language is a useful basis for coding the patient's body language in therapy and thus for getting in touch with her needs. This capacity to understand the baby's sign language and needs enhances our communication skills and attunement in other relationships.

This book acknowledges the impossibility of giving general guidelines to individual parents or of telling any mother how to look after her own baby. Guidebooks often drive a mother away from her own feelings and needs in a deleterious way. This is a book to feel and to reflect upon and is not to be taken as a set of instructions. No single formula works for every mother and baby, because she and her baby are unique, as is their shared experience long before birth. The key is therefore for a mother to look within and to discover and use her own resources. The picture on the front cover represents this concept beautifully.

Contradictory advice from nurses or the mass media is often confusing and disorientating. Instructions or medical prescriptions often interfere with the mother's developing relationship with her baby and thus lower her self-confidence.

In our Western culture, women are cast into a psychological state that introduces fears and insecurities to mothering. What could be a natural and enjoyable experience turns into something hazardous. Ambiguous pieces of advice are offered by different health professionals and the mother's confusion is no doubt reason enough for tensing up, which impairs her capacity to listen to her own feelings. For instance, if the baby goes on crying although her mother is trying to follow advice, the mother may become convinced that there must be something wrong with her and that she cannot be a good mother. The most likely result of this is a tension that locks her into a vicious circle. By contrast, the mother's ability to be in touch with her bodyself is of the utmost importance for being critical of advice and acting creatively instead of passively.

This book is intended for parents to read through while thinking back to their experience. It is a guide for discovering the space of their bodyself image, a space to sense, to feel, and to think about, in order to be able to have their needs met. I believe that it is only by acknowledging their own needs that parents can meet the baby's own needs and become attuned to her.

This book acknowledges the importance of birth institutions, which play a crucial role in child development, according to their capacity to give parents the opportunity to experience the birth fully and to think about, observe, and respect what their baby is. The mother's environment, supportive or not, affects her perception of her internal space, her body, and her baby. Improving the conditions of birth therefore means encouraging the rhythmic interaction between mother and baby, leading to greater likelihood of a fulfilled individual who may participate in creating a better society. This is one of the guiding principles of "active birth", which proves that the optimal approach to pregnancy, birth, and child-care is to allow the woman to express her entire bodyself and to use her own natural resources.

In active birth, the woman is free to move across the labour room, express the rhythmic movement of her labour and find her most comfortable birthing position, whether it is squatting, standing, kneeling, or lying down. In some hospitals, she can use the pool, either as a natural pain relief remedy or to give birth, allowing the baby a gentle transition from her primary watery environment (Balaskas & Gordon, 1990). The possibility of using the physical space to display her labour "dance" allows the woman to free her inner world. It is not pure coincidence that "emotion" contains the word "motion".

The woman's freedom to move during labour gives rise to a rhythmic or attuned communication with her baby during and immediately after birth, from which the baby is brought into the rhythm of life. When the mother does not feel secure and confident, both the progress of labour and birth and the earliest interactions with her baby are affected. The father's support plays a crucial role in the mother's emotional balance and consequently in the baby's healthy development. Birth institutions, as well as research projects, should acknowledge his role in pregnancy, birth, and child-care and his right to express his choices.

Respecting the baby means providing her and her parents with proper pre-natal assistance and a birth environment that gives them space and time to be themselves. An important contribution is made by those who assist mothers in giving birth and their ability to consider the baby as an individual with her own feelings. The first step consists in minimizing the traumatic effects of the transition from the intra-uterine holding environment to a world in which too often the baby is overwhelmed by harsh stimuli and accelerated rhythms. Second, the baby needs to be given the opportunity to reach out a little to explore the world as far as she is able and a chance to discover her own feelings as they arise (Bion, 1962). This means watching the baby instead of judging her or building up high expectations.

One of the baby's earliest interests is the exploration of her mother's body and the world around her. For instance, the breast is the baby's primary object, which "stands for" the mother, and through breastfeeding she has a learning experience—an experience of herself as well as of her mother. The infant's internal space, made up of emotions, feelings, and fantasies, takes shape through the earliest physical contact with her mother's body. Traumatic events in later life such as the loss of a loved person can attack that inner space and even rupture at a somatic level the internal container that holds the parts of personality together. Receptive parents allow the baby to nurture a solid inner space, enabling her to overcome the crisis, as they help her to get in touch with her own feelings. When the infant's emotional world is overlooked, she is unlikely to be able to cope with conflicting emotions or to make choices in accordance with her needs.

A receptive mother is able to be physically close to her baby and absorb the infant's fears and anxieties in her body, thereby relieving them. This impinges on the baby's way of monitoring her emotions and posture, as emotional tension displays itself through muscular tightening. Through this primitive bodily communication, the infant learns to trust her parents, which is the foundation for trusting herself and the world around her. This gives rise to a determined and assertive individual who is strong enough to cope with major life events. The internalization of a good relationship moulds a confident, flexible, and adaptable posture and enables the child to communicate appropriately in a wide range of ways through both bodily and verbal language.

The encounter between the mother's response and her infant's need, with an attunement to each other, makes the baby feel that she has a space in her mother's mind as well as in her body—in her arms or on her breast. When the mother's bodyself image is integrated, such that mind and body are in harmony, the pre- and post-natal baby occupies an equal space in her mind and her body. In other words, the developing baby needs to be sensed and thought about at the same time. Bion's term for the baby's space in the mother's mind is "maternal reverie" (1962). It seems to me that the mother's attunement to her baby must depend enormously on how she experiences her own bodily and mental space and on her attitude to the bodyself.

Research and clinical literature has paid very little attention to how the woman's bodyself image may impinge on her parental skills and on the quality of her interaction with her baby, which is what gave me the idea for this book. When the mother's integrated bodyself image and her associated self-confidence enable her to receive and contain her baby's fears, crying, and anger, giving her back these feelings in a renewed light rather than rejecting them, she allows her baby to acknowledge them through a mirroring process. If this process does not take place, the infant may escape from the frightening feelings and become unable to monitor them in later life. When the mother produces resistance, which hinders her from connecting with her emotions and inner child, her baby will have difficulty receiving back her own feelings and thus developing an integrated bodyself image based on a true experience of herself.

What happens between mother and baby is represented here by the relationship between a musician and her instrument. Her talent is maximized when the instrument's strings are tuned in order to produce the right notes. Neither mother nor baby is either just the instrument or the musician. They alternately play each other, as their interactions are two-way. There are babies whose capacity to respond and interact with their mothers readily inspires all their mothering capacities. Alternatively, there are babies who are so dissatisfied from birth that they evoke in their mother all her infantile anxieties and insecurities. For instance, the baby's cry can evoke primitive infantile fears in the mother or trigger projections associated to a negative meaning of crying, which do not relate to the baby's actual need. These babies may be attacked, rejected, or ignored if their mother is not in contact with those anxieties and, unaware of them, goes on projecting them on to her child. On the other hand, there are mothers who are strong and confident enough or who receive enough support to be able to keep coping and make an adjustment.

In this book, the relation between the woman's bodyself image and her parenting abilities is extensively considered for the first time. Consideration is also given to how the mother's attitude to her bodyself can affect the development of the infant body image. To nurture an integrated bodyself image and grow in self-confidence, a child needs a mother who values herself and has a fulfilled relationship with her body and self. A sense of guilt, hatred of life, or fear sends signals about self-esteem and about the importance of motherhood. For example, there is nothing "wrong" with being a working mother, especially if the first six or twelve months have been spent full-time with her baby. The important thing is for the mother to be feeling positive about her contribution to the workforce and her own life choices, as this provides a powerful model for self-confidence and success. The working mother has no cause to feel guilty, provided that she has time to spend at home and values herself and her role as mother in front of her child and thus sends positive signals. Parents teach their child assertiveness and self-trust through their confident posture and firm way of holding, as their attitudes and feelings constantly take shape through their muscular tension and body language.

What is "bodyself image"?

Any activity, whether it is lifting an arm, or walking, talking, going to sleep, learning something, thinking out a problem, or making a decision, involves an interrelationship between "mental" and "physical" processes and it is impossible to separate activities into either purely mental or purely physical. The distinction between "mental" and "physical" is merely a construct based on a particular observational perspective.

I call this unity of mind and body "psychophysical integration", which is one of the fundamental components of health. We experience this in our everyday lives. One example is the way in which anxiety can cause breathing difficulties, nausea, and stiff, jerky movements. Another example is the way in which we hold our breath when we are concentrating to try to solve a complicated mathematical problem. When we are afraid, we contract our facial muscles, producing the typical expression of fear.

Body image is the result of two activities: (1) the synthesis of sensory signals travelling from the body to the brain to produce a mental representation of the body's parts and activities; (2) the monitoring of the body's activities to maintain a correspondence between mental image and bodily attitudes. There is a constant interrelationship between the two processes. In other words, body image acts as a bridge between input—information from the body and its sensory channels (hearing, sight, smell, touch, taste, movements) to the brain—and output—mental control of the muscular activity involved in the postural attitudes.

Body image plays a fundamental role in modulating the relationship between posture, movement, and gesture, allowing the whole body to move in space. Posture is an integrated response to a variety of internal and external stimuli in the social and physical environment. It is the result of mechanical, emotional, and social factors. On the other hand, an individual's posture acts as a stimulus that can cause feelings of comfort/discomfort, confidence/insecurity, and stability/instability. For example, an individual shows "avoidance" behaviour through a backward posture, as her tension is pulling her backwards. Or, in a very different situation, an individual shows "approach" behaviour with open shoulders and chest and a "forward" posture.

Body image is therefore the way in which an individual organizes her muscular tension and uses her body and posture in accordance with her mental states and attitudes. Our attitude to our body reflects the way in which we think and feel. The way in which we view ourselves is reflected in everything we do—how we breathe, talk, eat, walk, sit, and stand up. It reflects the way in which we organize our self and body perception, our posture, or our bodyself image.

Babies are particularly sensitive to the close relationship between the mental and physical states of their caregivers. They sense their emotional state through their muscular tension and movements. They will sense if they are being held confidently or nervously, lovingly or rejectingly. A baby who is held in a confident, gentle, and sensitive manner will feel more secure and will learn to trust her parents.

A common complaint among mothers is strong tension in the upper arms, shoulders, and neck. This is often aggravated by an incorrect holding of the baby. An effective use of the arms that can provide a fulfilling experience of containment requires an effective use of the bodyself. The amount of tension that a mother may have in her whole body directly affects the sensitivity that she has in her hands, thus the quality of her touch.

Effective emotional support in pregnancy, birth, and child-care is aimed at leading a woman to get in touch with her bodyself, as the baby is dwelling in her body and needs a space in her mind as well. I believe that any deep therapy that acts on a mental level and ignores the active role played by the body leads a woman far away from a true connection with her baby. A woman communicates with her pre-natal and newborn baby through bodily cues such as breathing, touch, eye contact, movement, and facial expression.

I shall adopt the term "bow method" for a body image treatment that is aimed at increasing sensory and bodily awareness and thus enhancing the sense of self. I usually observe both parents and baby to observe how they organize their emotional and muscular tension while interacting with their baby. I shall provide a more detailed description of this method later in the book.

The mother's body image therefore displays itself through her movements, posture, gestures, and facial expressions and affects the development of the baby's sense of body and self. This relationship begins very early in intra-uterine life. When the baby is in the womb, many of her actions and rhythms are synchronized with those of the mother. Maternal and infant behaviours complement each other in several sensory and motor systems, thus increasing the probability of interaction. They interact as a single system, although this is subject to environmental influences.

The baby picks up the parents' attitude to their bodyself through her kinaesthetic sense and unconsciously learns to incorporate this into her own behaviour. Our muscular memory is very powerful in early life. If a baby experiences fear, anger, or distrust too often, her muscular activity and posture will be affected and these emotions will be stored in her muscle memory. The muscular system is a wonderful resource, enabling us to move, breathe, reach out, embrace, and kiss, thus to express our feelings and get in touch with our surroundings.

The human body has long been excluded from psychological and relational processes. The widely held view that any illness or difficulty should be classified as either "mental" or "physical" has long been predominant. This is partly related to conventional and religious factors and, more generally, to Cartesian dualism (Bermudez, Marcel & Eilam, 1995). Classical neurology considers the muscular system as a mechanism at the service of the mind. However, the mind plays a major role in whatever we are doing and a healthy, well-functioning mind can make effective use of information from the body and display itself via the body in a feedback relationship. Could we express a loving gesture, such as a kiss or hug, without the muscles that enable us to produce it? And if the muscles involved in these gestures have excessive tension, how can the message be communicated clearly?

The mother–baby synchrony seems to be innate and instinctive but in our industrialized society it is altering. This may be linked to a reduction of bodily contact and sensory communication between parents and babies—touch, eye contact, and attentive listening—which reduces the scope for getting to know each other through movements and bodily cues. It is often assumed that the mother will know instinctively how to handle a newborn baby but many women have never held one before and they feel tense and fearful. If they are in hospital, some women can be intimidated by health professionals who are the "experts" and trust themselves even less.

The bonding between mother and baby can be established before conception and during pregnancy. The woman's attitude to her bodyself plays a major role in shaping the bonding. To be able to feel and understand the baby's rhythms and synchronize (or attune) with her, the mother needs to be connected with her bodyself and know its rhythms. Her acceptance of the baby is linked with her self-acceptance. Very often, the inner ideal child nurtured during pregnancy prevents a woman from accepting and connecting with the real baby. Winnicott (1949) explains that the future mother's capacity to integrate the regressive feelings brought by pregnancy with outer reality is associated with a psyche—soma that loves and works in harmony with itself. Thailand offers an interesting example of the way in which the adjustment to the birth and post-natal period needs to be handled. For centuries, Thai mothers, upon becoming pregnant, have purchased a clay statue of a mother and infant. At the time of birth, the statue is thrown into the river; thus the image of the mother and infant before birth is destroyed, to be replaced by the reality (Klaus, Kennell & Klaus, 1996).

It is an essential principle of attachment that parents must receive some responses or signals such as bodily or eye movements from their baby to form a close bond. This sensitivity to the baby's cues is directly affected by the amount of bodily tension that the mother has—the less tension there is and thus the more integrated the body image is, the more open are the sensory channels and thus the higher is her sensitivity. A woman in Africa who carries her baby on her back or side is regarded as a poor mother if her baby

wets or soils her clothes, because this means that she has not anticipated this behaviour and held the baby away as would usually
occur.

This communication via body language is almost inconceivable
in countries where mother and baby are kept apart much of the day
and sleep separately at night. The primary movements and sensory
communication help parents to become more quickly attuned to
their baby and therefore to adapt their behaviour to her needs and
pace.

One observational study (Anisfeld, Casper, Nozyce & Cunningham, 1990) compared a group of babies who were carried on the
mother's body in a soft baby-carrier with another group that used
firm infant seats that provided less contact. When the babies were
three months old, the mothers using the soft baby-carriers were
more responsive to their babies' cries and other signals. When all
the babies were thirteen months old, the Ainsworth Strange
Situation Test that measures attachment security was applied, with
the finding that eighty-three per cent of the babies carried on their
mother's body in the soft carrier were securely attached, in contrast
to thirty-nine per cent of the babies from the group that used the
firm baby seats (Ainsworth, Blehar, Waters & Wall, 1978). These
findings suggest that early carrying (soft baby-carriers) is a simple
but effective way of establishing a healthy mother–infant relationship that affects the infant's future attachment and her physical and
psychological development.

The mother's increased capacity to attune to her baby through
physical contact can soften her habitual defences and bring her
more into touch with her feelings. The close loving contact with the
baby during breastfeeding can also be very pleasurable, sensual,
and affirming. For some women, it can be the first time in their lives
when they feel a complete self-acceptance, which can lead to a more
integrated and fulfilling bodyself image. This demonstrates the
parents' wonderful power and ability to change, grow, and modify
their attitudes and thus past experiences in conducting the relationship with their baby. Child-care can bring added benefits if
there is an awareness of the unity of self and body and of the role
of the muscular system and posture in emotional and relational life.

However, many women do not like their bodies at all at this
time, feeling plump, flabby, in pain and as if they belonged to the

baby instead of themselves. The bodyself image treatment is aimed at giving mother a sense of her self and body that is independent of her moods and her situation. The increased integration of the body-self image is passed directly on to the infant and is likely to be manifested later on in the form of a balanced emotional life and posture and healthy overall development.

The mother's increased sense of her own self will lead to an understanding and consideration of others and their well-being. In terms of the mother–infant relationship, if the mother has a healthy sense of her own body and self and is able to ensure that her own needs are met, she will be better able to love and care for her child. Her movements in handling her child and her loving gestures will be the reflection of her healthy self.

Having a clear sense of self helps the mother to become aware of her boundaries—of where she and her baby begin, who she is, and who the other person is. This enables her to have a healthy sense of separateness from other people and from her baby, which is essential for closeness and bonding and thus for nurturing a deeper relationship with her child. If the mother can learn to give herself the time and space for her own needs, her child will, through mirroring, learn the "otherness" of people, which is also fundamental in any healthy social interaction. However familiar a mother may be with babies, holding her child is such an emotional experience that she may still feel a little anxious. Sometimes there are persistent fears that have not been resolved during pregnancy.

In the latter half of the pregnancy, both parents undergo a kind of turmoil and self-questioning: "Will I ever get to be a parent? If I get to be a parent, will I have to be like my own parents?" Realizing that their only past experience with parenthood was their own upbringing can make them afraid of failure in the new task. They ask themselves: "Have we made a mistake? Do we really want this baby?" Pregnancy, like any other major change, is a turning point in an individual's life. The acceptance of life-change is closely related to the acceptance of bodily change, which allows the woman's body image to fluctuate and adjust.

We may wonder why the turmoil arising in pregnancy is so universal and mobilizes all the parents' available emotional energy, especially during late pregnancy and after birth, sometimes turning into a period of depression. The ability to adjust and apply this energy to parenthood and bonding with their baby is essential. Where the turmoil persists after birth and parents are not supported, the bonding may be altered, since parents' concerns and tension (acting through their bodies) can hinder their ability to sense the baby and get in touch with her needs.

I consider that this universal turmoil is linked to a process of rebirth, which mobilizes the parents' earliest experience of contact with their own parents. If a parent-to-be has lacked primary contact (they were not held properly, cuddled, touched securely, and so on), she is more likely to be overwhelmed by feelings of loss, grief, sorrow, anger, worry, and turmoil, which will affect the bonding with the pre-natal and newborn baby. Pines (1993) examines the ways in which the mind expresses itself through a woman's body and, conversely, how the bodily experiences impinge on the mind. She views mothering as an embodied three-generation experience.

Our primary feelings are stored in our muscle memory and shape our posture, breathing activity, bodyself image, and body language, alongside other factors such as genetic, cultural, and physical environment, diet, childhood illness, and injuries. Our bodyself image can be seen as the psychophysical expression of a conglomeration of all aspects of life.

Major life experiences such as pregnancy and parenthood raise unresolved issues related to our earliest experiences. A parent who was not handled sensitively as a baby, so that her muscles did not store loving sensations and experiences, is more likely to repeat what she received, as posture and body language are programmed to reproduce what was stored in earliest memory. The way in which someone was cared for affects their bodyself perception and image. Although later experience will be incorporated into past relationships, it cannot undo established patterns, only modify them over time.

The belief that parenting patterns are passed on may be well-founded. Many studies have revealed that the way in which we are cared for and nurtured as infants and children affects how we parent, as well as how we interact with other people in general (Klaus, Kennell & Klaus, 1996). The perinatal, pregnancy, and post-partum periods make early experience resurface unexpectedly, without the parents being able to recognize their source or their effect on how they monitor their bodyself.

Early care given to an infant is taken in via a complex mental and bodily process and affects her own parenting in later life. To give an example: Monica was born with a section of her oesophagus completely closed. She required feeding via a tube into her stomach and was never held in anyone's arms for feeding. At twenty-one months old, she had an operation—the passage was established and recovered. She was filmed over the next thirty years of her life and it was shown that in every feeding situation she repeated her own early feeding experience. She never held her doll in her arms as a little girl. Later, when she cared for her own four infants, she never held them in her arms. Her own experience in infancy became a model for her caregiving as a mother. This pattern may be carried into successive generations. Her four daughters held their dolls in a similar way to their mother.

The experience of touch with the baby may mobilize feelings such as anxiety, sorrow, and anger, and make a parent react with defence mechanisms and tightening of muscles. However, working through the contact with the baby can be a crucial path to exorcising ghosts from the past. It consists in a working through in the context of the present relationship, through self-investigation and observation, rather than a distant past. Merely going back to the parents' primary experiences at such a delicate time as pregnancy and birth may increase the suffering and worry and drive parents away from their relationship with their baby, which consists mainly of bodily rhythmic interactions.

There are many opportunities for growth and renewal and it is a principal aim of effective support to make parents aware of these possibilities. The experience of touch makes parents and their overwhelming feelings related to early experiences more likely to turn into something positive. Bonding can repair the traumas they may have suffered as children. The bond is experienced as a source of security and joy for both parents and baby and as a pleasurable experience.

This kind of support based on the "contact experience", which enhances parents' ability to respond to their baby's needs, is vital in decreasing the risk of post-natal depression. Baby massage is an effective tool that can complement a bodyself image treatment, and I will be discussing it in detail later in this book.

WINDOW ON TO THE WOMB

In my observational research and experience as a baby massage teacher, I have found that the mother's emotional and muscular tension affects her body and self-perception, posture, movements, and body language. It thus affects her perception of her baby and the progress of labour and birth.

The mother–baby relationship is shaped during pre-natal life and is exquisitely bodily. The mother's body is the visible metaphor for her feelings about pregnancy, birth, and her baby. Her bodyself image is a psychophysical process that continuously adjusts to the emotional and physical changes brought about by pregnancy, birth, and child-care. The way in which a woman perceives her bodyself image seems to impinge on how the baby is fed, held, nurtured, and loved.

Studies show that the womb, as recipient and source of signals, provides a sonorous environment and a learning ground for the unborn baby (Kisilevsky, Fearon & Muir, 1998; Lecanuet, Granier-Deferre & Busuel, 1991; Lecanuet, Granier-Deferre, Jacquet, Capponi & Ledru, 1993; Lecanuet, Granier-Deferre, Jacquet & Decasper, 2000). The baby's earliest perceptions concern rhythms: the mother's cardiac and respiratory activities, digestive sounds, voice, the rhythm of her body in motion and at rest, and a host of other more subtle rhythms. Their emotional content can be distorted or amplified by the mother's muscular resonance, which is an aspect of her attitude to her bodyself. This forms the primary dialogue between mother and baby, in which the mother's ability to get in touch with her own rhythms plays a fundamental role.

The sense of touch has been detected in human embryos less than eight weeks old. Although the embryo has no eyes or ears, its skin sensitivity is already highly developed. The pre-natal baby explores the womb through touch. Searching fingers reach out and touch from as early as the second month. First, they feel the soft texture of the amniotic sac, then the glossy surface of the skin (Valman & Pearson, 1980). After birth, the fingers will express emotions as well as receive sensations.

Touch is thus the very first sense to develop in the foetus and it is the most important form of communication that she has with her parents in her earliest days after birth. Infants are accustomed to the tactile stimulation of constant movement and they need to re-establish those rhythms after birth. In two recent studies (Hunziker & Barr, 1986), mothers in one group were asked to carry their infants each day in a soft-fronted pack, in addition to carrying during feeding or crying. These infants were compared with infants who were held and carried normally; at six weeks the infants who received the extra touching and movement cried half as much as others.

From the moment when the mother first perceives the foetus's responses to sound at around six months of gestation, the baby has already been listening to and feeling the mother's voice and move-ments. The newborn's body moves in rhythm with speech patterns, which means that she has long since imprinted the mother's vocal vibrations. In fact, it is her tone of voice that is more important, rather than the quality of her words. From the fifth month, the foetus is ready to hear, learn, and memorize. Her nervous system is stimulated by sounds and music.

Fascinating self-organizing processes occur in the developing foetal brain, through which nerve cells grow, migrate, and become appropriately interconnected, forming pathways between the brain and peripheral organs. A major change within the brain concerns the development of the cerebral cortex, which is fairly mature by twenty-seven weeks and exerts increasing control over the foetus (Fifer & Moon, 2003). Early in development, the foetus engages in constant movement. Later in development, clear sleep–wake cycles become established and behaviour is increasingly controlled by the cerebral cortex. The movements are important for the development of motor systems and sensory experiences encourage the develop-ment of sensory systems between eight and twenty-six weeks. The brain's environment and experiences at critical times will determine which connections are used and therefore which will survive (Solms & Turnbull, 2002).

The womb is therefore far from silent but is fully orchestrated: the rhythmic heart "boom" is a percussive pounding of blood, breathing rhythm, and incidental stomach rumblings, all occurring in close connection with the mother's emotional life (Liley, 1972). The baby begins to be aware of these sounds when the brain starts to interpret sensory patterns at around six months of age and can

Window to the womb. Painting by Antonella Sansone

detect a change in tempo. These capacities are signs of an autonomous core identity.

The pre-natal baby is able to "memorize" a tune and recognize it creatively. Sounds recorded in the water can have healing or soothing effects on the newborn by providing an experience of continuity with the life in the womb. One study (Olds, 1986) discusses the rehabilitation of a difficult baby (a baby whose mother had been sick during pregnancy) that was accomplished by recreating the intrauterine experience after birth when the mother was in good health.

Another study (Hepper, 1991) found that foetuses exhibited changes in their movements when they were played a tune that was heard during pregnancy. This was not the result of post-natal or genetic factors and was specific to the tune learned. Foetuses increased their movements on hearing the tune; newborns decreased their movements.

The womb is a long way from absolute darkness. The sudden intrusion of bright light into the calm darkness of the womb will penetrate a foetus's consciousness, even through closed eyelids. She may resort to thumb-sucking to adjust to the sudden change. Verney & Kelly (1981) encountered cases where, if the light could not be avoided by turning the head away, the foetus would put her hands up to her eyes to shield them from the light. When the eyelids open, the eyes can distinguish shapes at close range, so that by the time of birth the baby can see details of her mother's face from less than 30 cm away.

The pre-natal baby explores the uterine environment by tasting, thus by feeling pleasure. Our primary taste is the flavour of amniotic fluid. The taste buds are sensitive to the slightest change in its sweetness or—in rare cases—acidity, and it seems that by the seventh month they are well prepared to savour the first sweet drop of milk after birth. The mother's feelings can affect the sweetness of the amniotic fluid in the same way as they may affect the womb and pelvic floor muscles, and her whole posture.

The baby's pre-birth abilities make her fairly skilful in perceiving the primary caregivers and the quality of her interactions with them, as well as in experiencing feelings, tastes, and preferences. These primary interactions play a vital part in shaping the baby's core bodyself image and her initial relationship to the breast or to the mother in general.

The mother's internal world, the meanings she gives to her baby's movements and signals, contribute to forming the uterine environment, thus the baby's core personality, in the same way as her hormones and biorhythms do. Alongside her blood constituents, the pregnant woman creates the intra-uterine ambience with her feelings, breathing, attitudes to her bodyself, and motivation towards birth. For instance, if the mother is stressed out and her breathing speeds up, the baby reacts accordingly. If this becomes a habitual pattern, the baby's respiratory activity and posture can be affected, as can her emotional life. Piontelli (1992) considers that a warm and softly pulsating uterus or pelvis is shaped by the mother's feelings and acts as an emotional container to provide the best birth environment for the foetus. Therefore any study of the foetus's behaviour has to take the woman's own experience into consideration.

The fact that even identical twins are not exactly identical at birth suggests that they may experience the womb differently. They have the same genetic heritage but different weights, one's face may be bigger than the other's. Although they share the same environment, mother, and blood, they exhibit differences at birth. Different positioning in the womb may induce different perceptions of the mother's body in motion and at rest, and a different sense of boundaries. One may swallow and feed more than the other, or have more space to move and therefore more opportunities to improve her muscle tone. These primary sensory-motor experiences may sow the seeds of a different bodyself-perception. In fact, even twins with an identical gene pool can experience the womb environment in a different way.

The transition from the womb to the outside world is crucial. The breast is a prime example of a major source of nourishment or of life, as feeding occupies most of the newborn's life. If pregnancy or birth has been difficult and, in particular, if birth has resulted in complications such as lack of oxygen, separation of mother and baby soon after birth, or a very rapid cutting of the umbilical cord, there may be a disturbance in the adaptation to the external world and the relationship to the breast starts at a great disadvantage. In such cases, the baby's ability to experience new sources of gratification is impaired and in consequence she cannot sufficiently internalize a really good primary experience.

Furthermore, various factors such as whether the child is properly fed and mothered, whether the mother fully enjoys caring for the child or is tense and anxious and has psychological difficulties with feeding, influence the infant's capacity to take the milk with enjoyment and to internalize a good experience and relative security. The baby naturally experiences frustrations, for instance when she is hungry and is not being fed. The acceptance of frustration, based on her capacity to delay her need, very much depends, other than on the baby's character traits, on the mother's ability to attune to her baby's needs and contain her anxieties and fears.

The baby's extraordinary capacity to adjust is absolutely individual. There are babies who show panic reactions just at having their nappies changed or at being washed. They may display extreme psychophysiological reactions, such as accelerated breathing and heart rate. Parents play an important role in strengthening the baby's capacity to face the transition from the womb to the outside world and thus her capacity to adjust.

There are important things that a parent can do to help a baby who has difficulties during pregnancy or at birth. For instance, baby massage plays a key role in helping babies born by caesarean section to replace the stimulation of the uterine contractions they missed during birth. The contractions of the uterus during labour stimulate a baby's peripheral nervous system. This activates the child's survival system and strengthens her adaptive skills in preparation for her emergence into the world. The labour contractions are likely to have an intense massaging effect on the baby, which fosters her development.

Massage helps the baby to release endorphins or natural opiates. It also fosters breathing, especially in cases of lack of oxygen at birth, and encourages the circulatory and digestive systems, promoting easier feeding, bowel movements, and sleeping rhythms. The lovely interactions between parent and baby and their enjoyment of these nurture such physiological reactions.

Baby massage, with its multi-level communication between parent and baby—sensory, motor, and mental—can be of particular help to the growing number of babies who are born by caesarean section, born prematurely, or who have other kinds of difficult births or developmental problems (Speirer, 1982; Barnard & Brazelton, 1990; Field, 1990).

Pre-verbal communication

An attuned start in life

The following are two ordinary pictures of the newborn baby's amazing capacity to communicate.

1. When I entered the hospital room to listen to Clare's birth story, she was playing the same piece of Balinese music that she had played during pregnancy and labour. I noticed that her baby stopped breastfeeding and started crying. I thought he might have been disturbed by my voice or by the door opening. Then he stopped crying. As the mother began talking, the baby started crying again. When she stopped, he calmed down. The sequence continued for a while. During the gap, the baby decreased his movements and looked around as if he were searching for the

source of music, which he really appeared to enjoy. The tiny move-ments of his head appeared to be attuned to the melody. Clare went on telling me about her birth experience quite loudly and her baby immediately began to whimper. I commented that he was clearly telling her that he wanted to enjoy the familiar music. Then I walked closer to the baby and talked to him in a low-pitched voice, which became attuned to the music, as he went on with his tiny movements in rhythm with the tune he had learnt.

2. Patricia smiled at her three-month-old baby, who had been staring at her for a while. He smiled back and giggled. Then she spoke in a baby tone and he emitted a flow of sounds and really sounded as if he was telling her something. This gave me a first-hand observation of the mirroring process. I also reflected on the difference between the single vocalizations he made to me earlier on in the same observation and those he made to his mother—a more deliberate flow of sounds, a sort of melody with alterna-ting pitches and pauses. This showed the infant's early ability to discriminate between his mother's voice and someone else's, which means that he had been able to memorize the maternal voice pre-natally.

If the mother's rhythms and sounds are recorded in the baby's muscles and mind, they must affect the co-ordination of vocal rhythms between mother and infant and prepare for language. Research has found that the foetus's ability to discriminate between two low-pitched piano notes (testing cardiac deceleration) may play an important role in the earliest developmental stages of speech perception (Olds, 1985; Lecanuet, Granier-Deferre, Jacquet & DeCasper, 2000). This ability may be shaped by the rhythms of the mother and her surrounding environment very early on in pre-natal life. It is clear that rhythm is a fundamental organizing element of social communication. Breathing, vocal muscles, and posture are involved in the vocal emission and are channels of emotions. They are all aspects of the way in which the mother modulates her emotional and muscular tension and thus perceives her bodyself image.

Eye contact, touch, and vocalization are important elements in forming the bond between parent and infant and are an extension of pre-natal bonding. They have the power to release tension and reassure the baby. The baby develops confidence in her bodyself

image. Eye contact may be a powerful cue to the infant's physiological system; the signal received by the brain enables it to shut
down the production of stress hormones initiated during childbirth.
This is that infant has been symbolically and mentally perceived
long before being able to see the outside world itself. There is a
multitude of elements that help to build the bonding between
parent and infant: eye contact, skin contact, the parent's voice and
baby's response to it, odour, rhythms of communication and caregiving, the activation of maternal hormones by contact with the
baby, temperature regulation, and so on. The infant's olfactory
system is ready to function as early as seven weeks from gestation,
so it must be an important function for the newborn and it helps
her to identify her mother's chemical "signature". Unfortunately,
the infant's senses are often assaulted by artificial smells, which
inhibit this bonding mechanism.

These primary means of communication unfold in relation to
the mother's way of organizing her tensions and breathing—her
bodyself image, which moulds her loving gestures, and her whole
body language. The mother's harmonious body image impinges
on the unborn baby's core self-perception and after birth, it will
enable her body language to develop in a relaxed way and be
displayed through her way of holding, rocking, feeding, looking at,
and talking to her baby. It is like tuning a piano. The mother's integrated body image will allow her body language—voice, posture,
breathing, facial expression, and posture—as reflections of her
emotional state, to play the right tunes. Birth is thus a second
encounter between two or three individuals who have long been
communicating. The father's voice and touching of the woman's
abdomen, and the emotional content of these, are as important as
the mother's in organizing the baby's core bodyself image.

Given the baby's extraordinary sensitivity to vibrations and
rhythms, music, floating in water, and baby massage after birth are
powerful channels of primary communication. They have something in common with pregnancy. They all involve the primitive
part of the brain and induce regressive processes that cherish
primary language. In pregnancy, the body changes its physiology,
hormones, and size to become the container of a new life. In all
experiences, there is a renewed bodyself-representation. In pregnancy, there is an ambivalent perception of the internal and external

space: the abdomen expands both outwards and inwards. The baby is experienced as an object to retain and also as an autonomous individual, especially when her movements start to be perceived. This involves fairly intense work to adjust the body image to the internal and external space because it is important to accommodate the mother's integrated body image to the new event. The sensory-motor stimulation induced by sounds, contact with water, or skin contact with the baby during massage promotes an enjoyable feeling about the mother's bodyself image, a more harmonious experience of pregnancy, and an increasing acceptance of the changes brought about by pregnancy or parenthood. This healthy state shapes the infant's development.

Water, music, and baby massage provide an experience of contact, containment, and trust and can strengthen the mother's sense of boundaries. The aquatic environment induces harmony in our muscle tone and has a supportive effect. Muscles are stretched and elongated in the water and the body image can fluctuate. During pregnancy, mother and baby can share the same aquatic environment and this can boost their communication. Water myths often refer to birth and the mother-to-be can experience a form of rebirth that leads her closer to her baby's feelings and primary language. The woman's feeling of being taken in and massaged by the water is transferred to her pre-natal baby. This shared experience between mother and baby obviously does not exclude the father. Enjoying the effects of water allows her to share the woman's experience and thus to strengthen his communication with the baby.

The mother is not just a receptor but also a container, giving meanings to the baby's signals. Before seeing, the baby has long been seen and to become self-observant she needs to be felt and observed. The uterine environment is a space that needs to be filled with the mother's creativity in order for her to be able to contain herself as well as her baby. The regressive state of the pregnant woman seems to be adaptive and enables her to rediscover her primary language, identify herself with her baby through mirroring, and thus understand her cues and establish a rhythmic dialogue (Raphael-Leff, 1993).

Being able to figure out what the child is saying in her own language means being in tune with her feelings, needs, and her developmental stage. Play facilitates this matching process and it is the child's foundation for progressing in her development and learning. Other activities that do not involve play increase the distance between adult and child and hinder their communication. To rediscover the enjoyment of play, it is essential for a parent to abandon excessively intellectual structures. This means valuing primary body language—eye contact, facial expressions, touch, holding, smell, vocalizing, and movement.

Parents from industrialized societies often pay a high price for undervaluing these channels of communication. They are no longer "in touch" with their bodies, and therefore do not notice the early warning signs that they are misusing themselves when relating with their babies. We see the results of this in the extremely high incidence of communication problems between parents and children and developmental difficulties on many levels.

If the gesture of holding the child, for instance, is stiffened and restricted in its evolution by muscular and emotional tension, the signal sent to the child is distorted. It is therefore helpful to acknowledge the relationship between blocked gestures, emotional tension, and parents' posture while interacting with their baby. Very often, someone's posture reflects an attitude they have had about themselves that is no longer appropriate when dealing with an infant. These habits, accumulated over years, eventually become fixed patterns of tension in our bodies, which are reflected in our posture and the way in which we do things (Gottschalk, Serota & Shapiro, 1950). The parents' awareness of the intricate relationship of mind and body is fundamental to healthy communication with their baby. In addition, the child incorporates not only the physical movement of a contracted or tense gesture but also the psychological attitude of the people around her. Unfortunately, if parents and other role models have poor posture and body language, the same patterns can begin at a very early stage for the child.

The degree of support in the mother's environment affects her perception of her internal space and her baby, as well as her awareness of the continuous dialogue between mind and body. Improving the conditions of birth therefore means encouraging the rhythmic interaction between mother and baby, leading to greater likelihood of a fulfilled individual and thus of working to build a better society. This is one of the guiding principles of "active birth", described above, which has proved to be the optimal approach to pregnancy, birth, and child-care, allowing the woman to express her bodyself image in its wholeness and use her own natural resources. When the mother does not feel secure and confident, the progress of labour and birth is altered, as are the earliest interactions with her baby.

Baby massage

While studying and working on the Birth Unit, I made a discovery that changed the direction of my life. I became aware of the importance of traditional Indian massage, both for its soothing effect and for its role in non-verbal communication. An Indian mother sits with her baby across her knees, lovingly massaging her and singing. She offers her baby this beautiful gift of love and security, which helps to make her a compassionate human being. For infants, massage is much more than a sensual experience or a type of physical therapy. It is a tool for maintaining a child's health and well-being and it helps parents to feel secure and confident in handling their baby, promoting bonding and self-esteem. It can be an integrated expression of caring that contributes to both physical and psychological healing, not only for babies but for parents too. This art of massage enhances the relationship between parent and infant.

While observing baby massage classes, I became increasingly interested in body language, which plays a major part in mother–baby interactions. It is a language that we store in our muscular memory as infants and that affects our relationships in adult life. I witnessed the relationship between the mother's body language and the baby's—posture, massage movements, eye contact, voice, smell, facial expressions, and vocalizations. They combined to form a kind of dance. During massage, the signals exchanged between mother and baby go beyond the technique itself. These signals can prevent some developmental difficulties and be therapeutic for babies with special needs. As a sort of monitor of the rhythms between mother and baby, massage can be a vital part of the bonding process and act as an extension of the pre-natal environment and bonding. The mother actually begins massaging her baby long before she is born.

Rhythm is at the basis of social communication. During massage, mother and baby are organizing and co-ordinating five aspects of communication—sight, touch, smell, hearing, and taste—through a sixth powerful channel of communication, which is movement. The baby is reintroduced to a familiar world of vibrations and rhythms. Premature babies or babies with special needs benefit from this experience of continuation more than other babies and parents gain confidence in handling with them. The preemie's first contact with human touch brings pain—needles, probes, tubes, rough handling, and bright lights—all of a sudden after the warm protection of the womb. Many studies have proven that premature or underweight babies who are regularly and gently stroked and who regularly hear their parents' voices during their nursery stay progress rapidly in growth and development (Scafidi, Field, Schanberg & Bauer, 1990; Thoman, Ingersoll & Acebo, 1991; Anderson, 1991; Newman, 1980; Field et al., 1986).

Baby massage provided me with an interesting setting in which to observe the delicate interplay between the baby's development on all levels and the mother's tensions and ways of modulating her

Massage helps babies to develop open chest and fluent breathing, enhances the sensory channels and thus encourages visual exploration and at the same time bodyself perception and knowledge.
Photo by David Southwood.

touch and voice. This allowed me to assess the infant's extraordinary capacity to respond to body language, which is already formed at birth and seems to be the result of pre-natal rhythmic learning. The rapid improvement in growth and development of underweight and unresponsive babies to parents' regular stroking and voices demonstrates the physical and psychological healing effects of maintaining pre-natal cues of communication.

Parenting frequently brings tensions and fears. When a baby arrives in the world before she is expected or with some ailments, such as colic or chest infections, parents are thrust into cycles of grief: shock, denial, guilt, anger, depression, and fear. These feelings, especially depression, often create distance between parents and their baby, and the baby may be ignored as an emotional human being while adults around her focus on medical treatment. Through massage, parents can truly learn to listen to their infant's feelings and needs. The baby receives this message in her whole body and forms her feelings about herself and her body.

Massage fosters earlier development of visual attentiveness, indicating that the sensory system is interactive; the stimulation of touch encourages visual exploration and at the same time bodyself perception and knowledge. Massage thus helps babies to form an effective integrated bodyself image: this is important in establishing object-constancy, which allows the baby to confront the separation from the parent and begin exploring the environment.

The eye contact with the mother enhances self-perception through mirroring. As the mother touches the baby's foot, describing what she is doing, naming the foot,, and counting the toes, she cherishes her bodyself image and sense of boundaries. Talking to the baby about relaxing her feet (using some key words such as "relax" or "let go") as she touches fosters a secure feeling about her bodyself image in the baby. Through the practice, the baby will learn to anticipate being massaged as a pleasurable experience, a time to feel the security of her parent's loving touch. This also helps parents to become aware of their infant's body language and recognize her feelings by cues or signals and modulate their tensions while interacting with her. A parent who is attuned to how her baby looks and feels will often be able to understand her crying and detect illnesses in the early stages and whether she is tense or at ease. This fosters a true access to the baby's own needs and emotional life and thus effective communication. Mothers who have had meaningful skin contact during pregnancy and labour tend to have an easier labour and seem to be more responsive to their infants.

If the mother's touch, voice, posture, and body language in general are aspects of her attitude to her bodyself, the infant's body image is to a large extent moulded by that of the mother. By touching each part of the baby's body, the mother helps her integrate it with the rest of the body and to perceive it as belonging to a whole system. The mother's or father's self-image therefore plays a major part in the efficacy of the massage movement and has a powerful effect on the development of the infant's bodyself image. On the other hand, baby massage can help the mother to relieve tension, enhance, and integrate her bodyself image, mobilize her shoulders, chest and breathing, and smooth her posture. The practice of massage should come naturally but sometimes it does not because of blocked emotional and muscular tension that prevents the interacting gestures from evolving. The flow of energy in the body is essential for the parent to let the massage movements evolve freely and make the massage an expression of love. One of the most important aspects is keeping the massage playful, stopping when the baby starts to cry or terminates the "conversation" by abruptly turning away. It should use no more strength than that exerted by a balanced muscular tension flowing evenly throughout the body.

I shall examine the possible value of infant massage in enhancing the relationship and communication skills of parent and infant, particularly in the case of mothers suffering from post-natal depression. A fulfilling bonding is a source of self-esteem and the higher an individual's self-esteem, the wider the repertoire of bodily and verbal communication. A daily massage connects parents and baby in a way that is unmatched by any other type of interaction. The touching during massage has similar effects to the infant's sucking and licking of the mother. I have observed women with breastfeeding problems improving within a few weeks of a baby massage class. It is possible that the special closeness, skin contact, and massage movements increase the maternal prolactin levels in the same way as licking and sucking, instilling a sense of well-being in both mother and baby. This would be further proof of the psychophysiological rapport between mother and baby, which is formed pre-natally, and of their communication developed through touch and various cues.

Baby massage can improve breastfeeding and enhance pleasure and motivation in mothering, fostering a constructive bonding. Baby massage classes are especially well attended by breastfeeding mothers. Prolactin is a "love hormone": it seems to activate the close attachment between mother and baby. It can be increased by loving touch. I hope that this and other observations will also be borne out by further research. However, observational follow-ups are essential preliminary steps for developing this hypothesis.

CHAPTER ONE

Infant responses to parental contact

A baby's toe is minuscule,
but the feeling of grounding from the mother's touch
is enormous.

Parents' sensory cues—movement, touch, smell, sounds, and body temperature—can have regulatory effects on their babies. This is well documented among non-human primates. Some babies who are born with more vulnerable physiological systems may need the physical contact with their parents in a more crucial way. For instance, there are data to suggest that babies can be born with a weaker respiratory system that might cease functioning during deep sleep (McKenna, 1990). On the basis of some interesting data, I conclude that there is an adaptive fit with parent–baby contact and their bodily cues (McKenna, 1986; Trevarthen, 2001b). The parents' bodies, especially the mother's, act as a regulator of the baby's breathing, body temperature, and heart rate, particularly with premature and underweight babies.

The mother's body is the first environment for the unborn and newborn baby. There are data to suggest that bodily contact between parent and baby may prevent rare conditions such as SIDS (sudden infant death syndrome) or cot death, terms for a sudden and unanticipated infant death for which no cause has been identified. In the USA, two in one thousand infants die annually of SIDS and it remains the leading cause of non-accidental death for infants between the ages of one month and one year (Hoffman, Damus, Hillman & Krongrad, 1988). Interestingly, in Japan, where SIDS is quite unknown, babies usually sleep in the parents' room because of the small size of the houses. Obviously, this does not mean that all babies sleeping in a separate room are at risk of SIDS. Nor does it mean that all babies who have died of this syndrome lacked physical contact with their parents. Such generalizations are unlikely to be helpful. Instead, reflecting on possible links can help with prevention. Some SIDS researchers believe that the functional deficit involved may be quite subtle and that infants who die of SIDS develop differences from healthy infants during intra-uterine life.

One study (Howard & Hannam, 2003) discussed the association between post-natal depression and SIDS. Post-natal depression is consistently found in 12–13 per cent of mothers and is associated with deficits in mother–infant interaction. It is possible that mothers with depression are less attuned to their infants' cues and needs and are less able to respond appropriately to any changes in the infant. It is essential that these mothers and babies receive optimal care aimed at enhancing the mother's ability to synchronize with her baby.

Epidemiological studies consistently show that while rates vary significantly, SIDS victims belong to a wide variety of populations. SIDS occurs within all industrial cultures and races, and in rich and poor families, (Valdes-Dapena, 1980; Peterson, 1983; Hoffman, Damus, Hillman & Krongrad, 1988). It affects infants with diverse clinical histories during every season (although especially in winter, when skin contact is obstructed by the clothes and the baby's body temperature drops more easily) and at any time of day; while infants are in or out of the caregiver's sight; while they are in cribs, in their parents' bed and in car seats. Because of the multiple origin of SIDS, it would be impossible to control all the potential causes. What we can do is to improve the conditions in which infants develop before birth, as well as the environment in which they are nurtured and cared for after birth. This entails acknowledging the importance of the relationship that mother develops with her baby during pregnancy in shaping the intra-uterine environment and the baby's development.

The mother's imagination, mental representations of the baby, cultural beliefs, her motivation for giving birth, her expectations and self-esteem, her own previous intra-uterine life and way of being held are all elements that create the intra-uterine environment, as do hormones, bloodstream, diet, and so on. They contribute to shaping the infant's development. Every physiological process, such as the mother's muscle tone and posture, is mediated by her mental and emotional state and, in turn, these modulate physiological activities. Everything occurs in a circular feedback relationship. The complexity of the multiple interactions makes the mother–baby relationship subjective and unique. In this relationship, the father plays an important role through the contact with the mother and the support offered to her. There is no investigative access to this intimate and delicate relationship. A research project can study one or more factors and their correlation but they all interact with many others that are less apparent. Part of what is omitted is the whole subjective experience, the individual's feelings and relationships. This private space comprising mother, father, and baby is often neglected by research, perhaps because of its inaccessible subjectivity and uniqueness. Sadly, it is also too often neglected by the majority of birth and child-care institutions. It is a space that needs to be acknowledged on many levels of the child-care and parental network.

Sleeping together

Data concerning parents' and baby's sensitivity to each other's sensory cues and body language (Bowlby, 1969; McKenna, 1986; McKenna, 1990) indicate that sleeping in a separate room soon after birth may deprive babies of vital sensory cues that are more important for some than for others. This does not mean, of course, that if parents sleep with their children the risk of SIDS will be eliminated. Physical contact during sleep, which fosters tactile, vestibular, auditory, temperature, and carbon dioxide exchanges, induces infant alertness and thus helps to reduce what some researchers have

called "adaptive failure" at a crucial time in the baby's development. A baby needs a certain amount of carbon dioxide, which is
one of the physiological stimulations for breathing. She has very
sensitive receptors to carbon dioxide in her nasal mucus. Sharing
her parents' room is the best way to avoid carbon dioxide deprivation through their carbon dioxide exchanges. Another important
stimulation is the parents' touch and emitted sounds. Some babies
may miss the sounds of the womb—the mother's breathing, heart
rate, digestive sounds, and so on—more intensely than others.
Other babies may not miss them at all. The baby's individual
feelings and needs have to be acknowledged.

Three months before birth, sensory stimulation alone in the
absence of blood gas exchanges (oxygen/carbon dioxide) initiates
rhythmic breathing (amniotic or liquid breathing) in the foetus. The
mother's understanding of the infant's need for a smooth transition
into extra-uterine life may thus be significantly dependent on her
capacity to interpret her bodily signals. The mother needs to be in
touch with her own needs and body language, generated by the
interaction with the baby. Her capacity to respond effectively, or her
receptivity, requires a mutual understanding of codes.

An integrated view does not consider the baby in terms of how
industrialized societies define it either biologically or socially but
treats the baby's social, psychological, and physiological needs as
inseparable and interdependent. Parents tend to respond to their
baby's needs more according to cultural and lifestyle norms.
However, a baby's psychophysiological system seems to be more
biologically conservative and less autonomous during the first six
months of life. Physical contact, by inducing sensory stimulation,
acts as a synchronizer that promotes the stability of the baby's
breathing. Baby massage can act as a powerful regulator of the
baby's respiratory system because of the richness of the mother–
baby sensory exchanges that it entails. This can protect her from
environmental disturbances, particularly during the first six
months of life. Laying the baby on her stomach and massaging her
back triggers the reflex, when she has achieved this developmental
stage, to lift her head and chest off the floor. This strengthens the
back muscles and expands the ribcage and chest. As her chest
opens, she takes in more oxygen to fight disease and assist development. But, more importantly, she is training to assume a postural

attitude from which respiratory development will certainly benefit. It is important to do this for short, regular periods, as it reverses the foetal position to which babies are confined in the womb. On the subject of cot death, Peter Walker (1995), who pioneered baby massage in Britain, pointed out that putting babies on their stomach for massage was different from putting them in that position to sleep.

During the first few weeks of life, the newborn seems to have a natural immunity to cot death, possibly because of a "gasping reflex" that promotes oxygenation during periods of asphyxia. Breathing is still completely under the control of the primitive areas of the brain. Afterwards, however, the infant loses this reflex and becomes more vulnerable to breathing (apnoeas or periodic breathing). The baby's breathing can benefit from a regulatory entity such as a human body. This also applies to adult breathing. During contact, vibrations are passed on, synchronizing breathing. There are creative activities that maintain the baby's arousal and so stabilize her breathing, such as playing music or an instrument, or simply singing to the baby. These can be far more effective if the mother used to do them during pregnancy. These activities emit vibrations, which are not just auditory but proprioceptive; they amplify the effects on the baby's skin and muscular system, acting as regulators. Furthermore, they can mediate between mother and baby, facilitating their interactions. However, after nine months in the womb, no regulator is more powerful for the newborn baby than the mother's body. There is much research and observation to show the different ways in which parents and infants affect each other physiologically, socially, and psychologically (Shore, 1994; Feldman, Greenbaum & Yirmiya, 1999; Trevarthen, 1999). I have found significant support in this for my observational study (Sansone, 2002).

Movement and breathing

The effects of rhythmic rocking and movement on the human infant have been recognized since prehistoric times. Rocking stimulation can soothe as well as alert the baby, because of its effects on the reticular activating system (a substance linking the brain with the spine marrow). When babies cry, they are often asking to be rocked. They often stop crying when their mother begins to walk around and rock them. There is a position that Peter Walker (1995) calls the "tiger position", which seems to have amazing effects on most babies. Mother lays the baby stomach-down on her left arm (if she is right-handed), cradles her head and neck in the crook of her left arm, and lets her wrap her arms and legs around her arms, facing outwards. I have tried this position with several babies and taught it to mothers and, more often than not, it calms babies down. This position combines rocking stimulation with simultaneous gentle massage of the baby's stomach, which amplifies the soothing effect. The mother in motion produces a swinging pelvic movement that reproduces the familiar wave motion of the womb. The mother's breathing can also be reassuring for the baby, as it is likely to evoke that well-known rhythm sensed during intra-uterine life. The rhythmic movement and breathing sounds provided by the parent's chest movement, when the infant is held, particularly when parents and infant sleep together, can also benefit the infant's breathing.

During sleep, the infant feels the disruptive sleep movements and activities, which produce a feeling similar to that when she was sleeping or floating in the womb, providing her with a sense of security. Breathing is also dependent on body temperature, which in close physical contact is maintained by the mother's body. A preliminary study succeeded in stabilizing the breathing activity of some high-risk premature infants by placing mechanically breathing teddy bears in their cribs, which resembled the parents' chest movements (Thoman & Graham, 1986). The synchronized relationship between the mother's rhythms and the baby's breathing seems to represent an important transition from intra-uterine life for the baby.

The foetus's respiratory nuclei, located on the brain stem, develop structurally and functionally very early. The baby's breathing in the womb is connected with that of the mother. By six months of gestation, the vestibular system is well advanced. The infant's motor skills begin to develop before birth in relation to the movement produced by the mother's body. Thus, babies develop an interactive synchronization conforming to the mother's uterine biorhythms. This does not mean that the baby is asleep whenever the mother is sleeping. A baby also has autonomous behaviours. However, she lives in an environment in which stimuli such as hormones, temperature, bloodstream, water, sounds, mood swings, and so on contribute to moulding her responses and behaviours. Mutual synchronization of physiological rhythms is a fundamental process that mediates attachment or bond formation (Shore, 1994; Shore 2000 a, 2000b).

Touch and physiological changes

Touch affects breathing and is crucial for healthy development. By stimulating the skin, touch promotes a balanced distribution of muscle tone. It has effects on the hormonal and immune systems. Since emotional tension such as anger or fear displays itself through muscular tension, touch can prevent anger from building inside. Any sound in the womb, because it vibrates, is not just heard by the baby (her auditory system is well developed by six months) but it penetrates her skin and muscles, inducing or stopping her movements. Fully orchestrated, with a rhythmic heart "boom", a percussive pounding of blood and incidental stomach rumblings, the womb is far from silent. The pre-natal baby's brain starts to interpret sensory patterns at around six months and can detect a change in tempo. Core awareness does exist in the pre-natal baby.

Unborn babies can be extremely skilful in sensing the impulse of a song in their body; they can even determine the rhythms of their mother's body. This explains the newborn baby's amazing capacity to respond to, as well as determine, the rhythms and melodies of her mother's voice or a piece of music, just like a dancer, and suggests that the baby is born with a pre-formed system in her brain that can create a musical or rhythmic body.

Sound is therefore equivalent to touch. The feeling of being massaged originates in the womb, where the baby is massaged by the mother's or the father's voice, even by others' voices, by sounds surrounding the mother, the amniotic fluid, and the rocking from the mother's pelvis in motion, her breathing, and heart rate. Research shows that the foetal heartbeat and movements increase in response to sounds (Olds, 1986; Hepper, 1991; Lecanuet, Granier-Deferre, Jacquet & DeCasper, 2000). The foetus has specific preferences as to sounds, which can either please or disturb her and affect her heart rate and motor patterns. This means that melodic sounds and any tune enjoyed by the mother can act as a regulator of the baby's physiology and promote healthy development. Research shows that infants born to mothers with low heart rates sleep for longer periods, fall asleep faster, and cry less than infants born to mothers with higher heart rates (McKenna, 1986). I should re-emphasize the importance of considering research cautiously and avoiding generalizations. Evidence helps to understand a possible link, something that is likely to occur and is only a part of a more complex puzzle. Hypotheses and results may restrict the understanding of the whole phenomenon; nevertheless, they can be helpful in finding some important links. Consistently with the relationship between the foetal heartbeat and movements and sounds, Rubbing an infant's feet for about five minutes can reduce the duration and frequency of apnoeas. This helps to explain the full range of effects of massage on the baby's breathing.

What is termed "genetic" at birth is actually already environmental, as the mother's body is an environment for the baby and is itself affected by the mother's environment. A multitude of environmental factors, as well as the relationship that parents build with their baby through their own attitudes and expectations, and the baby's own activities shape the baby's personality in the womb. In regard to this, the following is an anecdote from my intra-uterine life, reported by my mother. She told me once that during her late pregnancy she often enjoyed lying on her stomach and feeling my kicking. I was surprised, as this is reported to be a fairly uncomfortable position for the majority of women in late pregnancy. For my mother, my kicking may have been a sign of liveliness, but for me perhaps it was a reaction to the pressure on my vital space. I also know that her labour was relatively short and that my black hairy head appeared unexpectedly when my father, who eventually almost delivered me, was in the room without the midwife present. If I look at my adolescent relationship with her, I see a possible link between that pre-natal behavioural pattern and my reactions to a possessive streak in her.

A further example of how during our pre-natal life we absorb attitudes, gestures, talents, and behavioural patterns through a form of mysterious non-verbal communication with our mother is the case of a one-year-old girl. She had just begun to walk, when I saw her taking her first steps on tiptoes and displaying a remarkable dance pose. Her mother said that she had first noticed this at home a few days earlier and had been amazed, since the child had never seen her dancing. Surprisingly enough, the mother had been a dancer. The complex amalgam of genetic and environmental factors makes the primary period of our life, including the pre-natal stage, the most fascinating phenomenon.

Separation

To understand the psychological effects of separation from the mother on her infant, it is important to know the physiological effects, as they are closely related. If we bear in mind how the mother acts through physical contact to regulate the baby's temperature, metabolism, hormone levels, enzyme production, antibody production, sleep cycle, heart rate, and breathing, we can envisage the impairment that can be induced by premature separation. Early separation from the mother may cause the infant to produce stress hormones (such as cortisone), which cause a drop in her body temperature. We can imagine the damage that can be caused to a pre-term baby who is whisked away from the mother to special care and will not see or feel the mother for hours and sometimes days on end. Studies on the macaque monkey (Reite & Field, 1985; McKenna, 1986) indicate that, when separated from their mothers, primates as old as four to six months also undergo a reduction of body temperature and can have disturbances in sleep, with decreased rapid-eye-movement sleep periods, changes in electro-encephalogram activity, alteration in cellular immune responses and increases in cardiac arrhythmia and adrenal (stress hormone) secretion and cortisone levels. When parents abuse infants by depriving them of bodily contact, babies can gradually lose weight even though they are being fed. Food intake alone is not enough to guarantee normal weight when there is no loving physical contact.

Research shows that mother's heartbeat soothes the infant and produces greater weight gain in early infancy and that mother's heartbeat is "imprinted" during intra-uterine life (Trevathan, 1987). Thus, carrying the infant on the left-hand side can reduce her anxiety. It has also been found that holding infants on the left-hand side may reduce maternal anxiety, and consequently, anxiety in the infant (McKenna, 1986). Babies who are attached by a carrier to the mother's chest may be soothed by the regular sounds of the mother's body. These data suggest that some infant disturbances may be related to sleeping too early in a separate room from the parents in Western and urban societies.

In the past, and still in non-industrialized societies with large families and community life, babies used to sleep with the parents and to be in constant contact with different family members during the day. Anthropologists have found that some non-industrial societies consider Western parents' urban style of sleeping separately from their babies prematurely as a form of abuse (McKenna, 1990). A baby sleeping alone may miss familiar stimuli and fall into a frightening silence that she is not used to, as for nine months she has been accustomed to an environment rich in sounds, movements, and skin contact with the amniotic fluid. Absolute silence can be the most terrifying thing for a newborn baby.

The essential task of the first year of life is the creation of a secure attachment bond between the infant and the primary caregiver. Premature and prolonged separation can thus have harmful effects on the primary relationship and on the child's development (Field, 1977; Thompson & Westreich, 1989). As soon as the child is born, she uses her maturing sensory capacities, especially smell, taste, and touch, to interact with the social environment. To interpret and decode the infant's capacities and needs through her bodily cues, it is important for parents to open their sensory channels by relieving emotional and muscular tension, since this acts as a barrier to communication. To meet her baby's needs and understand her language, it is therefore fundamental for the mother to be in touch with her own feelings and body language and to monitor and regulate her own affect, especially negative affect. The receptive parent creates a communication with her infant that flows between their bodies. If the parent's chest movement affects the infant's respiratory activity, especially during sleep, it is important that her breathing should be smooth and free from tension. This creates rhythmic interactions between mother, father, and infant, which prepare the baby for cultural adaptation. Through the early interactions and the mother's responses, the infant learns expectations and ways of responding and signalling effectively in a relationship, using a variety of communication channels. Rhythmic interactions are like a dance between two partners who can sense and respond in tune with each other's body language. Crying and clinging, powerful manifestations of the infant's non-verbal language, aid survival by maintaining closeness, but visual follow-ing, smiling, and facial expressions increase survival value by providing reinforcement through sensory and cognitive develop-ment. Moreover, survival and adaptive skills are important for living in society.

When a baby is pre-term and underweight

Pre-birth babies need the right degree of stimulation before they can respond. A mother may not provide enough stimulation for the baby to respond or she may be too stimulating. The parents of an underweight baby need to be particularly sensitive to the baby's signals and to attune their movements and handling to the baby's own needs and pace. These babies may take a long time to become accustomed to the rhythms of night and day. They are more attuned to intra-uterine life and may indicate that they are missing it through physiological disturbances such as breathing, eating, or sleeping problems. Even babies born on the due date who have had an easy birth can produce these signals. We have all felt homesick at least once in the course of our lives. Why then should a baby not feel nostalgic and unsettled after birth? Conversely, some babies may be looking forward to leaving the womb because of their curiosity or because they are so active that they need a bigger space. Adults are able to express their needs and feelings in language. Babies can do this only through bodily signals.

The baby's cry at birth is not just a reflex. As well as a sign of the birth trauma stemming from the overwhelming pressure of the pelvic canal, crying may be an expression of the baby's feelings about the transitional journey. Some babies are born crying, others are not; some are asleep while others look around straightaway. An experimental psychologist would say that a newborn baby's feel-ings cannot be tested. However, it has not been demonstrated that the baby has no feelings. Those who work with new parents and

babies, attentive infant observers, and observant parents themselves can provide significant details that prove the wealth of the
infant's emotions.

The pre-term baby has special needs because she has had to
spend days in an intensive care unit, separated from the mother's
body, isolated in a plastic crib or incubator under bright artificial
lights, often intubated on artificial ventilation tubes and catheters.
She has to obtain stimulation from a cold machine instead of the
warm maternal body. Such an unpleasant experience is likely to
affect's the baby emotional and behavioural development and
therefore her way of responding to her mother.

Institutionalized baby care, when the hospital takes over
responsibility for the baby and separates the baby from the parents,
who may feel powerless, plays a crucial role in shaping the relationship between mother, father, and child. The baby's trust in the
world, thus her sense of security, is shaped by these early experiences. Her perception of the primary environment as a secure or
insecure place is likely to affect her sense of identity and bodyself
image. The parents' role is crucial in reducing the baby's distress
through touching, cuddling, and holding. Infants have an extraordinary capacity to benefit from physical contact and lessen the
impact of a stressful experience.

The parents are affected by the hospital experience as well. They
may develop emotional and behavioural problems and even physical pain, and may need to be supported themselves. A major experience such as this may alter the perception of their identity and
bodyself image. A parent going through these feelings may be
unable to offer her baby appropriate stimulation. Feelings display
themselves through movements, tone of voice, facial expressions,
and ways of handling the baby, which are shaped by muscle tone
and posture. For instance, in a depressive state, movements are
generally slow, the voice is flat, facial expressions are locked and
immobile, while eye contact is poor and the level of responsiveness
is lower.

Early contact is facilitated when mother and baby can share a
room. Garrow (1983) pioneered an approach to helping parents to
adapt to a sick or premature infant at a hospital in High Wycombe,
UK. Babies have their mothers with them from the first hours of life,
no matter how seriously ill they may be. Fathers may stay the night

and young siblings may visit at any time. Some of the mothers' rooms are directly connected with the intensive care unit, so that parents can easily care for their infants. The mothers can eat together and thus share experiences and feel mutually supported. Parents adapt to caregiving tasks and to the birth of a sick or premature infant more quickly and smoothly than in situations where the mother could not be on-site. The High Wycombe intensive care unit has been used as a model by some high-risk nurseries in the USA.

In one observational study I carried out in a traditional hospital a woman who had a caesarean section because of pre-eclampsia said that she felt as if she had lost her baby, since she had been whisked away from her to intensive care. She did not see him for thirty hours because he was in an incubator attached to a heart monitor. This woman experienced an abrupt change from the feeling of the baby inside her, thus of fullness, to the feeling of emptiness, nothingness, and powerlessness. The mother's and baby's sense of belonging to each other is vital for the attachment bond to develop. It is not surprising that this woman became depressed.

Many professionals discuss post-natal depression too superficially by regarding it as a sickness that some women get because of the sudden hormone reduction or the relational or psychic dynamics of the new role. They split the syndrome from the social context, the labour, and the birth experience. The psychophysiological effects of an inappropriate birth environment, which can lead to a difficult parent–baby relationship, are hard to detect and they need to be acknowledged. There is a tendency to diagnose the increase of a child's breathing problems such as asthma, to draw up percentages, and link them with environmental changes in general such as pollution or chemicals in food, which would cause different forms of allergies. The impact of institutional birth experiences on the mother–baby relationship and consequently on their health and on the baby's development is usually overlooked.

In another study (Sansone, 2002), I followed-up an underweight baby who appeared to be disturbed by any sound in the days immediately following birth. The mother was having breastfeeding problems and struggling with giving the milk to her baby. One day she complained that the baby used to cry endlessly and would calm down only after being picked up, held, and rocked. During their first massage session, I led the mother to focusing on gentle, smooth touching and handling. The baby appeared to enjoy this and after a few weeks she gained a surprising amount of weight.

Mothers establish the picking-up pattern because they tend to pick the baby up whenever the baby is crying. Sometimes this is partly an expression of their own need to be held. Their love can hinder their realization that the baby is growing and needs to spend time on her own or needs special stimulation to get involved. In regard to the mother mentioned above, baby massage must have created a special space and time of containment for both mother and baby, thus dissolving the picking-up pattern. The woman, in fact, seemed to stop complaining about her baby's persistent crying. In addition, the special contact during massage helped to increase confidence in mother and baby and promote security and separation. The baby continued to appear a little anxious and sometimes irritable. At the age of six months, when she started to attend a mother-and-baby yoga class, she hardly interacted with the other young children. However, the frequency of her interactions increased noticeably over time. Soon I realized that the sharing experience was helping mother and baby to go through the transitional period of separation.

Research on stroking, cuddling, and rocking of underweight or special-needs babies started in the 1960s and showed that touch had a positive effect (Powell, 1974; Rice, 1977; Klaus & Kennell, 1982; Garrow, 1983; Field et al., 1986). It was found that babies who are touched more cry less, gain weight faster, and exhibit better motor, emotional, and behavioural development and learning capacities. Tender and caring touching, which does not entail any pressure on muscles but stimulates the nerve endings in the skin, can be done while a baby is still in an incubator and can be crucial for her to get over this. A care programme, aimed at binding the baby to her mother's breasts, like baby kangaroos in a pouch, can save many very underweight babies (Anderson, 1991). Although many survive because of highly sophisticated care facilities, "kangaroo care" can affect the relationship between mother and baby.

During my study on the Birth Unit in London, I met Andrea, who breastfed the first few days after birth and then developed mastitis, which prevented her from expelling milk. She was struggling to breastfeed, as she believed it to be the only gift she could make to her baby. The baby started losing weight and appeared sad

and irritable. I assume that this occurred, other than as a consequence of the change to formula milk, also because of the mother's
tension relating to her sense of failure and guilt. While I was listening to the woman's birth experience, it emerged that she had never
felt herself being "held" by her mother as a child. I linked this with
her remarkable tendency to leave her baby either to a midwife or to
me. The contact with the baby may have aroused her primary feelings that were acted out through the mastitis symptom. Mastitis
seemed to be a mind—body strategy to escape the anxiety. This case
is described in more detail in Chapter Two.

I proposed the "kangaroo technique" after talking about its
benefits. My goal was to encourage her to think of the various ways
of nurturing her little girl, such as touching, holding, massaging,
talking to her, which are more important than the milk supply.
Having her baby literally in skin contact with her body not only
helped the mother to tackle her striking feelings rather than fleeing
them by entrusting her baby to someone else but also allowed her
to get in touch with the real individual baby. Furthermore, this
helped mother and baby feel that they belonged to each other. I felt
that this was a critical time, when she needed to overcome her anxiety about contact by, and only by, getting in "contact" with her
baby. A few months later, I saw her interact with the little girl
during the post-natal class. She appeared to make regular eye and
skin contact and to enjoy and benefit from it. There is plenty of evidence from observational and research study of the healing effect of
attuned touching and holding (Montague, 1978; Trevathan, 1981;
Cunningham, Anisfeld, Casper & Nozyce, 1987; Field, 1995).

The baby's crying at night may express her longing for physical
closeness to her mother. Sleeping together can be a healing solution.
Sleeping alone in separate rooms is a recent historical innovation
from the nineteenth-century industrial revolution as a result of
increased economic prosperity. Traditionally, large families took
sharing the bed or at least the room with the baby for granted.
Sleeping together can be a useful solution for the mother as well.
She does not need to get up; she can just cuddle, massage tenderly,
and let the baby suckle whenever she needs to. Even having the
baby in a cot close to the bed can be a good solution. Parents can
reach her without getting out of bed, so that the baby can feel and
hear their movements, sounds, and thus their presence. After a few

The infant/child's need for physical reassurance is paramount for his healthy overall development. Nikolas smiles at his mother who is delightfully smiling and chatting with him.

Photo by David Southwood.

months, the child will naturally express her need to sleep in her own bed and room.

Many mothers are concerned about getting their child into bad habits or disturbing their partner's sleep. Some of their reading may push them to conform to standard child-care practices and make them feel confused and guilty. A sense of guilt is far from helpful. The mother's trust in herself and her capacity to rely on her own feelings is the key thing to getting attuned to the baby's own pace and needs. It is also a prerequisite for enjoying every experience and achievement with her. This entails detachment from others' judgements.

Touch and communication

Physical contact such as kissing, cuddling, holding, and stroking encourages infants to thrive. If they are deprived of this, their physical, emotional, and intellectual potential is impoverished.

Western societies have become so impersonal and desensitized to the value of loving touch that many mothers are discouraged from expressing this from the earliest moments of birth by having their babies whisked away. Depriving any mammal of the opportunity to feed or feel her offspring makes the mother likely to reject her newborn. Unlike other mammals, who are on their feet a few minutes after birth and independent within weeks, human development is extremely complex, which is why human babies remain dependent for a longer period.

The newborn baby's need for physical reassurance is paramount for her healthy psychological development. Touch is the most developed of the senses at birth and the primary tool of communication. It is regarded as the "mother sense" and plays a major role in the parent–child relationship. It is no coincidence that we use

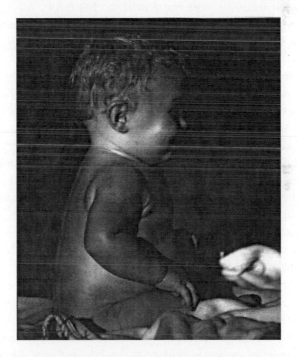

The child's emotional states are imprinted in the muscles and are visible in his movements, gestures and postures. The emotional state of a confident and resilient child is directly reflected in his upright, open and secure posture.

Photo by David Southwood.

expressions such as: "to have the feel of", "to be in touch with", to describe human relationships in terms of our sense of touch. The way in which babies are touched and held has a remarkable effect on the development of their personality. Cuddly toys are obviously poor substitutes for loving human contact. Massaging the baby provides the best way of getting the feel of her, getting to know her, and becoming able to handle her with more confidence. It can ease the parents' as well as the infant's anxiety and increase mutual and self-trust in all of them. Massage has the potential to bring fathers more in touch with their new baby and helps them to retrieve feelings often neglected in men by our societies in favour of cultural stereotypes. It is a playful way of making a father feel involved in the child-care.

The benefits of a period of close physical contact are supported by research from all over the world. In his book, *Touching* (1978), Ashley Montague includes some anthropologists' observations on Balinese children and the Arapesh in New Guinea, the Netsilik Eskimos, the bushmen of the Kalahari, and the Ganda children of East Africa. These studies on the babies of these cultures, who are cradled, sung to, stroked, caressed, and carried by their mothers and other family members, show that their overall development appears well advanced. Jean Liedloff, in her book *The Continuum Concept* (1986), reports her observational work of two and a half years, living with the Yequana Indians of South America. Liedloff describes how the instinctive maternal and parental capacity, if it has not been impaired by their childhood experiences, is aroused by the newborn baby and helps them to respond properly to the baby's emotional and physical needs. Liedloff highlights the period of physical contact following birth and its profound effects on the personality of parents and child.

The primary touching and holding and early infancy and childhood experiences shape adult personality and behaviour. Any emotional response of the baby intensely involves the whole body. Her emotional states are imprinted in the muscles and are visible in her movements, gestures, and posture. For instance, the emotional state of a confident and resilient child can be directly reflected in her upright, open and secure posture, and fluid movements. Whether touching a child and helping her to sit, stand, and walk forms an everyday part of child-care, it is the quality of contact and help that really matters. What makes a child progress in her achievements is the emotional message that is sent while she is being handled. Under some circumstances, when for instance it is difficult to maintain regular baby–parent contact because of illness or premature birth, the quality of contact can do much to compensate for the quantity.

The mother's touch

The mother, who may be exhausted or incontinent, and who is dependent on the nurse and the doctor for skilled attention in many different ways, is at the same time the one person who can properly introduce the medical care and staff to the baby. She knows how to do this not through any training or cleverness but just because she is a natural mother. Her touch, eye contact, and voice are the key healing things in the medical programme. They are part of the mother–baby relationship and its uniqueness. Medical staff must facilitate this relationship as a major part of the treatment. The parents' and baby's natural skills cannot unfold if the mother is afraid for personal reasons or because of excessive medical control, or if she does not see her baby when she is born, or when she is ill in hospital, or if the baby is brought to her only at times stated by the authorities to be suitable for feeding purposes. It just does not work that way.

The following account is a woman's experience of her child's illness (meningococcal disease). The case gives remarkable evidence of a mother's receptiveness and self-confidence as an active participant and crucial figure in her child's healing process. It highlights her intermediary role between the medical staff and the child's individual needs. Her capacity to rely on her own feelings and intuition was important in encouraging the staff to listen to her and to accommodate the medical treatment to a sensitive and creative recovery programme. The key points that were implemented concern important issues with which this book is concerned. The following is the mother's faithful account.

Surviving Evan's illness (meningoccocal disease)

- Trusting the Mum's intuition/instincts

- Demanding/persisting in getting a diagnosis
- LOTS of skin contact, including massage, holding and touching

- Sleeping together (especially during illness and recovery)
- Bathing together
- Returning to full-time breastfeeding
- As much direct physical contact with his Mum as possible during medical treatment
- Encouraging Evan to scream or cry out when a painful procedure is taking place
- Asking all medical staff to look at him *before* handling him
- Never leaving Evan alone with anyone he does not know
- LOTS of cuddling and playing (whenever possible)
- Music and laughter in the hospital room
- Mum helping with undoing bandages, giving oral medication, and taking Evan's temperature
- Encouraging the caregivers Evan has got to know to be, if possible, assigned to his room again
- Refusing any "UN-gentle" treatment

Continually reminding Evan how much he is loved!

CHAPTER TWO

A psychophysiological theory of emotions

Our body is involved in our relationships as much as our
mind.
The two levels of our being are inseparable
and a circular relation exists between them.
They are split only by language and concepts.
While thinking, speaking, dreaming, and interacting
there are changes in our breathing, muscle tone,
posture, and facial expression,
—throughout our body language.
They are powerful forms of non-verbal communication.

P sychological phenomena emerge from the complex interaction between systems in the body and the brain. The body
image exists in the neocortex, which is the outer layer of the
brain. It is a process involving the deep brain, the skeletal frame,
the muscular system, and all bodily activities. The neocortex is a
highly sophisticated entity that collects, assembles, associates,
analyses, and stores data provided by sensory organs. The subcortical nervous system or primitive brain is closely connected with
the hormonal and immune systems, our emotions and instincts.

There is continuous interaction between the neocortex and the primitive brain. Information travels along the spinal cord and reaches the hypothalamus, which controls the autonomic nervous system (Luria, 1973). The hypothalamus is closely connected with the limbic system and together they form the locus of emotional centres. They form a complex network that can be conceived as a "primal adaptive system". The right hemisphere in particular contains an integrated map of the bodily state and plays a primary role in the regulation of fundamental physiological and hormonal functions. Since the hypothalamus-pituitary-adrenocortical axis and the sympathetic system are both under the control of the right cerebral cortex, this hemisphere is thus primarily involved in the survival functions that enable the organism to cope with stress.

Drawing on Bowlby's notion that the infant's "capacity to cope with stress" is associated with certain maternal behaviours (1969, p. 344), the attachment or bonding relationship directly shapes the development of the infant's right-brain stress-coping systems that operate at unconscious levels.

The right cerebral cortex contributes to the development of mother–infant interaction and shapes the capacity for biological synchrony, the regulatory system of attachment. This biological synchrony provides the basis for the empathetic perception of emotional states. The right brain (non-dominant hemisphere) stores not only the representation of visceral and somatic states, and of the bodyself, but also an internal model of the attachment or bonding relationship and affect-regulation strategies.

Neuropsychological studies now also indicate that the right hemisphere, not the verbal-linguistic left hemisphere that develops later, is the site of autobiographical and bodyself memory, where our past experiences are stored (Fink et al., 1996). I speculate that it is in the neocortex-subcortical nervous system that the repertoire of the mother's body language is stored—her gestures, facial expressions, touch, smell and posture, which contribute to forming the infant's bodyself image and posture. Freud (1923) deduced that the unconscious system appears very early in life, well before conscious and verbal functions. The internal psychic systems that he described can now be studied by neuroscience. The connections between the highest centres of the autonomic nervous system with the limbic system and the hypothalamus and the cerebral locus of drive and emotional centres support Freud's idea of the central role of drives in the unconscious system, which he considered to be the mediator between the somatic and the mental (Freud, 1915c).

There is a third system, usually overlooked by affective neuro-science, yet significantly involved in the neocortex—deep brain relationship. It is the muscular system, which modulates the relationship between the neocortex and the primitive brain. It can also be considered as a portrait of our emotions, body language, and gestures. The muscle tone modulates the activity of the sensory organs and the information pathway that runs from the periphery of the body to the brain and vice versa, via feedback. The muscular system is a sort of window between the external environment and the central nervous system.

The three systems—neocortical, subcortical and muscular—are inseparable and should be understood as a whole. Therefore, the perception of our self and body, as well as all psychological phenomena, is an integrated psychophysiological process. If sensory perception is analytical and fragmented, so is the general perception of emotion. The latter is a synthesis of all the information that feeds back via the neuromuscular system to our brain and vice versa. When the three levels are persistently in conflict, for instance when one inhibits the other, dysfunctions and disease develop. Disease is here considered as a condition of imbalance that leads to a distorted perception of the bodyself. An example of one of the three levels inhibiting another is when an idealized representation of birth, associated with high expectations, induces fear of an unpredictable labour experience. Fear increases muscle tone throughout the body and may have paralysing effects on the labour process. The result is a distorted perception of the bodyself and consequently of the birth process. Fear can also interfere with the central nervous system and inhibit the hormone secretion necessary for the normal process of labour.

CENTRAL NERVOUS SYSTEM
NEOCORTEX (representations, beliefs)
SUBCORTEX (emotions/instincts)
MUSCLE SYSTEM

To give birth, the woman needs to release certain hormones. The birth functions are located in the primitive structure of the brain, which can be conceived as a gland that releases hormones. The hypothalamus and the pituitary gland are the main parts involved. During the birth process, as well as during sexual intercourse, cortical inhibitions may be operating. When a woman is about to give birth, she needs to reduce cortical activity, i.e. intellectual processes. This explains the particular state of isolation and envelopment that the woman experiences in labour. This state is so delicate that one question or word from a midwife can alter the process. Environmental factors such as bright light or a sense of being observed, particularly with a camera present, can also disturb the labour and birth process, as is common in many traditional hospitals, because they activate the cortex and thus have inhibitory effects. Sadly, in most traditional hospitals there is no sensitivity to the woman's fundamental need for privacy and security during labour. Any sense of danger or insecurity triggers a release of adrenaline, which interferes with the labour process.

Studies on child development usually overlook the importance of the birth environment in encouraging a healthy relationship between mother and baby. It is clear from some Asian and East African cultures how rituals and beliefs concerning the period preceding birth, even conception, sow the seeds for birth (Maiden & Farwell, 1997). For one East African tribe, the child is born the first time that she is a thought in her mother's mind (Hopkins, 1999). When a couple wishes to conceive a baby, the woman goes out into the bush and sits alone under a tree. Here she waits and listens until she hears the song of the child to whom she will give birth. Conception occurs, in the eyes of these people, at the moment that this song is heard and the soul of the child is visualized. The mother then teaches the song to the father, so that the child's spirit is called to them during lovemaking. These traditional beliefs show that mental representations can affect conception, pregnancy, birth, and parenting. Expectant and new parents can adapt this idea to the births of their own children. If nowadays birth has become more complicated, this is partly because the rituals and beliefs around it, which sustain the mother's self-confidence, have been replaced by unnecessary fears and medical intervention. These can interfere with the natural processes of pregnancy, birth, breastfeeding, and early interactions with the baby. Even conception and ways of making love are being disturbed by new kinds of tension.

Nowadays, in Western societies there is a lot of planning around pregnancy, birth, and breastfeeding, as well as excessive control on the part of professional obstetricians. This generates many preconceptions about the birth scenario. I remember a woman anxiously asking how to register the baby at the office when she was only two months pregnant. Intellectual processes can inhibit emotional-instinctual behaviours, create expectations, and distort the woman's perception of her own feelings and bodyself. The most important consequence is a reduction in the woman's potential and confidence in natural resources that are fundamental in labour, early parenting, and in life in general.

The role of every professional working with parents-to-be should be aimed primarily at boosting parents' self-confidence and autonomy in handling professional knowledge with criticism. Words spoken by doctors often have a negative effect on the mother's emotional state, her self-confidence and, thus, her capacity to prepare for birth. We will never know the impact of a certain word on foetal development because it is intimately linked with the mother's personality and the level of her self-confidence. The way in which a word is absorbed and impinges on the baby's growth will probably remain obscure to pre-natal research.

The acquisition of an integrated model of emotion helps us acknowledge that even a sentence spoken by a professional can have a powerful resonance on a woman's pregnancy. For example, some common words are inappropriately used when the medical staff do not really know the physiology of the placenta. It is therefore not just a failure to view the human being as a whole system with different interacting levels, from cellular to emotional, but also an inability to interpret a positive sign. For example, a woman is told that she is diabetic because her blood glucose level has increased. The production of glucose during pregnancy is something natural and temporary. It reverts to the normal level after pregnancy. This happens because the placenta manipulates the mother's physiology via hormones because the foetus needs more glucose. So there is no need for diagnosis but it may be worth simply suggesting that the woman does not consume too much sugar and takes some exercise. Most doctors still misinterpret the subtle signs of a placenta that is functioning well for something pathological.

Misunderstanding may also arise concerning uterine bleeding during early pregnancy. Many doctors, especially in some traditional societies, still prescribe bed-rest in this event. The woman's sense of responsibility is then extremely delicate and even a confident woman would be unlikely to take the responsibility for making her own decision not to rest. However, immobility may increase the woman's anxiety level, induce negative thoughts, and thus reduce her confidence and ability to enjoy pregnancy. Unnecessary bed-rest may be useless and even dangerous for other reasons. It can have negative effects on the foetal vestibular and sensory system. The mother's motion, in fact, provides a vital stimulation for the baby's vestibular system and general growth. Stimulation from maternal behaviour and physiology may impinge on the foetus's behaviour and morphology by provoking respiratory activity, swallowing and movement. Pre-natal stimulation can promote pulmonary development and neuromuscular activity associated with breathing before the onset of post-natal respiration. Depressed motor activity is therefore associated with numerous morphological anomalies and developmental delays (Drachman & Sokolov, 1966; Moessinger, 1983). Unnecessary bed-rest could therefore deprive the foetus of vital sensorily evoked behaviours.

If modern medicine took into account new data and observational outcomes (Klaus & Kennell, 1982; Klaus, Kennell & Klaus, 1993), much more would be done to improve birth conditions and reinforce the mother's positive attitude to birth. Unfortunately, it is much easier to maintain what has been established in books than revise it.

To go through the wild, primitive experience of labour and birth, a woman needs to abandon her mental structures, intellectual background, and rigid defences. This entails the rediscovery of the primitive language of instinct and intuition, so as to be able to encounter the baby's primitiveness. A mother, immediately after birth, should be naturally able to take the baby in her arms and on to her breast and to find a position in tune with the baby's sucking (Oakley, 1985). On the other hand, babies know how to find the breast after birth. Why is there an increasing need today to learn how to breastfeed? One reason may be that intellectual processes tend to dominate our "primitiveness". It is not by chance that many aspects of sexual life have been distorted, because it is often overplanned, overcontrolled, or intellectualized, resulting in reduced interest in emotional life and probably in sexual and fertility problems.

Difficulties in conception and long-term IVF programmes are frequently followed by eventual unassisted conception, once the couple gives up planning. The path to health is aimed at channelling the emotional and instinctual life with a moderate and balanced control that is in tune with our planning and our intellectual life. To find this harmony, it is fundamental for a parent-to-be to listen to her own instincts, feelings, and needs, to trust them and to shape her potential with creativity. The need to labour in isolation in the forest, which some aborigine women show, can be considered a typical instinct. Some Western women manifest this need, which Michael Odent (1990), the French natural childbirth pioneer, calls a trace of the nesting instinct, as all animals prepare the place where the offspring will be born.

Another invention of industrialized societies and an expression of over-professionalized pre-natal care is the use of ultrasound scanning. Excessive ultrasound scanning, apart from its negative effects on foetal growth, may alter the woman's beliefs and imaginative system, and consequently her emotional state. However, every individual case needs to be taken into consideration, as for some women seeing through the scan that the baby is growing healthily can be reassuring. Nevertheless, I regard the mother's self-confidence, enjoyment of, and positive attitude to pregnancy as the best source of healthy foetal development. Therefore, scans should be prescribed only in case of genuine need or on specific request.

It is because of the complexity of the interactions between emotions and instinct and other levels of human functioning that it is reductive to stick to a single definition of emotion or any other process. Definitions are made by specialists who study one piece of a complex puzzle. We can describe some physiological or behavioural aspects of a certain emotion, such as facial expressions, respiratory, cardiac, and postural changes, but we cannot easily give a precise definition of the whole emotional process. My aim is to shed some light on its intricacies.

Emotion has too long been relegated to the background in cognitive science. Emotional neglect and its consequences for development have been overlooked in neuroscience until recently, although the effects of emotional deprivation have always been central to psychotherapy. Affective neuroscience integrates aspects of human functioning into its conceptual models, which include the main subjects of clinical interest (emotions, relationships, the construction of meaning and of internal working models). Brain functioning is conceived in a new way and bridges between disciplines are being constructed (Olds & Cooper, 1997). Major neuroscience researchers such as Damasio (1999) and LeDoux (1996) have contributed to integrating neuroscience with psychology and psychotherapy. Emotion cannot be reduced to a few simple elements, but involves facial and other motor system changes, physiological and autonomic changes, cognitive processes, and subjective feeling.

Emotion is a subjective process involving different levels—cellular, hormonal, nervous, muscular, and behavioural—holding the whole system together and reflecting fundamental adaptive integrations. The psychological level is the most complex, as it is the result of an intricate interrelationship between all levels. For example, fear involves a neural circuit in the brain, a hormonal process such as adrenaline release, with its effect on pupil size, heart rate and breathing rhythm, body temperature, hairs, muscle tone, posture, and facial muscles (Ruggieri, 1987). The subjective feeling of fear is the result of all those changes. The facial expression of fear is also a warning, adaptive signal with the social function of alerting others to a possible danger. When we are joyful, the physiological and psychological picture is obviously not the same; immune system, cells, hormones, breathing, and heart activities work in a different way. The perception of our self and body and the overall subjective experience of joy are different from those induced by fear.

The concept of emotion and instinct according to an "integrative" theory includes the neocortex, the primitive brain, the muscle tone and posture, the whole body's activities, and the individual subjective experience, which is the result of all these activities. Definitions built up by different approaches or disciplines are conventional and often create artificial barriers. Very often, the definition of instincts is based upon the distinction between "ontogenetic" (innate) and "phylogenetic" (acquired). The capacity to learn is innate. For example, the baby is born with the instinct to suck at the mother's breast. Yet, her innate interactions with the mother are soon a cultural experience. When the baby is born, she comes from an environment where she has already learned a great deal. The human being is predisposed to learn from intra-uterine life onwards and to record experiences not only in her brain but also in her muscles and posture. The recorded experiences shape her attitudes in conjunction with genetic heredity. Therefore, what moulds the genetic component is the individual's life history and her way of relating to the environment.

By considering the womb as an environment, we envisage that the foetus's genetic pool is shaped by its primary experience. Much scientific literature still creates a split between "emotional" and "physical", neglecting the major part that the body plays in emotional processes. Indeed, we could not feel at all without a living body. Our earliest experiences play a crucial role in shaping not only our attitude to life but also our immune system and cellular functioning. For instance, where two individuals are born with a genetic predisposition to develop the same disease, one may develop it while the other may not, according to the different environments in which they have grown up and their differing emotional experiences. Before a symptom becomes manifest, there is a psychophysiological network that has already shaped an individual's lifestyle.

A rollercoaster of emotion

To understand how emotions affect the progress of pregnancy, birth, and early parenting it is worth describing the physiology of emotions.

Emotional behavioural patterns in response to external and/or internal stimuli (thoughts, memories, unconscious drives, dreams, and so on) alter the level of arousal-activation through muscular tension, breathing, and cardiovascular changes. For instance, anxiety and stress alter breathing by inducing hyperventilation (Suess, Alexander, Smith, Sweney & Marion, 1980). These changes feedback via the nervous system to the central regulator, such as the hypothalamus, amygdala and so on, which is located in the deep brain. The regulator induces a behavioural response in order to re-establish internal equilibrium or turn one emotion, thus the psychophysiological condition, into another.

Therefore, there can be interplay between different emotions. An alarmed state, such as anxiety or fear induced by harm, can turn into an impulse of flight or anger, which does not necessarily manifest itself in flight or aggressive behaviour. For example, someone may feel paralysed or dominated by a situation. Prolonged anger or fear, when unbearable, can induce the central regulator to turn it into a more bearable emotion such as sadness. It may occur that one emotion is not commuted into another but becomes chronic, as an individual's typical retreat. When anger is not acknowledged and is locked inside, it can turn into depression.

When we come across a new stimulus, we tend to develop a widespread non-specific response (alarm) that lasts until we recognize the stimulus. This occurs in the orientation reflex. The recognition, through the association of the new object or event with what is already familiar to us, is a cognitive process that relates to the process of learning, understanding, and representing knowledge. A cognitive solution, therefore, can also re-establish internal equilibrium. Acknowledging the anger can help to bring it out and channel the energy in a constructive and creative way. Another possible response to a new stimulus can be surprise, which can be either pleasant or unpleasant. It appears after the stimulus has been recognized.

A prolonged alarmed state induces a general psychophysiological response characterized by psychological and muscular tension and alterations in respiratory and cardiac activities. This is an anxiety state. Anxiety can be described as a fear without a recognized object. The stimulus that induces this state can be a mental representation, an unconscious disguised element, a recent impression, a somatic need, or a stored sensation or experience. Anxiety is a state of instability in which the choice of response is very important for re-establishing equilibrium. The balance promotes an integrated perception of our bodyself or body image. When anxiety or any other emotional state is locked in our body by resistance and does not find a channel of release, it displays itself through a prolonged contraction (excessive muscular tension), which prevents the free development of our gestures and alters the perception of our bodyself.

Moreover, whether the stimulus is perceived as threatening or not, anxiety or alarm can turn into fright, attack, flight, or cognitive redefinition, according to the social context and the individual's own strategies. A conflict, which is a cognitive ambivalence, can prolong the alarmed state. Anxiety can also evolve into anguish and depression, when an individual, unable to choose an adaptive response, inhibits the excessive arousal by enhancing muscular tension. This is what occurs in paralysing sadness. In this instance, muscular tension acts as a defence mechanism. The Latin derivation of the word "anguish" (cognate with *angustia* and *angor*) sheds light on its physiological basis. It corresponds to a painful sensation of constriction and immobility in the ribcage, or to a feeling of tightness, especially in the chest or throat and, consequently, to constricted breathing. In psychological terms, anguish is an alarmed response of the ego to a presumed danger. Long considered the centre of love and courage, the area of the chest is also associated with grief and longing, and the great wave of breath that precedes our feelings of elation or self-satisfaction is the same wave that breaks into tears of sorrow. The rhythm of breathing and the heartbeat, residing in the chest, converge into the pulse of life. Either way, the way in which we manage our emotions converges with the rhythm of breathing.

To sum up, some psychosomatic disturbances and body image distortions are the result of repeated emotional, behavioural, and postural patterns that have not found healthy adaptive responses. The acknowledgement of our emotions and needs, dependent on our ability to feel and interpret our body cues, allows us to free ourselves from repeated patterns and make adaptive choices. In disease, the symptom is a psychosomatic strategy, a warning signal that something in our lifestyle needs to be changed. Inhibited emotions such as anger or rage express themselves through high muscular tension, associated stiffness in posture, and a disharmonious body image. Repeated patterns are associated with a rigid representation of self that restricts an individual's potential. Our body image is the mental representation of our self in relation to our emotional and social relationships and of our body in relation to space. It is the way in which we manage our boundaries in relation to our bodyself, emotions, and social environment. Some postural patterns and gestures partly reflect the way in which we represent and programme ourselves in relation to physical and social space.

The objective of a physiological description of emotions is to make it easier to understand how a pregnant woman's emotional state can affect foetal development and early mother–baby interactions. When a woman, for instance, feels dominated by a situation that she has no way of changing, this can be a risk factor for the pre-natal baby. Cortisone, the hormone released in a stressful situation, is in fact an inhibitor of the foetus's life. Therefore, a woman needs to enjoy her pregnancy to reduce the level of cortisone. Further-more, the feeling of being dominated is likely to be manifested in a muscular constriction of the chest, constricted breathing, restricted gestures, and stiff posture, which affect the baby's growth as much as the cortisone does. The mother's body, in fact, is a container of her feelings other those connected with the baby. To free herself from an overwhelming situation or bouts of suppressed crying, she needs to mobilize her breath and generate life and feeling in herself and the baby alike.

With an open chest and shoulders, combined with a relaxed stomach, an individual can inspire the maximum volume of oxygen, the very pulse of life. To breathe is to feel, and the word "inspire" means both to "breathe in" and to "arouse feeling". As the foetus's breathing depends on the mother's breathing, the mother's respiratory pulse fosters both hers and the baby's feeling. By contrast, to breathe little is to feel little, and one of the ways in which our bodies cope with trauma or stress is to inhibit the breath to diminish the sensation of pain. In the same way, the mother's abdomen, in which the baby resides, is an emotional centre. It tight-ens in response to fear, stress, and anxiety and relaxes with tran-quillity and enjoyment. As a centre of intuition and feelings, it often predicts an outcome of events more accurately than our intellect. Recent medical findings reveal the nerve cells in the small intestine to be nearly as numerous as those of the brain itself. The digestive system is regulated by interconnected cerebral systems that are the centres of emotional processes (Ruggieri, 1987). In the cerebral cortex, there are areas directly connected with the organs contained in the abdominal wall and metaphysiological studies (Wolf, 1966) indicate that interpersonal and emotional situations can modify the colon activity and its bloodstream. Because of this, the abdominal area is now known as "the little brain". In the East, the abdomen has long been venerated: by the Japanese as the *Onaka*, the honoured middle; and by the Japanese and Chinese as the centre of *Chi*, a source of great energy utilized for self-healing and self-defence. As a container of the growing baby, the maternal abdomen, combined with her open chest, is a source of great energy for the baby. I shall explain more extensively how this powerful source for the baby is created by the mother's fluctuating body image, leading to a feeling of elation and inner contentment.

The blend of emotion

Emotions produce non-verbal affective signals such as facial expression, gestures, vocal tone or prosody, and a postural pattern, in accordance with the individual's culture and the social context. The right hemisphere seems to contain the vocabulary for these non-verbal signals. This finding is consistent with Bowlby's (1969) suggestion that human feelings are detected through facial expressions, posture, tone of voice, physiological changes, and tempo of movement.

A facial expression occurs through the complex interaction of facial muscles. A face can also express mixed emotions or, under other circumstances, a specific emotion can hide another emotion. For example, it is possible to hide sadness or anger with a smile. This occurs when an individual feels that a certain emotion is inappropriate for a particular social situation, when there is an emotional conflict, so that she needs to inhibit one emotion, and when an emotion cannot display itself freely because of an unconscious mechanism such as repression.

Internal states can be completely visible in our face, gestures, movements, and posture. Emotions vibrate through our body and can be sensed as well as seen. Particularly sensitive to vibrations, the baby senses the caregiver's mental and emotional state through the way in which she is held, touched, talked to and looked at. Observing face-to-face communication between mother and baby, Trevarthen (2001b) notes that proto-conversation is mediated by eye contact, vocalizations, hand gestures, and movement of the arms and head, all acting in co-ordination to express interpersonal

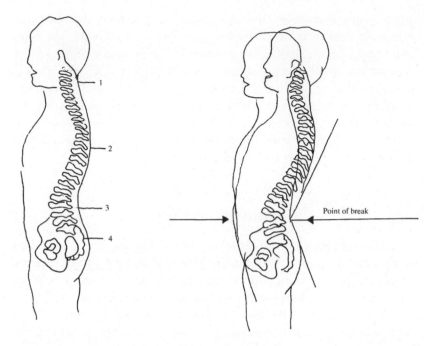

Figure 1.   The "point of break", where tension accumulates, hinders the evolution of a gesture, movement, facial expression, and alters the tone of voice, weakening their communicative power. Once we have focused on the source of tension we can free the gesture or emotion, and divert it in a positive direction.

awareness and emotions. He indicates that the development of the infant's brain requires brain-to-brain interaction and occurs in the context of an intimate and positive affective relationship. In other words, it is the caregiver's emotional availability and consistent bodily expressions that seem to be the most central feature of early experience in promoting development.

We receive, therefore, many cues to interpret someone's face as sad, radiant, or bored. We can see joy, indifference, interest, excitement, torpor, and so on. Moreover, some significant signals are transmitted through posture, for instance from a forward or a backward posture, from their gestures and their whole body language, which informs us about their emotional state. To make things more complicated, our perception of someone's mental or emotional state is also affected by our own feeling, our mental representation of her, our stereotypes, and cultural beliefs. We all tend to project our feelings on to other people, in other words, to imagine that other people have the same feelings. This striking phenomenon can be particularly dramatic when the person on to whom we project reminds us of someone much closer to us, such as early infantile figures. This person represents a surrogate of primary influences. Either way, the mental state and behaviour of the person we project on to is influenced by our projections as well. This circular process is at the basis of empathetic perception of other people's emotional states and, the ability to share another person's feelings and emotions as if they were our own.

The mother's capacity to get in touch with her own affect and to acknowledge and monitor her projections on to her baby helps her to understand the baby's needs and feelings through her body language. This will enable her to access the infant's internal world in an empathetic way.

The baby's feelings manifest naturally. They reside in her movements, gestures, facial expressions, and vocal utterances and crying, as evidently as in her chest and respiratory rhythm. On the other hand, the baby leads the mother and father to connect with their own feelings, rediscovering their childhood resources and new unknown abilities. This fluctuating communication between parents and between them and the baby can enrich their personalities and strengthen their identities. The child's physical, behavioural, and emotional development will then benefit from the parents' fulfilment, and a personality all of whose facets make up an integrated whole will thrive.

If the caregiver feels rejected by the child, it is important to acknowledge this feeling and stay with it rather than being frightened and consequently denying it. Realizing that it is a natural parental feeling is the first major step to working it out. One of the consequences of denied emotions is the transmission of "inconsistent" or confusing messages. Motherhood has often been considered a romance by literature and the mass media. In real life, moments of romance alternate with bouts of overwhelming feelings. A parent may feel rejected by her crying baby and find it difficult to love her. This may be accompanied by overwhelming feelings of guilt and self-perception as an awful mother. The unexpressed anger can further increase her tension in a vicious circle and affect the

Journey into Mothering. Painting by Antonella Sansone.

relationship not only with the baby but also with her partner through her body language. She may direct the unexpressed anger towards an unsupportive husband, or towards the baby. If she is ashamed of these intense emotions and anxious to protect her baby, the anger is introjected and turns into depression. Acknowledging the blend of emotions and sharing them with the partner can help to elaborate and channel them in a constructive way. Being honest about their own feelings is a crucial path towards effective communication between parents and baby that promotes healthy child development.

Drawing on Ruggieri's (1993) description of the physiology of anger, it is experienced as a "break-point" in the body and an attack on our integrity, since tension is concentrated in one part or in the whole body. The break may be experienced as a locked chest and constricted breathing. To acknowledge the anger, it is worth focusing on the "break point", where tension accumulates in our body (Ruggieri & Moria, 1994). The "break point" hinders the evolution of a gesture, movement, facial expression, and alters the vocal tone or prosody, restricting their communicative power. Once we have focused on the source of tension, we can free the gesture, thus the anger, and divert it in a positive direction. Listening to music or playing an instrument, even a very simple one, singing, or vocalizing with the baby's screaming, dancing with her, and breathing deeply can help to relieve the break points and distribute the tension throughout the body.

Some women are locked into fixed emotional and postural patterns that have their roots in their earliest experiences. A compulsion to repeat, which overrides the pleasure principle with the force of the repressed feeling, can be observed to some extent in all human beings. Dealing with the baby may contribute to reinforcing this compulsion if the parent does not work through it and discover a creative strategy. If it is not elaborated, the anger is stored in the muscle memory, shaping gestures and posture, thus restricting the perception of the bodyself.

The mother–baby interactions offer a natural vivid setting to see how the mother's emotions, feelings, and mental states take shape through her movements, gestures, and posture. This striking phenomenon formed the starting-point and a principal subject for reflection during my observational study and support work at the Birth Unit. The case I am about to describe concerns a woman who, worried about her baby's persistent crying, handed him over to me, after which he eventually calmed down. Then I observed her posture: her shoulders appeared closed and raised and her neck was pulled into her shoulders. I listened to her voice, which sounded fairly tense. I thought that her body and voice were transmitting vibrations to the baby and that the baby had calmed down because he had passed from tightened to more relaxed arms that were not involved in the overwhelming emotion. I regard therapeutic work aimed at a bodyself-knowledge and focusing on the recognition of the physical signals of emotions as the path to resolving some kinds of repeated patterns and communication difficulties between mother and baby.

Creative visualizations, in the sense of a body image treatment, can be powerful strategies for relieving tension. The brain sends messages to the muscles even if the body is stationary. These are processes that can bring about changes in breathing, heart rate, and muscle tone; they can therefore have effects on the emotions. For instance, a woman can visualize the anger as a wave flowing out from her body together with each deep outward breath. When she breathes in, she can visualize fresh water that purifies her body. She can really feel the sensation of the water. This can lower her body temperature, which has been increased by the anger. She can imagine flying with clouds, for instance. The white colour and the blue sky affect her body and thus her affective and mental state.

Breathing and posture change with our emotions: thinking, imagination, movements, and visualization can bring improvements. The rhythm of breathing, and the whole area where it resides, together with the heartbeat, with the heart having long been considered the centre of love and courage, are also associated with grief and longing. To breathe is to feel, to perceive our body-self, and to be receptive. It is a window that connects our inner world with the one outside. While breathing, we are taking in not just oxygen but information from the environment, our body-self and our inner world. Conversely, to breathe little is to feel little.

A mother whose breathing is smooth and deep is more likely to be present with the baby's feeling and experience, connected with her self and body, and able to sense her cues and interpret their meanings. A mother who is listening to the rhythm of her breathing and visualizing a wave going through the body is enhancing the perception of her self, her body, and thus her baby. As a result, her receptiveness towards the baby thrives.

Shouting, screaming, singing, dancing, playing an instrument, swimming, painting, and so on are all activities that can provide the mother with a space in which to play. Through singing, for instance, she can relieve tension in the jaws and the whole face and free and strengthen her breathing, whereas facial muscles remain contracted when anger, rage, and aggressiveness are stored inside, affecting the communication with the sensitive baby.

Writing about her feelings can also be a creative way of letting emotion flow. Putting her emotions, thoughts, and sensations down on paper can be a way to acknowledge them better and reflect on them. Taking just twenty minutes a day to write about a traumatic or upsetting event can bring about dramatic improvements in breathing by helping relieve internal stress. However, she must write expressively; she needs to say how the event affected her feelings. The mother can write letters to her baby in which she explains her anger, love, shame, and the blend of emotions. When the child is able to read them, the relationship with her mother will be strengthened. Obviously, there is no reason why the father should not be involved in this activity. This will enable the child to get to know the parents' inner world and her own inner child, through a journey into the past that will give her a sense of continuity between present and future, or a sense of history. Thus the continuity between being parented and parenting is deeply established.

Sending cards and letters to my two-year-old niece, Rossella, living in Italy, for example, is a way of keeping our relationship alive. At her age, it is not enough to see me two or three times a year to internalize me. But writing letters and cards will demonstrate, when she is able to read, that her aunt living in London has been in contact with her.

When attending to her vital space and her bodyself, a woman may find herself moved or crying. This is a sign that she is getting in touch with her self and inner child. She may discover unknown feelings and, terrified, she may retreat from them. It is constructive to indulge them, whereas flight builds up defence mechanisms that are physically experienced as tension, stiffness, restricted gestures, and pain. This is a healthy form of crying that releases the anger that has been diverted, and the tension that then flows out from her body, and frees the spirit of life itself.

CHAPTER THREE

Skin contact in primary relationships

For the young baby, moving into the unknown world
is possible only when there is a secure matrix
to which the infant can immediately return at any moment.

One of the baby's most primitive and fundamental needs is to find a containing caregiver to be held by. Bick's hypothesis (1968) was that, in the very young baby, the parts of her personality as well as her body have no interconnecting binding force. Due to this fragile psychic skin, which functions as a container of the parts of the self, the baby fears spilling out in a state of non-integration. She therefore depends on an object (the mother or the breast) that contains her fears. The sense of being held gives the baby security and establishes the foundations of her self-confidence. The baby is born with integrative competence, but needs an intuitive caregiver to attune and resonate with her psychophysiological states to maintain an integrated self (Papousek & Papousek, 1987). The infant acquires understanding of the world through communication and collaboration with sensitive primary figures.

I consider that the psychic skin is equated by the baby with the physical skin and that skin experiences, through touch, affect the

Touch should neither be too gentle nor too hard but firm, in order to nour-
ish in the child a sense of security and confidence in his bodyself. Mother
should use the whole secure hands, and not just the fingertips, to feel the
baby and let the energy flow.
            Photo by David Southwood.

development of the baby's personality. The primary function of the
skin is to contain. It functions as a boundary. Through the contact
with the mother, the baby introjects the experience of being held,
which strengthens her psychic and physical skin and her sense of
security. This relates to a process called "projective identification".
By introjecting a containing object (mother, breast, and all the experiences with her), the baby cements an internal space and identifies
with that object and with the experience it provides. An ideal containing object is the nipple in the mouth and the mother, with
all the forms of containment she provides while cuddling, gazing,
talking, bathing, massaging, and so on
    The baby searches for an object—a light, a voice, a smell, or
other sensory objects—that can hold her attention and thus be experienced as holding the parts of her personality and body together.

A four-year-old boy who had missed maternal containment because of some difficult circumstances and developed an intense fear of the dark one day drew a tree with a source of bright light. The light was for him a substitute for the mother that enabled him to hold himself. Any containing object is experienced by the baby physically as a skin. If the mother is absent, either physically or emotionally, and thus unable to contain the baby's needs, the baby has to find ways of holding herself to survive. For instance, she can relate to the light and smile and coo at it. The light may be experienced by the baby as a substitute for the mother. She may focus her attention on a sensory stimulus and feel held together. She may engage in continuous bodily movements that can act as a containing skin. An extreme example is seen in infantile autism, when the child focuses on a stimulus or produces rocking movements and switches off from the rest of the world.

An absence of sound and movement can be experienced by the baby as a hole in the skin and in the self. It is well known that babies continuously need to follow moving objects, both by looking and listening. Sounds are in fact vibrations that produce changes in the baby's muscle tone and are experienced as movement. Another form of self-holding is tightening the muscles, clenching sets of muscles together in a rigid position. This mechanism can involve not only skeletal muscles but also the smooth muscles of the internal organs, so that the spasm might result, for example, in colic or constipation.

If these defensive survival mechanisms persist because of the mother's inability to meet the baby's needs, for instance when she is tired or depressed, they may become part of the baby's character. These mechanisms can impair the baby's trust in her parents and consequently in herself, as well as in the world around her. This impinges on the development of harmonious posture, motility, and gestures, and on body language in general. Therefore, the defensive mechanisms are likely to impact on the child's social and communicative abilities.

The perpetuation of these survival mechanisms, through a disturbance in the primary skin function, can lead to the development of a second skin, a tough and rough skin, a type of muscular shell that can be identified with a rigid posture. Dependence on the primary object is replaced by pseudo-independence, a substitute for the containing mother. True independence comes from good attachment and reliable dependence.

The primitive fear of a state of non-integration, thus of dependence, is present to some extent in all human beings. The issue of independence from and dependence on beloved caregivers accompanies us throughout life. It may impair the child's development when the defensive mechanisms become persistent because of the lack of a receptive parent who is able to meet the baby's own needs. The capacity to tolerate separation and overcome loss and mourning originates in this primary encounter between needs and responses. This encounter also gives rise to meanings, which are fundamental to the ability to elaborate mourning and loss. For example, a baby was trembling, sneezing, and making disorganized movements. The family had moved to a new house that was in an incomplete state of repair. This severely disturbed the mother's holding capacity and led her to withdrawing from the baby. She began feeding while watching television, or at night in the darkness without holding the baby. This brought about some somatic disturbances. The father's illness made matters worse and the mother had to plan to return to work. She pushed the baby into pseudo-independence, severely refusing to respond to the crying at night and tending to stimulate the child to aggressive displays. At seven months old, the little girl was hyperactive and aggressive and was called "a boxer" by the mother. She built up a muscle pattern as a form of "self-containment", or a "second skin".

Another example concerns the survival mechanism provided by a visual stimulus. A mother looked tired and depressed. She had talked about her feelings of isolation when with her baby. After being bathed and fed, the baby was brought by the mother into the kitchen and placed in her baby seat. Meanwhile, the husband returned home from work and started telling his wife about some incident there. The baby began to make louder and louder noises as she was ignored. The mother went to the baby, picked her up, and then put her back in her chair. She turned back to her husband, who also wanted her attention. The baby wriggled in distress, looked upwards, and began staring at the light. Her face and body relaxed and she smiled at the light. The mother's expression was hurt, almost distressed and she seemed to be wondering why the baby was doing this. She was afraid that something was wrong and that her intolerance might have caused that baby's behaviour. She also felt rejected by the baby. This is an example of how a visual stimulus can become a substitute for the mother. A baby can experience the loss of the mother's attention like being dropped. She suddenly can feel that she is not being held and is falling down, so that she needs to hold herself together by finding another object to cling to.

Mutually synchronized interactions are fundamental to the infant's ongoing affective development. If attachment is an interactive psychobiological synchrony, stress is defined as an *asynchrony* in a sequence of interactions. However, a period of re-established synchrony allows for stress recovery. The key to this is the mother's capacity to monitor and regulate her own emotions, especially negative emotions. A fundamental function of attachment is to promote the regulation or synchrony of biological and behavioural systems within the organism. Mutual synchronization of physiological rhythms is an essential process that mediates attachment formation (Shore, 1994, 2000a, 2000b). In other words, in an attachment bond, the mother is attuning and resonating with the rhythms of the infant's internal states and then regulating the arousal level of these positive and negative states. Attachment therefore concerns the regulation of emotional states, aimed at minimizing negative emotions and facilitating opportunities for positive emotion. An early relationship and attachment bond are internal processes that shape the infant's nervous system and all the psychobiological systems. These systems require interaction with the environment to establish networks and mature. Evidence now clearly indicates that these earliest emotional non-verbal interactions also affect the development of the infant's consciousness and verbal development (Trevarthen, 2001b; Trevarthen 2002). I equate such a complex coherent brain organization with an integrated bodyself image.

All adults can experience infantile feelings of helplessness, bringing back echoes of not being held and asynchronized communication. In extreme therapeutic settings, this can lead the patient to holding herself together. The same may happen to a new mother and father whose baby arouses their primary feelings of not being held. At first, these survival measures are adaptive. Gradually these defence mechanisms can structure the character, if they are not followed by re-established synchrony that allows for stress recovery. Some will lead to socially adaptive behaviour and special abilities;

others can block emotional development and lead to disintegration of posture and motility on the one hand, and of communication, behaviour, and abilities on the other.

I should emphasize the difference between "non-integration", which is a passive experience of non-containment, and "disintegration", an active defensive splitting process in the service of development. The baby's attempts to hold herself together when distressed are no different from the adaptive mechanism used at times of crisis when an adult experiences non-integration.

Behaviour in a patient, such as refusing to speak, holding back from expressing feelings, muscle tightening and postural stiffening, constant talk, jumping from one subject to another, being busy all the time, can be seen as defensive attitudes, attempts to hold the self and the body together. In psychotherapy, they oppose the analytic relationship, while they express the patient's need to hold herself together and her fragility. The analyst thus feels rejected by the patient. The analyst's feeling of rejection can lead the patient to reinforce the defence mechanisms, as she feels that she cannot rely on someone to understand and hold these primitive anxieties.

A similar phenomenon occurs when the mother, as in the example of the baby staring at the light, feels rejected when the baby turns away from her. She may have felt guilty and afraid that she has damaged the baby by causing her to smile at the light. But if she understood the baby's attempt to master her environment, she would not feel guilty and she could meet the baby's need. In the same way, only a therapist who understands the defensive function of the patient's behaviour and helps her through the transitory states of non-integration, rebirth, primary dependence on the maternal object can strengthen her internal fragility. The therapeutic setting therefore becomes the containing object.

Studies of attuned communication (Shore, 1994) between an empathetic mother and her baby indicate that the emotional synchrony is exquisitely non-verbal and that *resonance* is more than with the baby's mental states with her psychobiological states. The mother acts as a regulator of the infant's physiology. Psychotherapeutic work with parents, or parents-to-be, and infants thus implies the therapist's capacity to *attune* to the parent's psychophysiological state, acting as a regulator of her physiology (Lyons-Ruth, 2000).

The role of baby massage

In nearly every mammal birth studied, close physical contact has been found to be essential both to the infant's healthy survival and to the mother's nurturing capacities. In one study (Hammett, 1922) with rats, when pregnant females were restrained from licking themselves, their mothering activities were significantly diminished. Moreover, when pregnant female animals were gently stroked every day, their offspring showed greater weight gain and reduced excitability and the mothers showed greater interest in their offspring, with a more abundant milk supply. Another study (Harlow, 1959) showed that for infant monkeys, contact comfort is even more important than food.

There is evidence pointing to the same conclusions for human beings. Studies with premature babies have found that daily massage is of invaluable benefit (Field et al., 1986). Twenty premature babies who were massaged three times a day for fifteen minutes each gained forty-seven per cent more weight per day, were more active and silent, and showed better neurological development than infants who did not receive massage. Furthermore, their hospital stays averaged six days less.

The natural sensory stimulation of massage speeds myelination of the brain and nervous system. The myelin layer is a fatty covering that encases each nerve. It protects the nervous system and speeds the transmission of impulses from the brain to the rest of the body. The process of encasing the nerves is not complete at birth; stimulation speeds this process, thus improving brain-body communication. In psychological terms, this enhances integration between mental and bodily processes and therefore the integration of the bodyself image.

The parts of the brain beneath the cortex, the *brainstem,* and the *hypothalamus* are involved in the body's self-regulation, in emotion and communication. The cranial nerves are initially involved in self-regulation of visceral functions, such as circulation of the blood, breathing, eating, and digestion. Vocalization, speech, and facial expressions are produced through muscle systems that are controlled by the cranial nerves. We can then see the relationship between emotions, muscle systems, and visceral functions and how they are involved in relationships and communication. The baby is born with a vital need to have these systems nurtured by mindful sensory stimulation. Skin contact, sensitive touch, and eye contact strengthen the relationship and integration between emotions, muscle systems, and visceral functions.

The cranial nerve system, in particular the brainstem and the hypothalamus, are also involved in the development of the body-self image. This system is well formed in a seven-week-old human embryo, long before the cerebral cortex has even begun to form. Studies on embryos' brains (Trevarthen, 2003) indicate that the *emotional system* or the brainstem/hypothalamus self-regulatory system monitors cortical development and this process continues throughout life. This system controls attention, muscle tone, and motor activity. Emotional systems thus influence cognitive development and also language, contrary to some theories that it is the other way round. This physiological description of the nervous system helps to explain all the potential benefits of mindful touch and massage on the child's overall development.

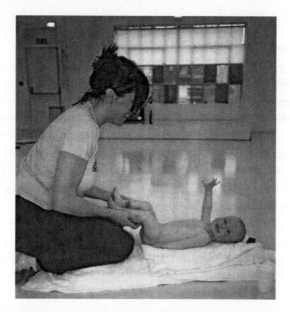

The synchronization of massage movements facilitates attuned communication and interaction between mother and baby. When there is rhythm, massage is a dance.

Photo by Antonella Sansone.

Loving skin contact and massage benefits the mother as well. Mothers who receive meaningful skin contact during pregnancy and labour tend to have easier labours and are more responsive to their infants. By regularly massaging her baby, the mother sets up a cycle of healthy responses in both the baby and herself, which improves her parenting skills day by day and enhances her baby's well-being and the relationship between them.

The baby's skin experience during massage impinges on the whole development of the child, from the biological to the psychological level. As the baby's skin is smooth and moist, and continuously renewed through the constant regeneration of healthy cells, regular massage with a pure organic oil, which makes the movements smoother, penetrates the pores, and cleanses the skin of its dead cells, fostering healthy growth. It also helps to preserve the skin's elasticity and resilient qualities. By regularly massaging her baby, the mother stimulates survival mechanisms such as the circulatory system, digestive and excretory processes, and the immune system, which are not fully developed at birth. She also encourages muscular co-ordination and flexibility.

However, these biological effects are not the only benefits. As our body's largest visible source of sensory perception, the skin provides a principal means of communication. As a protective covering, it allows the body and self to accommodate to the immediate environment. As an extension of our nervous system, our skin receives warmth, cold, and tactile impressions and reflects our emotional and physiological changes when it tingles with excitement, blushes with embarrassment, turns livid with anger, white with fear, and so on. The skin exhibits symptoms or signs as indications of well-being, illness, or infection. As a barrier against invasion by micro-organisms, the baby's skin acts as the primary defence against surface injuries and infections. In the same way, it can act as a defence against internal emotional injuries such a lack of holding and touch. When these injuries and baby's resulting fears are persistent, the primary skin function fails and the baby is compelled to develop a second protective skin, a substitute for the primary skin, a sort of shell. A second skin is expressed in excessive muscular tension, rigid posture, and disrupted movements.

Gentle stimulation of the baby through the skin begins in the womb, through the amniotic fluid. In the developing embryo, the outermost of the three embryonic cellular layers, the ectoderm, becomes the central nervous system and then develops in the form of skin to cover the body of the foetus. Major stimulation of the baby through the skin begins with the strong labour and birth contractions. Like massage, the descent through the pelvic canal sends firm, muscular impressions that stimulate the peripheral and autonomic nervous system, and the principal organs for survival.

The protective function of the baby's skin begins during the very early development of the foetus. The vernix caseosa (a white, greasy substance) covers the baby's skin to protect it from the amniotic fluid. The vernix, together with other secretions, helps to facilitate a smoother descent through the birth canal. Although most hospitals remove the vernix from the baby soon after birth, keeping the vernix provides a protective layer. No less importantly, it maintains a familiar and thus reassuring element for the newborn. Sadly, these primary moments after birth and its effects on the baby's feelings and on her emotional development are usually neglected. The vernix and the psychological effects of its presence after birth may seem irrelevant to adults. However, they may bring paramount benefits to some newborns.

What is regarded as a small and unimportant thing by an adult can be fundamental for the vulnerable baby and contribute to the development of a healthy physical and psychic primary skin. The feeling of missing something, together with an unfulfilling holding experience may compel some babies to develop a defensive second skin. Many tribal cultures leave the vernix on for two or three days or wash the baby by hand with warm water and replace the skin's cover by oiling it. Soap is not used, as it dries the skin and removes its natural protective elements and secretions. However, most importantly, soap introduces a strange chemical element that could cause some babies irritation or discomfort, or lead to prolonged crying. The baby's emotional reaction to a minor element such as a smell or an irritating product can be remarkable. In the West, the vernix, which is a rich source of vitamin K, is removed and then, paradoxically, vitamin K is given by injection or orally immediately after birth. Interestingly, in hospitals that do not routinely remove the vernix, the incidence of skin infections in babies has been significantly reduced. Maintaining the vernix on the skin has been found to be particularly helpful for underweight or premature babies at the Birth Unit at the St John and St Elizabeth Hospital in London.

Given the wealth of the baby's skin experience, we can understand the multitude of benefits that "sensitive" touch and gentle massage can have on the overall development of the infant and, more directly, on the development of a healthy primary skin. Baby massage can promote the internalization of containing objects during a playful and enjoyable time. The mother's touch, smell, voice, talking, eye contact, and facial expressions and the baby's vocalizations and cues are containing objects for both mother and baby. The mother's closeness to the baby provides a containing experience in itself, an experience of integration or wholeness that is essential for the development of the baby's sense of identity and self.

Baby massage fosters co-ordination of movement and senses and therefore improves posture and body communication. Co-ordination provides security and experiences of wholeness, while trembling and disorganized movement are induced by fear and mistrust. Observing the behaviour of a considerable large number of babies while being massaged in a class, I have come to the conclusion that baby massage has the potential to contain the primitive anxieties and fears of the newborn's non-integrated states. The mother's closeness, the nipple in the mouth, together with her holding, voice, and familiar smell, are optimal objects that contain and create boundaries. Baby massage gives a unique experience of closeness. The communication between mother and baby is triggered through a variety of channels: skin contact, smell, warmth, eye contact, interplay of facial expressions, vocalizing, movements—all these sensory ways of holding the infant's attention are therefore experienced as holding the parts of the personality together.

In regard to the warmth produced by massage, the hypothalamus, the primitive brain, stores the body temperature experience. One of my most vivid childhood memories is the warmth of my mother's body on my cold feet. The feeling obviously went beyond the physical sensation itself. It gave me a reassuring sense of all the parts of my body and self being contained together. The tactile information travelling from the peripheral body to the brain promotes the process of mental representation of those parts, which

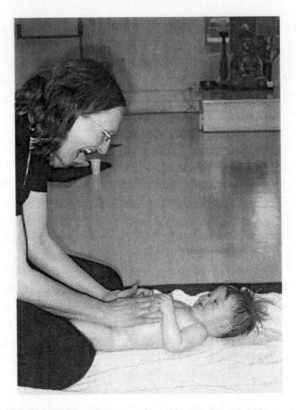

During massage the infant experiences, through her mother's voice, smile, touch, her own resounding vocalization and the mother's echoing, her primary external space, which is increasingly becoming her own internal space. Fiorence appears to be in tune with her mother's enjoyment of massaging.

Photo by Antonella Sansone.

are associated with warmth. The baby's representation of the self or parts of the self is by no means disconnected from her bodily experiences. Touch, therefore, provides nourishment for the sense of each part of the body belonging to the self. This process is related to the baby's sense of belonging to her mother, without which the introjection of the mother would not be possible.

The infant's non-integrated state is related to her as yet undeveloped perception of each part of the body (and of the self) as belonging to herself as a unity. Massage, providing playful closeness between parent and baby, can foster the internal reinforcement of good and enjoyable objects. An external object—the mother's smell, eye contact, voice, touch, massage and so on—becomes the baby's own, occupies an internal space and is experienced by the baby as an object that contains the parts of the body and the self and provides unity (Winnicott, 1962). The introjection allows the baby to have the perception first, then the fantasy, of an internal and an external space, a process that is crucial for the development of the sense of boundaries and identity. It is a fantasy, a concept of space, that takes shape from a concrete internal and external space, both of which are modulated by the parent's interactions with the child. The baby's internal space, made of emotions, feelings, needs, and fantasies, is projected on to the mother—and in a different way on to the father, who gives them meaning by interacting with and containing them, so that the baby can reflect on herself and develop a sense of self. The mother also projects on to her infant her inner world, feelings, reveries, and expectations, giving shape to the infant's internal world and to her way of responding. Every intro-jected experience that meets the baby's needs strengthens her trust in her parents, paving the way for good relationships and construc-tive social experiences.

During massage the infant experiences, through her mother's voice, her own resounding vocalizations and the mother's echoing, her primary external space, which is increasingly becoming her own internal space. When she starts crawling, walking, and running, thus moving in a larger space, her way of managing the physical and social space will be shaped by the earliest emotional space. Every expression of her body, at rest or in motion, will be a reflection of that internal space and, at the same time, a response to the surrounding environment. The gentle smooth massage of the skin and muscles strengthens the physical as well as psychic skin and, therefore, its boundaries, sowing the seeds of a flexible and adapt-able identity. Massage, for all the enjoyable and playful experiences provided, becomes for the baby an internal object that will mould her gestures, posture, behaviour, and interaction with the social environment. The infant identifies with the object and this identifi-cation contributes, alongside other factors, to shaping her person-ality. For instance, a girl will be likely to mother as she has been mothered or she is likely to handle her doll in the way she is handled by her mother. If she has experienced being contained, she is likely to be able to contain. Many abusive adults have experienced violence as children.

Breathing plays a crucial role in the formation of the infant's perception and conception of an internal and external space. Breathing is not just a chemical exchange between our body and the environment but an activity involving our feelings, thoughts, muscle tone, and social relationships. To "breathe in" or "inspire" is to "arouse feeling" and an internal mental space is nourished by the rhythm of breathing. Either way, the baby's internal world regulates her breathing. If this world is not "inspired" by the parent's containment and receptiveness, the baby is deprived of a vital source for expanding her breathing. By contrast, to breathe little is to feel little, and one of the ways in which our body copes with trauma, loss, and grief is to inhibit the breath so as to diminish the sensation of pain. The mother's physical and emotional closeness and her satisfactory interactions contribute to modulating the baby's breathing.

The reason why I refer to the *perception* of an internal and external space instead of a concept of space is that perception comprises both the skin/body experience and the mental process (representation of the space), as the two levels are inseparable. The concept of *receptive* mother instead of Winnicott's concept of the "good-enough mother" (Winnicott 1960; Winnicott, 1963) contains her perception of the self and body, her physical and psychic skin, her own feelings and inner child and her attitude to her bodyself image. To get in touch with her baby, a mother needs to be in touch with her own feelings and needs, her inner child, and her own need to be mothered. The concept of *receptive mother* thus implies her perceptive awareness of the baby.

However, the mother's success in attuning to the infant's cues is also related to the infant's unique personality. The baby's character or, for instance, the degree of enjoyment in being massaged, does also affect the mother's way of massaging and responding. There is nothing given or taken for granted. It is a learning process through which parent and baby get to know each other. Failures on both sides are unavoidable and essential steps to getting to know each other. Acknowledging the constructive function of mistakes and misunderstandings, rather than building up a sense of guilt, makes mutual growth possible and facilitates a healthy development of the relationship. By contrast, feelings of rejection and guilt arrest the process by locking the repeated patterns in.

When the mother is empathically attuned to the baby's inner state, the resonance amplifies the affective state in the mother–baby dyad and its biological regulatory system. This synchronization facilitates attuned communication and interaction. On the other hand, misattunement indicates stress or desynchronization within the dyad. By re-establishing attuned interactions, the mother alleviates distress and reinforces positive affect in the infant. This re-establishes the synchronization.

Certain life events can severely disturb the mother's holding capacity and lead her to withdraw from the baby. Distress can disrupt a mother's ability to focus on the baby's experience. Some examples of her "absence" are regularly feeding while watching television, in the dark without holding the baby, or while arguing with her partner. When other times of connection do not compensate for this, the baby is deprived of a containing, integrated experience, which may cause somatic disturbances. Failure in the internalization of containing objects because of the mother's distress can lead to disturbances in the primary skin function, formed by the primary objects, and consequently to the development of a defensive "second-skin". Through the second skin, dependence on the (impaired) object is replaced by a pseudo-independence and inappropriate use of the personality, resources, talents, gestures, posture, movements, and social boundaries. The second skin is a substitute for the containing function of the primary skin.

Mindful baby massage can strengthen the primary skin and so the infant's trust in her mother and consequently in herself, acting as an antidote to a second defensive shell. Massaging the baby can also have healing effects on the mother (Field, Pelaez-Nogueras, Hossain & Pickens, 1996; Sansone, 2002). It enhances the mother's tolerance of closeness in cases of distress because her defences subside. Defences manifest themselves through body language such as muscular tightening, avoidance of eye contact, vocal tension, or reduced holding, and are sensed by the infant as a lack of containment. Not only does mindful baby massage provide a unique time of closeness, but it gives the parent the opportunity to enjoy a playtime, therefore, to relieve any tension caused by a stressful incident or difficult primary experiences.

Lack of holding as a baby may be at the root of a parent's own intolerance of physical closeness. I remember a woman in a baby massage class handling her baby and dropping her on the floor like a sack of potatoes. Baby massage can help parents to improve the quality of touch and strengthen their own primary skin experience. It can be a means of self-containment. The catastrophic anxiety of not having being held as a child seemed to have led one woman, Andrea, to develop mastitis, so as to be unable to breastfeed and be too close to the baby. Her intolerance of physical contact, which gave rise to excessive anxiety, was visible in her remarkable tendency to hand the little girl out to either a midwife or me. The conflict at the basis of her disturbance consisted in her sense of fail-ure at not being able to breastfeed and her unconscious strategy of avoiding breastfeeding by developing mastitis in order to escape the overwhelming feeling this caused.

The mother's conflicts, such as those just mentioned, can lead her to develop symptoms that impinge on the baby's experience of the primary skin. Massaging the baby can help the mother, under some circumstances, to get over conflicts related to her own early life or ones induced by a Western lifestyle, which for instance drives many mothers to return to work too soon after giving birth. No less importantly, the group experience during the baby massage class creates a community environment that res-ponds to the new mothers' needs for containment. The nuclear family of the industrialized society submerges a mother and her baby into isolation and is unlikely to meet her need for containment and mothering. The class provides something of what the extended family used to do in the past.

Case histories describing the skin experience

Andrea

The following case is a vivid illustration of how lack of holding can cause a mother's intolerance of physical contact. The day after Andrea gave birth to a baby girl, I went to visit her in the hospital at her request. While telling her birth story, she did not make eye contact. I had noticed this during a pre-natal class. Her eyes moved around quickly, while she kept saying that it had always happened in her life that she found the right people in the right place, and that on that day, for example, there was the right midwife to help her breastfeed. I focused on her way of viewing her experience with extreme optimism and control. I also noticed that she had not mentioned anything about her feelings or bodily experience during labour, such as breathing or contractions, pain or worry. After a while, she asked me to pick up the baby saying, "She likes you; she remembers you very well", recalling when I held her baby a few hours after birth. Then she got out of bed, sat on the rocking chair next to me, and prepared for breastfeeding. I held the baby out to her; then she lifted her top and adjusted the baby to her breast. I did not notice any sign of discomfort in her facial expression or the position of her shoulders, as I had noticed in most first-time mothers in the very early stages of breastfeeding, either because of the milk expulsion or the unknown breastfeeding positions. Nor did I see any change in her expression. She displayed a "rigid posture". The arm that held the baby looked contracted and fairly geometrical and, together with her shoulders, reminded me of a ballerina pose.

Two days later, Andrea left the Birth Unit. One day I saw her coming back to it crying. The midwife noticed my puzzled expression and said, "It must be post-natal depression". After a while, another midwife told me that she had got mastitis and needed to spend a few days at the hospital. The day after, I had just arrived at the Birth Unit when I saw Andrea walking towards me holding the baby out. I was surprised at the way she gave me the little girl straightaway without asking. She just said that she needed a shower. I witnessed the same pattern "handing over the baby-needing a shower" in other instances. After a while, she came out of the room and walked back and forth along the corridor to reception a few times. She was holding her breasts with both hands and with an expression of pain, as if she were carrying a tray with crystal glasses in mid-air.

I visited Andrea the next day. She appeared to be delighted to see me. The baby was lying on the bed next to the mother's left side, as her right arm was on a drip. She appeared particularly glad when I approached the baby. She pointed out that she had always refused drugs and made a gesture of taking the tube off. Nor did she want to give any *"drugs"* to the baby (referring to formula milk). Mastitis was preventing her from breastfeeding, as the milk had stopped flowing. She said, "I wanted an active birth because I believe in nature. I've always thought that the best gift I could give my baby was breastmilk". I said that she had lots of gifts to give her baby, such as holding, touching, and cuddling, which were more important than the milk itself. For the first time, there was a silence. Her face suddenly became pale and her voice trembled. She was close to crying but she tried to hold it back.

Mastitis did not seem to be her central problem but a symptom or a psychosomatic strategy to avoid contact with the baby, which perhaps aroused unbearable intense emotions. This was consistent with her tendency to give her baby either to the midwife who attended her birth or to me. Over time, I came to see in her determination to breastfeed anger, struggle, and a sense of failure at not being able to do so.

When I asked Andrea if the woman I had seen leaving the room before was her mother—an indirect way of finding out about her primary relationships—she shook her head and began talking about her. "What I remember about her is going out with a friend of hers, walking around and liking the shops. My sister doesn't mind taking drugs, having sex without any precautions and yet, to my mother she has always been the perfect daughter". A midwife had told me that when her mother came to visit the baby she did not touch the baby but only repeated: "Sweetie! Sweetie!".

Then she talked about her experience as a dancer, saying that she had taken it up at a very young age and given up because of some knee problems. When she recovered, she took up contemporary dance, which she enjoyed a great deal. But her mother wanted her to be a ballerina. Then I discovered that her father was alcoholic and liked going out with different women. "He used to say that I was not a good daughter. I didn't want to go to his funeral", she said.

I asked her about her feelings while breastfeeding. When I observed her breastfeeding in the Birth Unit room, her arms and shoulders seemed immobile and stiff and her posture resembled that of a ballerina. She did not say anything about her feelings except, "When I went back home after the delivery, before getting mastitis, I used to breastfeed on a "Victorian bed", with lots of cushions and in a ballerina pose. And now . . . lots of problems". A picture of her mother arose from her gestures and words. McDougall (1989) describes how people who develop a psychosomatic symptom as a result of their incapacity to articulate the emotional suffering may unconsciously evoke in others the feelings that they themselves have repudiated. In fact, they frequently behave as their parents did when they were young. McDougall explains that because emotions are psychosomatic, the incapacity to be in touch with the child's emotional needs may lead the child to develop the symptom as a defence against the emotional suffering.

The baby looked tiny, sad, and stressed. I thought that Andrea needed to be encouraged to hold her baby and to make as much contact as possible with her, especially at this early stage of development, in order to trigger healthy interaction between them. I believed that working on the bodily contact and exploring its meaning, would enable the mother to face and overcome the crisis, and thus nurture the baby. My goal was to facilitate the establishment of the biological regulatory system of the mother–infant dyad, so that synchronization could facilitate attuned communication and interaction. In the same way, psychotherapeutic work with parents and infants is a process of sensing and communicating emotional states alongside the exploration of meanings.

My first step was to enhance Andrea's awareness that mastitis was not her true problem. After a long silence, I smiled, stroked the little girl, and said: "Don't waste time struggling with yourself for not being able to give her your milk. She needs your presence, love, holding, and touch more than your milk. As long as you struggle, your baby and yourself are missing something irreplaceable". Then I left them together.

I saw her a few more times in a baby massage class. Her anxiety about contact with the baby had subsided and there was a variety of interactions between mother and baby. The baby was apparently growing well and Andrea appeared to enjoy being with her.

Susie, Sarah and Ana

The other cases I shall present are from my work experience as an assistant and observer in a baby massage class. This special setting allowed me to observe the parent–baby interactions in the course of their development and the bonding process by observing the parent's posture, massage movements, eye contact, and voice, as well as the baby's movements and vocalizations. Their interactions during the class take the form of a dance. Mindful touching of every part of the baby's body naturally conditions the whole holding experience, and smooth and secure massage movements and rich pre-verbal communication between parent and baby provide the baby with a containing experience, a solid primary skin that contains the parts of the baby's personality as well as those of her body. On the other hand, I see in baby massage, with its closeness, skin contact, and playfulness, a way for parent and baby to get to know each other and synchronize, hence a vital part of the attachment bond, bringing security to them and instilling a sense of well-being.

1. Susie's interminable chatting and very sharp tone of voice seemed to be preventing her from getting in touch with her baby girl. Most women appeared quite happy to have a playful time with their baby. They settled on the floor in a semi-circle, each woman facing her baby, nearly ready to start the massage routine. There were eight mothers that day. I paid attention to some babies who, as they were being undressed and naked, smiled and giggled, quickly moving their tiny bodies and kicking, as if they knew what was awaiting them.

Then Susie, who had been interminably chatting at a remarkable speed and in a sharp and intense tone since her arrival, caught my attention. She was complaining about how many times a day she did the laundry for all her kids. "I certainly cannot expect any support from my husband", she said. I noticed her complaining about the laundry and various other things in the breastfeeding support class. She did it in a very humorous way, which was amusing, and at the same time irritating because it interfered with the group dynamics. Her little girl Sarah gazed into the air. Then she began to show increasing signs of discomfort that soon turned into crying. Susie kept talking in the same way, regardless of the group. She appeared not to be connected with her baby. I could see how hard it was for her to relax and let her energy flow from her hands to massage her baby.

Susie picked up her baby who was now crying and brought her to her breast, saying "shut up" in such a funny way that a few women tried hard to not to burst out laughing. I saw in the baby

Sarah's crying, standing out against the background of a joyful concert of babies vocalizing and babbling, and in Susie's chatting while women were engaged with their babies, the isolation of the mother–baby dyad. When Sarah was on the breast, she did not calm down. Susie made a further attempt, pushing her on to her breast. The baby went rigid and I thought that she might be sensing the mother's tension in holding her. Here we could see how the mother's milk flowed together with her feeling.

I approached Susie and talked to her in a slow, low-pitched voice in the hope of modulating her tone. I invited her to find a comfortable position and focus on her breathing. Then I talked to the baby very quietly, touching her tummy gently. Sarah was about to stop crying. Susie's face had changed colour and expression. I asked her if I could show the slow gentle massage movements, so I joined the group in the same routines. Sarah appeared to enjoy the drawing of the leg hand over hand through my palms and fingers from the thigh to the foot, while talking to her slowly and smiling. Susie was watching in amusement. I smiled and let her continue, while Sarah was exercising her legs by repetitive kicking and by making some sounds with her mouth.

Susie and Sarah attended the baby massage class for four months and now that Sarah is over six months old they come to the baby gymnastics class fairly regularly. I think that that time, when she was struggling with the baby's crying and I simply played with my voice to modulate hers, she had an important insight. She still entertains the group with some funny family stories but she has become much more an observer of her baby. Obviously, she has not continued to attend the baby massage class just to learn the technique, as a couple of sessions may be enough to learn the basic routines. Instead, she has learned over time and through the containment of the group that there is much more to it than the technique.

This case illustrates the mother's provision of physical and emotional containment to the baby through her touch, tone of voice, smile, eye contact, and holding. Susie's fast speech acted as a sort of shell, a second defensive skin that was preventing the baby from having a containing experience that could keep the parts of self integrated. Ruggieri & Frondaroli (1989) indicate a possible connection between style of contact and prosodic characteristics. Although loud and fast speech with a low level of contact can sometimes express a positive attitude to contact, it is also possible that, in Susie's case, the velocity of speech represented a form of physical barrier. The case also highlighted the function of the group to hold the mother's as well as the baby's feelings and to enhance their self-confidence.

2. The next case shows how emotional difficulties during her pregnancy affected a woman's interactions with her baby. Sarah held her little boy Louis as though he were something precious and fragile. I noticed that each movement occurred in slow motion and disjointedly. She sat in the corner at the end of the semicircular group, slightly behind it, and undressed her baby. She appeared shy and embarrassed. She looked at me, as I had noticed her doing in the breastfeeding class, uncertain what to do. I made encouraging eye contact with her while she began to undress her baby. The way in which she laid her baby on the floor and touched him appeared really peculiar. She seemed to be straining every movement in order not to hurt him. Her arms appeared quite stiff, her chest closed and her shoulders raised, as though she needed to protect herself.

I observed the same phenomenon when I saw Sarah breastfeeding. The shoulder of the feeding breast appeared locked and the neck pulled down into the shoulder. Her face appeared quite tense and preoccupied, giving me the impression that she was somehow far away from the baby and absorbed in emotional difficulties. There was no smile.

Louis's naked body appeared still and his eyes fixed in the air. He did not kick or stretch his legs as babies usually do during massage or even when they anticipate it. Nor did he make any vocalization. Sarah did not talk to her baby; neither did she make eye contact. She used her fingers instead of the whole hand to massage. Although the teacher recommended using the whole hand in order to feel the baby and transmit the energy, she kept using her fingertips. She really seemed afraid of damaging her baby's skin. Sarah glanced at me as if she was asking for help. I went over to her, smiled, and said that she could use a firmer touch as the baby would enjoy feeling his skin being stroked. Aware of the function of her muscle tension as a shell, and to make her aware of that, only when I felt I could, I gently laid my hand on her shoulder, releasing her tension, and letting her breathing go. Her expression turned quite intense. When I touched the baby, with the mother's consent, he did not respond with the particular joyful movements that other babies usually produce. I thought that both mother and baby could benefit from this special playtime of close mutual contact with individual counselling.

During our meeting, I gathered that Sarah had been abandoned by her husband when she was two months pregnant and that he had never seen Louis since then. She was living with her parents and expressed to me her need to have a private space with her baby. It took some time to obtain a single-parent housing allowance from the government.

Sarah attended baby massage classes regularly for the first six months and then she took up a mother-and-baby yoga class. The first time she came to the yoga class, the seven-month-old Louis appeared a fairly unconfident baby. He did not interact with other children during the first few weeks. He clung to his mother all the time. At the age of eighteen months, he was a sociable and talkative baby. Sarah appeared a fairly receptive mother. She recently started to attend a music class with Louis.

The group experience provided an important form of containment for the mother's emotions, from which Louis's development benefited. I witnessed times when the women's talk about life in a couple induced a strong feeling of solitude in her. Nevertheless, sharing difficulties with other women freed her from isolation. Furthermore, Louis's interactions with other children in a place that felt safe and the playfulness of the yoga class for both mother and baby gave him the opportunity to experience himself at his own pace and to gain self-confidence. In some way, the group was for Sarah a substitute for the lost partnership. She increasingly gained in self-confidence and overcame her depression.

3. I shall now briefly outline the case of an underweight baby. I followed up Ana in the days immediately following birth. She was disturbed by any sound. Samantha, her mother, had breast-feeding problems and was struggling with giving her the breast milk, which did not flow abundantly. A few times she complained that her baby was crying continuously and would only calm down if she was picked up, held, and rocked. The pattern of picking the baby up whenever she cried seemed to be more about the mother's own need to be held and her fear of separation from the baby. She was undergoing treatment for breast inflammation. Because her

problems seemed more emotional and relational, I thought that the baby massage class could create a special containment for both mother and baby and so dissolve the "crying–picking up pattern". There is considerable evidence that babies who are touched more gain weight faster and show better motor, emotional, and behavioural development (Field et al., 1986; Scafidi, Field, Schanberg & Bauer, 1990; Anderson, 1991).

A care programme aimed at bonding the baby to his mother's breast, like a baby kangaroo in a poncho, can save many very underweight newborn babies. The caring touch of massage throughout the body, by stimulating the nerve endings in the skin, can have even further benefits, providing an experience of integration of the parts of the baby's body and self.

When I met Samantha I explained to her all the benefits that she and her baby could obtain from a baby massage class. At first, she appeared a little sceptical. During the first massage session, I encouraged Samantha to focus on smooth and gentle touching. The baby's tiny body appeared to enjoy it and after a few weeks she had gained weight noticeably. Samantha remained fairly apprehensive with her baby, but I noticed that she did not complain about the crying–pick up pattern any more. The special contact during massage contributed to increasing the mother's and baby's confidence, promoting security and separation. Eight-month-old Ana recently started to attend the mother-and-baby yoga sessions. She still appears a bit anxious and sometimes irritable when she interacts with other children. Nevertheless, belonging to a group is helping mother and baby as they go through the transitional period of separation.

CHAPTER FOUR

Body image

While musical notes of a universal sweetness
were coming from mothers and babies of an African tribe
to spread over monuments of differing beauty and history,
I thought that we are all indeed so close to one another,
and that there are situations and languages more able than
others
to make us close.
We just need to perceive them.

All the sensory information (tactile, proprioceptive, visual, auditory, olfactory, vestibular) from the peripheral body is synthesized in the cerebral cortex (the outer layer of the brain), producing a body image. This information plays an important role in organizing posture and motor activity, both involuntary and programmed. Muscular activity is regulated by reflex pathways (involuntary) and volitional patterns located in the cerebral cortex.

The process of synthesizing the sensory information and all bodily activities begins in the primary stage of life. An attentive observer will notice how a mother during massage or any physical contact with the baby modulates her sensory channels through her voice, touch, eye contact, skin contact, facial expressions, and posture. This impinges on the infant's whole body experience and her representation of the body's boundaries and activities. Primary relationships modulate the infant's physiological activities such as breathing, heart rate, muscle tone, body temperature, postural attitudes, and motor activities, providing the baby with the formation and representation of a primary skin. In other terms, they act as regulators, in the same way that cerebral centres do. This complex process begins in the womb, as the mother's interactions with her baby, and more indirectly those with the surrounding environment, shape the foetus's overall development.

Colwyn Trevarthen (2001b) contends that babies are born with innate regulatory capacities that motivates them to engage in relationships. He stresses the fundamental role of emotion and relationships in the infant's development. To move her whole body in the space, when she starts crawling and then walking, the baby needs, as quickly and effectively as possible, cerebral and bodily information that may be representative of the body as a whole. This process leads to the development of an integrated bodyself image. This applies to adults as well but for a developing infant this process is far more delicate. Ruggieri & Sera (1996) suggest that to move her whole body, an individual needs to use certain bodily "points of reference", which regulate and balance the position of the body at rest and in motion. These points can be perceived visually or kinetically and are present in both real and imagined movements. Through her attuned bodily communication, the mother contributes to organizing the child's points of reference, therefore, her movements in space and her way of monitoring her posture. The basis of this process is the infant's trust in her parent, which forms the foundation of her self-esteem. This psychophysiological learning process relies on the mother–infant relationship and the child feeling "supported" by a key figure leads to self-support, grounding, and independence.

I am interested in exploring the relationship between posture, movement, primary interactions, and trust. Trust is a psychophysiological learning process that manifests itself in an integrated and flexible bodyself image. Baby massage and mother-and-baby yoga classes later on are ideal organizers of the baby's points of reference.

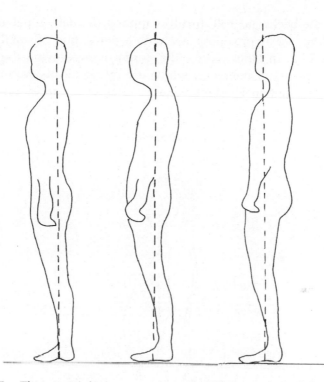

Figure 2. The gravity line passes through different points of the body. This is because we balance and counterbalance the gravity line to adjust the diversions caused by postural patterns.

Once the baby is able to crawl or to stand, with hugs and kisses a parent can engage her in some simple games to maintain the flexibility of her spine. Bending backwards is a movement that children enjoy from a very early age. This movement keeps the front of the body, the abdomen, chest and shoulders open and relaxed, and strengthens the back, organizing the focal points. This is of great importance for good posture.

However, these benefits would not be possible if the child did not trust her parent. While doing the bends, the quality of touch and the way of "bouncing" the baby are paramount for attuning to the baby's pace and increasing her confidence. After having rolled the baby back through her arms for the very first time, a parent will notice her mixed facial expressions, partly of enjoyment, partly of fear of the new hazardous experience. However, if the parent, soon after the backward roll, firmly supports the baby's pelvis while standing, she is providing her with a perception of stability and grounding. In other words, the parent is organizing the baby's bodily points of reference, which are by no means disconnected from her emotional and relational key figures or earliest caregivers.

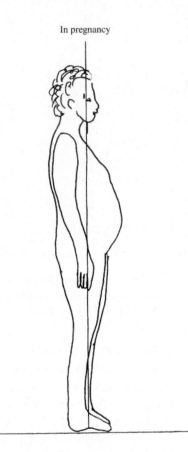

In pregnancy

Figure 3. The extra weight in front makes the body tend to fall forwards. The muscles at the back have to work more to maintain the balance. The way a woman compensates for the increased muscle activity will reflect her bodyself image. A tendency to over tense posture, resistance to the emotional and body changes, low "trust" in herself and self-support, produce excessive tension to balance the force of gravity and hinder the BI harmony. As a result the pregnant woman is likely to pull her head and upper back "backwards" creating a vicious circle which further hinders the BI fluctuation

For instance, a major important point is the abdomen, the centre of life and stability. By supporting the baby's pelvis in the backbends, a parent is also partly organizing the baby's posture, shaping her trust in herself and in the world, thus providing not only a bodily and emotional experience but also a social one.

Each movement or gesture of either the mother or the baby is associated with the basic muscle tone, which is the source of information for modulating our postural attitudes. This basic muscular activity occurs in close conjunction with the parent's and the baby's own emotions, feelings, and reveries. The primary function of bodily points of reference as organizers of postural attitudes is apparent in some clinical exercises. For example, when an individual is asked to change the parts of the body used as focal points in her movements and at rest, important changes occur in her feelings about tension, pleasure, and stability. This finding has been demonstrated by some research by Ruggieri et al. (1986).

The woman's use of new perceptual points during pregnancy, resulting from the major postural and emotional changes that modify her bodyself image, contributes to organizing a core of reference points in the pre-natal baby. To move her body into the space, the pregnant woman needs to deploy new information from the body and thus a new representation of her self and body. The body's focal points are not easily identified because they operate unconsciously. Their roots reside in the mother's primary "trust" experiences. The woman's trust in herself is fundamental to accepting the new physical and emotional changes, adjusting the body to the new state and therefore developing harmonious movements. Her attitude to her bodyself shapes the relationship with the baby and her development from conception. Rigid resistance to the changes induced by pregnancy can cause muscle tightening, stiff posture, restricted movements and gestures and, as a result, inappropriate use of the body's focal points. This may impinge on the baby's motor activity in the womb and thus on the organization of her primary postural attitudes. The foetal environment is enveloped by the placenta and the uterine wall, a smooth muscle whose activity corresponds to the mother's mental, emotional, and physical state.

The "Leicester Motherhood Project" is consistent with this line of thinking. The project was designed to investigate, in a controlled prospective study, the effects of raised maternal age on woman's experience of motherhood (Berryman & Windridge, 1995). While the studies compared older (thirty-five-year-old plus) and younger mothers, it was found that differences between the groups could not be attributed to biological age *per se*. The observed differences recorded in this study revealed that in the context of the care of new mothers, older women may differ from younger women in a range of attitudes, needs, and behaviours that alter the experience of pregnancy and motherhood. The mother's attitudes, developing in relationship with her primary experiences and life history, can be a more powerful factor than ageing in the experience of pregnancy for her and her baby, and in her parenting.

According to a psychophysiological or integrated model of body image, the distinction between body image and body schema does not hold. The cortical representation of the bodily experience is multi-dimensional and as fluctuating as the bodily functions. Feelings and sensations continuously provide feedback via our nervous system to the brain, including during sleep. Body image cannot therefore be considered a static mental representation of our body. In many kinds of psychophysiological disturbance, such as anorexia, the body image is perceived as rigid and is resistant to bodily and emotional changes. At the basis of the overwhelming fear of consuming food and thus putting on weight, a major feature of anorexia, there is an altered body image that has its kernel in the primary "trust" experiences.

In Fisher's view (1986), an individual may continuously and simultaneously be monitoring different aspects of her body such as its position in space and the integrity of its boundaries. According to Ruggieri's integrative model of body image (Ruggieri & Sera, 1996), two activities develop in the cortical area: (1) synthesizing the sensory information from the body to produce a complete representation of its structure and activities; (2) modulating the activity of the bodyself to maintain a correspondence between the cortical image and the body's activity. Between the two processes there is a continuous feedback relationship. The cortical image acts as a regulator of muscular, respiratory and cardiac activity, tone of voice, postural attitude, gestures, and movement.

The right hemisphere is, more than the left, deeply connected not only with the limbic system (particularly involved in emotion) but also with both the sympathetic and the parasympathetic branches of the autonomic nervous system. Therefore, the representation of visceral and body states, and thus the body image, is predominantly under control of the non-dominant hemisphere. The right cerebral cortex rather than the left seems to be the site of an integrated map of the bodily state and to play a primary role in the regulation of important physiological and endocrinological functions. As the limbic system is also connected with the hypothalamus-pituitary-adrenocortical axis, the right cerebral cortex seems to be primarily involved in the vital survival functions that enable the organism to cope with stress (Shore, 2001).

In accordance with Bowlby's view that the infant's "capacity to cope with stress" is related to certain maternal behaviours (1969, p. 344), the attachment relationship shapes the development of the infant's cerebral stress-coping-system that acts at an unconscious level, and of the infant's representation of bodyself states. The brain, and the right hemisphere in particular, stores an internal model of the attachment relationship containing strategies of psychophysiological regulation that operate particularly in stressful situations. The infant's bodyself image thus takes shape in close relationship with the attachment model. The seeds of this may reside in pre-natal life.

Bodyself image displays itself very early in life through all the aspects of body language. Body image plays a fundamental role in the movement of the whole body into the space, modulating the relationship between posture and movement. Bodily activities, such as muscular tone related to postural attitudes, movements, gestures, breathing and so on, are thus partly the reproduction of the cortical image of the bodyself. The representation of bodily activities is formed in relationship with the earliest experience of "pleasure", which opens up the sensory channels and the mind. Consistently with this, Ruggieri's research and clinical work (Ruggieri & Sera, 1996) has found that when the individuals are asked to change some perceptual points of reference, and consequently their postural attitude, changes in their subjective feeling about muscular tension, pleasure, and stability or instability are reported.

The experience of pleasure involves respiratory, cardiac, and muscular changes, and results from the synthesis of sensory information with bodily or mental activities. Because of this synthesis, pleasure is an integrated experience of mind and body. There are immense benefits for a woman and her baby from enjoying her pregnancy and the relationship with her baby. The mother's enjoyment and expression of her love are shown in the way she handles her baby in all the day-to-day details of maternal care (Abram, 1996). Muscle tightening, as an expression of a second defensive skin, due to a primary skin impaired by a lack of containing experiences, diminishes such experiences of pleasure.

Fear and anxiety have the same effect. In fact, the associated high muscular tension hinders the flow of information between body and mind and inhibits the fluctuation of the body image. Posture is shaped not only by primary experiences; it is also continuously modulated by the environment and social relationships. Either way, posture and body language affect interactions in the present. Breathing, muscle tone, and body language, as well as body image, are organized through a long process that starts very early in conjunction with the pre-natal and post-natal environment. Breathing and posture are like the bed and banks of a river that determine the course along which the water flows; they gradually erode and shift but this is a slow process.

This line of thinking may raise a question as to the part played by genetics. An individual's genetic background is moulded by pre-natal and post-natal primary experiences. Genetic and learning processes are inseparable and interrelated. The mother's belief system, alongside other factors, has a significant impact on her emotional state and her body image and influences foetal development in conjunction with her genetic inheritance. Unfortunately, a large number of researchers and child-care professionals still overlook this subtle linkage.

Body image, movement, and gesture

A gesture is a psychophysiological pattern that involves our muscular activity, emotional life, and belief system. When restrained by excessive muscle tension, a gesture can reflect inhibited emotion. In the long term, this phenomenon affects our well-being in the same way that a part of the body does when it stops functioning properly.

To restore a fragmented gesture, a physiotherapist as well as a psychotherapist will find it very helpful to bear in mind the close relationships between the different levels of functioning. There are still many physiotherapists who believe the cause of back pain to be necessarily localized in the back. They therefore manipulate this area and do not even consider that a different area or an emotional disturbance might be involved.

The communicative function of a gesture also has to be considered, as it is a powerful cue in the repertoire of body language. Freeing a gesture from its inhibiting source, both at the emotional and the muscular level, means enriched and effective communication, smoother posture, and a larger repertoire of movements and expressions. It often creates a feeling of fulfilled internal space that allows a richer perception of the external social and physical environment.

These considerations, which concern human beings of all ages and all levels of well-being—physical, emotional, behavioural, and communicative—point to the importance of unconstricted caring gestures from a parent while interacting with the developing baby. The infant's gestural language is shaped by the way in which parents deal with their body language in the course of their interactions with her.

Any gesture or movement evolves through a balanced interplay of all parts of the body. While some muscles contract, others relax during a movement. For a gesture to evolve smoothly, everything needs to happen in harmony. The same occurs with facial expressions. However, if a muscle or group of muscles produces a prolonged contraction rather than contracting and relaxing alternately, the evolution of the movement, gesture, or expression is constricted. The excessive tension prevents the muscle from passing through the relaxed phase. In clinical work, we often find emotional blockage at the basis of this pattern. Some individuals use held-back patterns as defensive adaptive mechanisms to repress feelings that they are unable to acknowledge.

Smooth and balanced posture and movements require a rhythmic sequence of muscle contraction and relaxation. In most psychosomatic disturbances, these rhythmic patterns are altered. A prolonged muscle contraction (due to excessive tension) can be conceived as a "break point", a point that alters the natural evolution of a movement or gesture, the perception of the body and self, and therefore hinders the fluctuation of the bodyself image. We can change the way we use some parts of the body by acknowledging the emotional link. As a result, we can improve the general use of our body and self and experience a greater freedom of gesture. The sense of self will simultaneously change, as the use of our body is a reflection of our self and vice versa. Breathing will change as well, and the sensory channels open wide. The sensory channels are the windows that put us in touch with the environment, enhancing our perception of it as well as of our bodyself and enriching our communication skills.

Visibly, some individuals use a very small percentage of their potential. They have grown so accustomed to their habitual uncomfortable posture that they are not aware of the multitude of mental and bodily strategies. Learning occurs together with feelings and dramatically involves the body and the muscle memory. This is especially visible in the young baby, whose learning involves the whole body in a dramatic way. What we learn is recorded in our feelings and muscle memory and it manifests in our posture, gestures, and the way we deal with relationships. For example, a baby records the mother's voice not just by hearing it but also, and more importantly, by sensing the vibrations and rhythm of the sounds in her skin and muscles. She records its emotional quality. Together with her touch, eye contact, facial expression, and smell, the mother's voice modulates the baby's muscular and emotional activity, as well as other physiological activities such as respiratory, cardiac, and digestive functions, and by doing so she shapes the baby's posture and gestures.

The repertoire of the mother's body language which contributes to forming the infant's bodyself image and posture, seems to be stored not just in the infant's brain but also in her body. This complements neuropsychological studies that now reveal that the right hemisphere and not the verbal-linguistic one, developing later, is the site of autobiographical and bodyself memory (Fink et al., 1996; Shore, 1994; Shore, 2003). Emotional and muscular systems thus have a formative influence on verbal and cognitive development, in contrast to previous theories. Cognitive psychology, seeking to explain psychological processes in terms of processing sensory information, may be losing ground.

By acknowledging their own feelings and body language, parents undertake a journey through the exploration of the bodyself's creative potential. This refers not only to parents but to all human beings. The primary muscle memory, where our earliest experiences are recorded, shapes the image of our bodyself and, likewise, the bodyself image affects our movements, posture, and body language. These processes in childhood have an impact that endures into our adult lives, which thus cannot be understood in isolation from them.

Posture: from the primary experience to pregnancy, labour, and birth

An individual's posture is a response to a wide range of internal and external stimuli, mechanical, emotional, or social. Posture can also act a stimulus for inducing comfort or discomfort, stability or instability. These feelings impact on our close and social relationships. Emotional and postural balance is related to a fulfilled and integrated personality. I shall illustrate this concept with a spectrum ranging from "immobility/rigidity" to "escape/avoidance", with "stability" and dynamism at the centre.

```
                        Stability
Escape/Avoidance ──────────* *──────────Immobility/Rigidity
                        Dynamism
```

The capacity to "stay" and "be present" is not meant just in psychological terms. The "dynamic stability" is linked to continuous minor changes in muscle tone and a fluctuating body image, which allow the body and self to counterbalance gravity without excessive resistance. This process makes an active birth successful, when the woman in labour can play with her bodyself and gravity in a sort of rhythmic dance. These small changes in muscle tone allow an individual to produce the tiny swinging movements that are necessary to exert a force to balance and counterbalance gravity. Rigid resistance to these movements by muscle tightening or postural stiffness leads to useless effort and wasted energy. Immobility, as a consequence of excessive tension, hinders the appropriate expression of emotions and locks gestures and movements.

Conversely, flight is usually a response to anxiety and fear. Like immobility, it hinders communication.

For a pregnant woman or new mother, it is crucial to accept the bodily and emotional changes and the new responsibilities. Self-acceptance can enrich her sense of identity, which will enable her to sense and understand her baby's needs and all aspects of her personality. In this process, being able to find "self-support" through some external support from a familiar environment is very important.

The human posture does not allow static support. The body weight rests alternately on different points of the feet, allowing our body to be cushioned. The feet are an important base of support and the sense of grounding pervades the whole body, which is reflected in a confident, balanced posture. The toes spread for stability. Their sophisticated sensitivity and co-ordination are constrained in civilized life by shoes and loss of contact with the ground. The result is the inability to rely on them as a base of support for an effective posture. The smoothness and harmony of posture and its relationship with the feet is noticeable in women from Bali while walking. They articulate their feet, alternately flexing and stretching their toes.

A balanced posture requires an effective bodyself support (both psychological and postural) for relief of excessive tension. There are four primary interrelated aspects of posture—support, balance, weight, and gravity. The perception of our weight is related to our muscular tension. Effective support in our bodyself impinges on our weight perception, as it favours an even distribution of tension. An obese woman can demonstrate good posture if her self-acceptance lets herself produce gestures and movements that are free of tension. Conversely, a slim woman is likely to perceive her body as heavy if she produces high psychomuscular tension. Her movements will generate effort and tiredness due to wasted energy and her posture will look heavy.

The capacity to find effective support in our bodyself is connected with self-trust and takes shape during our primary experiences. The special attachment that develops between mother and baby is the baby's first experience of being entirely loved and of trusting another human being. This unique relationship is likely to mould the way in which the baby will deal with other people throughout her life. The baby searches for a balanced posture and before she can walk she uses her parents' hands, the wall, or other objects to help herself stand. She will be able to stand up and walk independently as she finds a form of self-support and masters her posture and movements in the space. Holding and sustaining the infant in her earliest experiences is a crucial way for the parents to help her to find a pivot in her own bodyself, from which self-trust builds up. This learning process is psychophysiological, as it involves the baby's sensory, motor, emotional, and relational experiences. Sitting up, crawling, standing, walking, manipulating objects, and speaking are developmental stages undertaken with the mediation of the primary relationships.

The child needs to experience her "self" and her abilities by going through each stage at her own pace, without being pressurized. Only by doing so can she acquire the belief in a true "experienced bodyself". The meaning of the word "experience" from its Latin derivation, is "trying to do something". It refers to the intention to know something, like the French word "experience" which means "experiment". In this process of self-experiment, parents are attentive observers, helping when the child signals her need for help. It is far easier to help a child to retain her natural good posture and skills than to regain them. By helping the child practise her amazing flexibility, for instance, by massaging or taking her to a mother-and-baby class, or simply being with her while playing at home, the parent helps her not to lose it. The upright posture, never witnessed in the animal kingdom, offers major advantages, allowing free movement in any direction and freeing the hands for creative achievements. On the other hand, this posture can lose its balance and advantages quite easily. For instance, sitting on the lower back (as most of our furniture encourages) is detrimental to good posture. This hinders the movement of the spine and has a major effect on bodily activities and learning abilities. A healthy mind develops in a healthy body and vice versa, and this is especially true in the first three years of life, when the child undergoes crucial developments and her actions are closely related to her emotions and mental states.

Sitting, like standing, involves balance; to find a balance and sit unaided, the infant must feel securely grounded. This state derives from a secure relationship with her parents, and is related to the parents' self-confidence, which expresses itself through a secure and firm touch while handling the infant. To establish the foundations of good posture, a parent needs to help the child practise sitting upright and the subsequent achievements by observing her. This allows the baby to observe herself, thus to frame her body image. This integrated map will simultaneously help her to develop more fluid, co-ordinated, and intelligent movements. The child's body image is like the prow of a ship. It needs a skilled captain to guide it in the right direction.

Parents, by being present at each of the baby's achievements, enable her to accomplish a secure and balanced position. During mother-and-baby yoga classes, in which mothers and babies freely play together and practise yoga, I came to see the importance for a baby of "staying" with every position and movement achieved, in order to be able to move confidently to the next step at her own pace. More importantly, the attuned presence of the parent and the support from her at a time of enjoyment shared with other children encourages the child in her achievements.

Trusting the caregiver is a key process for the development of the internal parental model. It enables the child to master the anxiety of separation and grow in confidence, as she feels them inside her and is aware that they are always present and will never abandon her. Once able to master this primary anxiety, she will grow independent, to move, explore, and experience a broader and richer space, which, along with the primary objects—mother, father, and any time of contact with them—nurtures her internal space. The separation anxiety, rather than being stored in the muscles, is thus relieved through creative movements, exploration, and play. This strengthens the child's ego and her relationship with reality. An ego that is open to enrichment from experience is likely to manifest itself in smooth and comfortable posture. Interestingly, the word "comfortable" means "with strength", since "*com*" means "with" and "*fort*" means "strength". A body that retreats in fear of falling increases tension and tightens its muscles and posture and this restricts its potential. In this instance, the child's defences against her fear may make her appear clumsy in all her movements, acting as an impediment to her development.

The foundations of this primary period are laid during pregnancy, when the relation between balance, weight and gravity is paramount in finding an effective self-support in the body. The centre of gravity moves further forward and away from the spine. The extra weight in front (baby, placenta, and breast) makes the body tend to fall forwards. The muscles at the back have to work harder to maintain balance and the woman tends to pull her back backwards and to curve the spine to compensate. However, this causes backache and strain, impacting on her emotional and mental state, the baby's ability to accommodate to the pelvic space, and the relationship with her.

Pregnant women are usually recommended to keep the back as straight as possible and to tighten the abdominal muscles when standing or walking, to lessen the protuberance. I believe that this postural process correlates with the woman's attitudes, motivations, emotions, and reverie. For instance, rejection of the emotional and bodily changes, low self-trust and self-support, or fear are generally associated with excessive tension and postural tightening to balance gravity. This makes a pregnant woman feel heavier and tired, which may alter the perception of her body image. As a result, the pregnant woman is likely to pull her head and upper back far further backwards, setting up a vicious circle that is going to hinder her body image from adjusting to the new state. Her withdrawn posture in this case is a concrete portrait of her emotional retreat.

A postural pattern such as closed and lifted shoulders, a constricted chest that inhibits breathing, and neck pulled down into the shoulders is the portrait of fear, anxiety, and lack of self-trust or external support. Panic attacks are also characterized by altered breathing. The pattern described above may be persistent in pregnancy and thus affect the labour and birth process. Breathing, labour contractions, and gravity work in synchronization. To let her body be guided by the process of labour, a woman needs to feel and balance gravity effectively. In order to respond to that need, it is worth finding support in her feet and a steady grounding. The conscious perception of the bodyself can enable a woman to be led by gravity and by her breathing, as by a sea current. Resistance to the flow of gravity, however, may prevent the uterine muscle from stretching, relaxing, and contracting alternately and the pelvis from dilating in rhythm with the breathing and the baby's movements.

Shoulders, pelvis, and feet work together as important key body points. During my observational study in pre-natal yoga classes, I found significant links in some women between immobilized ribcage and shoulders and emergency caesarean section that was due to incomplete dilation of the pelvis. Shoulders and pelvis work together during labour and tightening of the shoulders and chest, with resulting constricted breathing, prevent the pelvis from opening. This could hinder the birth process. When I listened to these women's birth stories, I found that their reports focused upon pain and fear. Very few details of breathing, labour contractions, or the baby's movements emerged, while generally these were vivid in the birth stories of women who gave birth without complications. Taking into account the complex significance of birth in a woman's life history, presumably some women can develop resistances to giving birth to their baby and so to separating from them. These psychological resistances impact on the entire body, altering the birth process.

In order for the mother to be able to express her bodyself harmoniously and to resonate and dance with her baby in labour, it is essential that she feels secure in the birth environment and receives appropriate emotional support. An experienced doula (supportive lay woman), midwife, or nurse will calmly and intensely help her to cope with labour and will be a reassuring and constant presence for both parents. This key figure, whom the mother-to-be can trust and feel supported by, will enhance her natural abilities. It is important that she sees the midwife throughout her pregnancy in order to build up the trust and internalize a maternal model that is calm, nurturing, accepting, and holding. In one study, (Sosa, Kennell, Klaus, Robertson & Urrutia, 1980), the "doula"-assisted mothers showed more attuned interaction with their infants, with more smiling, talking and stroking, than the mothers who did not have a doula. In another study (Wolman, Chalmers, Hofmeyr & Nikoden, 1993), the supported mothers developed relationships with their babies significantly more quickly than the non-supported mothers. They also reported picking up their crying babies more frequently, showed a more positive attitude to mothering, and perceived themselves as more attuned to their babies.

Imagination and visualization

Imagination induces a form of cortical activity that, through the nerves, modulates muscle tone and breathing. Therefore, it has effects on posture and bodyself image. When we visualize something, particularly when we are emotionally involved or it has a particular meaning in our life, there are changes in breathing, heart rate, body temperature, and muscle tone.

We should remember that basic muscular activity even at rest is rhythmic and involves different muscles. The proprioceptive signals do not reach the cerebral cortex at the same time. The muscular system is continuously traversed by minor motor activities throughout the body that are like a whole wave passing through it. The optimal postural tone is the result of a fluctuating activity of alternate contraction and relaxation of small motor units. This physiological synchronization can be equated with a fluctuating body image, whereas high tension hinders the wave-like activity of the small motor units, restricting the perception of the bodyself. As a result, the perception of the surrounding environment is also impoverished. The objective of the imagery techniques is to find a new effective base of support in the bodyself (self-trust) and a new postural tone. They can be part of a programme of body image treatment aimed at enhancing the perception of the bodyself and the feeling of fulfilment and integration, and at encouraging an individual to explore her own creativity and resources.

To highlight the power of visualization, I shall report part of one woman's birth story: "I couldn't let my body go, I was afraid of not being able to manage it. But it was when it was suggested that I visualize a wave going down through my body that I felt I was being led by it. I felt confident enough to cope with the contractions and the pain". The visualized wave acted as a trigger for the labour process. Interestingly, while talking, she was reproducing with her hands and arms the wave movement as perceived inside her body. The whole gesture was one of containment. She was drawing a picture of her feelings. An increasing number of women receive epidural analgesia or other kinds of medical intervention as a method of pain control. In some situations, the sensation of the contractions causes enough pain to be intensely uncomfortable. However, many women are not aware of the powerful natural resources of their bodyself. Every technological innovation needs to be assessed not only for the risks and benefits but also for its effect on the birth experience and on the interactions between mother and baby (Fox, 1979; Sepkoski, 1985; Murray, Dolby, Nation & Thomas, 1981). Babies whose mothers have an epidural often have difficulty in catching on to breastfeeding. Some mothers also feel that they have been deprived of the birth experience because they cannot feel their body or their babies' movements fully and cannot control the labour process. Epidurals may counteract the release of oxytocin that naturally occurs at birth and that encourages close interaction between mother and baby.

Visualization can help focus on feeling and enhance awareness of what is happening to the bodyself in labour. It can be used to lower the level of anxiety about pregnancy or labour and birth. In fact, a high level of anxiety and fear, as a state of general arousal or alertness, disorientates and therefore alters the perception of what is happening to the birthing bodyself. Imagery can help to reactivate the sensory channels and connect them with the cognitive and emotional processes. A smell, even the memory of a smell, can induce the visualization of something associated with it, and a feeling or sensation. Sound or touch can have the same power. A particular way of touching our skin can arouse an intense feeling, the seeds of which are stored in muscle memory during our primary relationships. I assume that some likes or dislikes of certain sounds, tones, or rhythms have been channelled by the earliest voices and vibrations imprinted on our bodyself during primary life. As an example of how the sight, smell or visualization of a certain object can trigger an emotional or physiological process, individuals who are allergic to roses can experience an asthma attack just by looking at a paper rose, or others, sensitive to vapours, can experience an asthma attack when watching a steam train at the cinema.

Imagery can provide a means of exploring our potential and rediscovering the wholeness of our being, freeing us from repeated, unconscious patterns. If emotional tension is reflected in muscle tightening, locked gestures, and constricted breathing, some imaginative exercises can help to relieve anxiety, distress, depression, headache, backache, and so on. Imagination can in fact adjust the muscle tone, bringing changes to the bodyself representation. Any kind of body image rehabilitation needs to focus on the bodily cues, as any change in the body representation derives from a modification in muscle tone and posture. In a breathing rehabilitation, the client, by touching her chest, abdomen, and all the muscles involved, feeling their movements and possibly observing them in the mirror, can enhance the awareness of the physiology of breathing. The therapist's touch, in a proper setting, can bring new adjustments to breathing and the body image. Some individuals get so used to an unhealthy way of breathing and body image that they do not realize this until they experience modifications. The new experience adjusts the mental representation of breathing and the body image, which in turn will feed back the peripheral sensations. New perceptions will arise, leading to a revitalized breathing.

Freeing ourselves of repeated behavioural or postural patterns implies a capacity for self-observation. While practising breathing rehabilitation, if the woman feels any resistance to mobilizing the chest and freeing the breathing, she may need to look into herself and explore the emotional connection with the muscular tension. For instance, if there is any locked-in anger, visualizing the anger flowing from the body with each wave-like breath is a means of relieving it. She can imagine walking, running, or dancing in a meadow or flying in a sky with clouds. Any imagined movement has the power to release the tension, since the brain sends messages to the muscles even if the body is stationary.

Colours can also help to change body temperature, muscle tone, and breathing: clouds and sky can give an individual fresh energy and lower the body temperature raised by the anger. Colours can induce emotional states, calmness, lightness, excitement, and so on. These imagery exercises, done once a day, can help the individual to find a private space for the self, a dimension for self-discovery.

The parent-to-be can benefit from the discovery of the internal space of her bodyself. This space is fundamental to communicating with the baby in the womb and to building up a triangular relationship with her. The mother's bodyself, and indirectly the father's, contribute to moulding the space of the womb. Imagery and visualization can be a vital bridge for communicating with the baby, especially during pregnancy and labour. It is worth practising the imagery exercises with a therapist or support figure who is specialized in observational and body image techniques at first, in order to become able to use them alone.

CHAPTER FIVE

Voice and body image

We teach love with our gestures, more than with our words.
We love through touch and breathing;
the child feels whether the hands are loving
or whether they are careless, or rejecting.
Muscles obey our intentions and feelings
Words can lie; muscles and gestures cannot.
Hands can be distracted, as can our brain.

Colwyn Trevarthen (1999) has made rich use of micro-descriptions of mothers and infants in "proto-conversation" to explore the dynamics of the infant's first relationship. His study of communicative and co-operative exchanges between infants and adults brought about radical change, undermining the reductive cognitive perspective and the classical psychoanalytic models. Since the late 1970s, he has conducted research that reviews the very young baby's emotional, communicative, and relational capacities. In contrast with the idea of babies as unskilled, Trevarthen sheds light on the baby's innate musical intelligence, narrative awareness, and capacity to engage in relationships.

The sounds a mother makes, including "motherese" or baby talk, vocalizations, and rhythmic songs and rhymes, are an important element of bonding. From the moment that she first responds to sound around seven months' gestation, the infant has been hearing her mother's voice. Her body moves in rhythm with her mother's speech patterns, and the high-pitched tone her mother uses when talking to her is particularly reassuring.

If mother sings a song or tells a story during daily massage, the infant will learn to associate certain sounds with massage; by repeating her name and using the words "relax", "you are safe", she is teaching her how to release tension. Through mirroring, the mother is also nurturing her sense of self. The baby acquires knowledge about her own body and self as her mother shows her how to relax a tense arm, or helps her to release painful gas. Therefore, the rhythmic pattern of bonding unfolds day by day and a real mutual trust develops.

In the particular case of infant massage, daily massage enables a parent to understand the baby's body language, her rhythms of communication, her threshold for stimulation, and how her body looks and feels when she is tense or at ease. The mother's awareness of the baby's cues and her extraordinary sensitivity to her body language helps her to regulate her vocal tone and muscular tension while interacting with her. A true communication is initiated based on this rhythmic modulation.

The mother's voice plays an important role in getting in touch with her baby, with its tone, pitch, and rhythm, acting as a melody. This can have the same effect as a lullaby. Babies move in rhythm with the mother's voice. Listening to music, as well as to the parent's voice, is an active process involving the baby's whole body and inducing muscle tone variations. Listening is like dancing, although the body expresses only minor movements and looks stationary.

I often observe mother–baby proto-conversation. Very often "motherese" sounds, such as "ch ch ch ch . . . ch ch", are accompanied by a gesture such as holding the baby's foot and bouncing it in synchrony. The mother's sounds are like an instrument such as a percussive drum. The baby, at exactly the same time, is cooing like a flute, clarinet or cello. Mother–baby proto-conversation involves a form of dance that is not unlike jazz or tango. The mother's voice and her graceful gestures play with the baby as if she were a resonating instrument. The whole conversation appears like a sinusoid or a display of pitch curves with rising or falling curves of sound. Music has many features in common with mother–infant proto-conversation. A piece of music without words tells a story that is mainly sensed and interpreted, just like mother–baby proto-conversation. Therefore, like an orchestrated melody, the mother's voice is tremendously communicative and affects the child's development.

Using music and dance in a clinical research study at the University of Rome (Ruggieri & Guistini, 1991; Ruggieri & Katsnelson, 1996), we found changes in body temperature, breathing, muscle tone (shown by electromyography), posture, and pain relief. One individual may feel the vibrations produced by certain musical notes in specific parts of her body in a different way from others. Some observational and research evidence (Vernon, 1933; Il'ina & Rudneva, 1972; Ruggieri & Katsnelson, 1996) made us hypothesize a link between the sensitivity of specific parts of the body and certain musical notes. We found, for instance, that generally low-pitched notes reached lower parts of the body. This finding needs to be tested by further research. The relationship between body image, voice, and posture is a new field of investigation and our results show significant links.

An individual's receptiveness to specific musical sounds may be associated with her unique way of monitoring her muscle tone throughout the body, thus by her posture. The earliest sounds the baby encounters, which usually come from the voice of a primary caregiver, are recorded in the baby's muscles and skin and may later orientate her sensitivity and preferences to sounds. A high level of tension in the caregiver, expressed through a tense voice, will act as a barrier to vibrations. Vibrations can also modify posture, either reducing or increasing muscle tension. For instance, during baby massage, pleasant rhythmic tunes in the background may inspire smooth movements.

Voice expresses emotion by tempo, volume, timbre, or "voice quality". Voice can give us information about the degree of tension or relaxation. High tension in the motor system in the mother's throat, where her sounds are being made, also manifests in the way she holds her baby. Lynne Murray of the Winnicott Unit in Reading studied the relationship between sounds emitted by a depressed mother and her baby's responses, and compared these with the relationship between sounds emitted by a happy mother and her baby's responses (Trevarthen, 1999). Both cases were recorded when the baby was eight weeks and then six months old. In the earlier recording, the depressed mother was unable to communicate with her baby, but four months later she had recovered from her depression. When she was depressed, there was a dramatic drop in the pitch range of her talk with her baby and the content of her sentences was quite negative. When she was happy, she talked to her six-month-old baby playfully, and the pitch of her speech was much higher.

Voice is not just heard but sensed. Listening to music or a voice is an experience of contact, which has the same effect as touching and can have the power of modulating a relationship, just like an orchestral conductor. Moreover, voice is not just sounds or vibrations producing muscle tone variations in the speaker and in the listener. Vibrations are modulated by emotions, so through them the baby connects with the mother's internal world and recognizes the quality of her emotions. The voice, its tones, and energy level communicate emotion and have a direct effect on the baby. Movements, gestures, eye contact, and voice are all conditioned by emotions. For instance, a depressive state characterized by low muscular tone manifests itself through slow movements, a flat, low-pitched, and monotonous voice, and reduced eye contact. Numerous studies illustrate the sensitivity of young infants to the quality of their interpersonal engagement. The infant internalizes the mother's mental state and the reciprocal effects on the relationship, which impinges on her development (Murray & Stein, 1991; Murray, 1997a; Murray, 1997b). Hopkins (1990) describes cases in which a slumped and resigned state or lack of physical vigour in the infant are a response to inadequate holding and handling, reflecting the mother's state.

I shall report the case of a baby who peed on the carpet during a post-natal class. Her mother appeared quite annoyed and the tension in her facial expression was fairly evident. As she started talking to the baby in a very sharp and irritated way while cleaning him up, he burst out crying. Many babies cry while their mothers are changing their nappies. The baby might have been sensing the changes in her touch, handling, voice, and facial expressions. Conversely, I have seen babies enjoying having their nappies changed, while their mothers play with vocalizations and funny facial expressions or when music is on.

Sometimes her voice does not express what a mother would like it to, because, for instance, of tension in the jaw, lips, neck, chest, or abdomen, as the whole body is involved in speaking. In labour, for instance, the sound vibrations produced are directed towards the areas that are more involved in the process. Deep downward sounds are connected with abdominal breathing and, when labour runs smoothly, are likely to be attuned to the contractions and the baby's movements. By contrast, screaming in fear produces opposing upward vibrations, which travel away from the body. Moreover, screaming mainly involves the chest, increases its tension, breaks breathing down, and prevents the vibrations from reaching the baby and thus facilitating her descent. Lack of correspondence between the actual emotion and the voice quality due to excessive tension causes miscommunications that impinge on the child's development.

The baby senses the mother's emotions through her vocal and muscular vibrations. Breathing plays an important role in producing sounds and letting our emotions flow. Excessive tension may inhibit communication. For instance, when we talk to a distant individual we tend to raise our pitch, but, beyond a certain limit, this has the opposite effect to what is intended. Too high a pitch travels a shorter distance, because we produce unnecessary tension that breaks up vibrations. Likewise, when we quarrel, communication can break down for two reasons: the tension kills our vocal sounds and prevents us from feeling the vibrations of the other person's voice; the other person's tension also increases and so we may both remain locked behind our barriers.

By contrast, a clear and long-lasting sound is produced by balanced muscle tone and low pitch, particularly when they are full of emotional content. Our muscle tone can be equated with the strings of a piano, which can be in or out of tune. Deep sounds, accompanied by deep breathing, can help relieve tension and let emotions flow out; therefore, they can have a healing effect. Producing primitive sounds that involve the whole body can be an effective exercise for relieving tension not only in the jaw but throughout the body. The changes that the mother has undergone during pregnancy and delivery, the demands of caring for a new baby, and the lack of sleep all contribute to a tension and anxiety that can become habitual in the early months of parenthood. In fact, it is essential that mother feels what is happening to her body—when she is tensing up or holding her breath—in order to be able to relieve tensions. Babies are amazingly sensitive to every nuance of the caregiver's communication. If the mother says "relax" with a furrowed brow or sharp voice, the message sent by the furrowed brow or tone of voice is much more powerful than the words.

In "active birth", a woman during labour is encouraged to do whatever she feels like doing, to move and produce any sounds freely and to let all her energy flow. Deep sounds facilitate the contractions and the baby's descent through the pelvic canal, as they involve the abdominal muscles and breathing. A woman in labour can be helped by imagining that her deep sounds, breathing, and contractions have a massaging effect on her baby. Downward labour sounds can be considered signs of the mother's focus on her bodyself and on her baby, the connection between mind and body, and her presence in the labour and birth process. The abdomen is the centre of emotional life. Excessively high and sharp sounds, such as those produced by screaming from anxiety or fear, mainly involve the chest. The vibrations go upwards and away from the mother's body, turning into wasted energy. The woman is not producing a useful force that helps her body and baby to work, but is producing effort, which has an inhibiting effect.

Excessive anxiety may result from an element of disconnection between mind and body. Voice is thus an expression of the body image. A mother's attitude to her body and self during pregnancy, labour, and birth will contribute to shaping the quality of her holding, massaging, and talking to her baby and of every moment of contact. The continuity from pre- to post-natal experience is provided by the mother's unique bonding with her baby. This connecting thread is supposed to begin before conception and have its roots in the woman's relationship with her body and self. This relationship, subject to continuous adjustments during pregnancy, shapes the woman's sensitivity to the foetus's cues and establishes an intimate form of communication. The ability to attune to her own bodily rhythms and thus to those of the baby allows the mother to nurture a mental representation of the baby that is closer to the real individual baby.

The newborn baby is particularly sensitive to sounds. Her earliest channels of communication are touch, hearing, and smell and through them she gets to know her primary caregivers and external environment. This is probably why a particular sound, smell, or way of touching can evoke an image, a strong sensation, or emotion with what is often an underlying unconscious origin. The baby's proprioceptive system is extraordinarily active and responsive since her time in the womb. She can feel the sounds of her parents' voices just as she perceives light, especially when the mother's abdomen is exposed to the sunlight. The unborn baby is responsive to her mother's voice, its nuances, and its inflections. She can also hear and feel sounds from the environment around her. One woman in a post-natal support group told me that her baby was soothed by the sound of the loo flushing. The babies of another mother calmed down at the sound of the hairdryer, the vacuum cleaner, or the ticking of a clock. These were probably familiar sounds for those babies that they had heard regularly throughout intra-uterine life.

Research shows that a newborn recognizes her mother's unique voice and is soothed by it and drawn to it where there is a range of voices present (Hepper, 1991; Hepper & Shahidullah, 1994; Righetti, 1996; Sansone, 2002). She can also recognize the music her mother enjoyed playing during pregnancy. Early sounds affect the baby's future preference for pitch and pieces of music. In this regard, I shall provide an anecdote from personal experience. My sister-in-law used to play the piano when she was pregnant, both as a teacher and so as to share her enjoyment with the baby. We were having Christmas dinner when Rossella, three months old, began to cry intensely, probably because she was disturbed by the noise. Her mother picked her up and walked to the next room, where some classical music was playing. Rossella instantly calmed down and appeared to be comforted. She showed a rather evident sense of orientation by searching for the source of the sounds, which probably reminded her of the haven of the womb. Sounds are vibrations that seem to modulate muscle tone. Rossella was probably reacting not just to the sounds of the music but also to the vibrations that penetrated her whole body like a lullaby, with the same effect as rocking. She also responded to being carried and rocked, and she may have experienced the same movements induced in the womb by the mother's motion. The vibrations of the sounds and the motion recreated a familiar environment for her.

The sense of *kinaesthesia* is the first and strongest that the foetus develops. All babies are highly responsive to being rocked, which reproduces the pre-birth movements of the mother's pelvis. Rocking with the arms is usually a waste of energy for the mother, as a lot of tension is concentrated in the arms and may be sensed by the baby, providing an uncomfortable position. Walking and gently swinging the pelvis are more likely to soothe the baby. Babies respond in the same way to being caressed, probably because the skin contact with the amniotic fluid and the small wave movements had a caressing or massaging effect.

At birth, sounds that were muted and soft because of the surrounding fluid often strike suddenly and forcefully and what was a gentle touch turns into an explosion for the baby. The foetus is immersed in a world of sounds, vibrations, and movement. After birth, when the baby encounters immobility and absolute silence, this must be an extraordinarily terrifying experience. For nine months, the baby has been moving and sensing sounds. Even while the mother was sleeping, the baby moved around in the amniotic fluid, along with the rhythm of the mother's breathing, her diaphragm, and her voice. The baby has never been alone; she will react to stillness with movement and may feel very frightened. Some babies can be paralysed by the immobility and loneliness. Might this sense of loneliness be enough to cause some babies to stop breathing?

The babies' need for movement and communicative displays can be clearly seen in their sensitivity to the human face and its wide range of expressions. Babies have the power to stimulate movement in adults, triggering a mirroring process. Movement, sounds, and expressions are forms of communication for the baby. Have we ever thought that babies can have a healing effect on adults through the mirroring process that they can trigger? Mothers sometimes say during baby massage classes that they get such pleasure from massaging their babies that it is like an art of meditation in movement, a gentle exercise for mind and body that leads to a sense of peace and harmony. This is consistent with the feeling I had, when observing them in baby massage classes, that mindful contact with the baby could help some new parents to integrate their bodyself image and their babies to develop a harmonious bodyself image.

Playing some music that she likes during pregnancy can enhance the mother's communication with the baby and strengthen the bonding. Playing the same pieces of music in the early post-natal period can provide the baby with an experience of continuity. Music induces changes in muscle tone and feelings, so it stimulates movement in the mother and consequently in the unborn baby. Movement is a form of communication. The unborn baby's inner ear is fully developed by mid-pregnancy and she is able to hear sounds outside the womb and to sense them even earlier. The mother's enjoyment of her attunement to the music is a medium for communication. Listening to music is a personal experience involving both mind and body, and the woman's own tastes and feelings are essential for the vibrations to reach the baby.

Some mothers find pieces of music that they regularly used to play during pregnancy have the power to soothe their babies after birth. A woman was struck by her baby's changes of facial expression and bodily movements while she played a piece of music that she had played pre-natally. The baby showed a strong orientation reflex towards the source of music. Other women are fascinated by their babies' movements while playing some music that they played during pregnancy. Further research may show whether the pre-natal baby's facial expressions and movements change with external stimuli such as music.

Every baby reacts in a unique way to music and to her parents' voices, but all babies produce clear facial expressions and postural changes in response. Depending on the pitch, a piece of music or voice can have a soporific instead of a stimulating effect. The baby's vocalizations, like music, can induce a wide range of responses in the mother, modulating her muscle tone and affect, and thus her bodyself perception. This impinges on the interaction.

Through touch and sounds, parents can rediscover their body language and enhance their communication with their baby. They can talk, sing, and vocalize in a soft soothing voice and the baby will be likely to move in tune with them. Every element of the interaction involves a vibration, with a gentle massage effect on the skin that shapes the relationship. The mother's voice can act as a lullaby, which is an ancient way of comforting babies with rhythmic sounds. It provides vestibular and muscular stimulation. It is music in terms not only of performance but of the pleasure and quality of melodic vibrations it transmits to the baby. Voice can create a form of play, especially if combined with singing, rocking, or dancing. The mother's voice, as well as any familiar piece of music, helps the newborn to overcome the crisis of separation from the womb and adapt to the new environment through an experience of continuity.

Playing music in a group of mothers and babies can have a far more powerful effect, as the vibrations merge with group dynamics. In a group, particular psychological phenomena occur. Bion had this intuition (Bion, 1948). He verified the therapeutic power of the group on individuals. In the individuals who form a group, specific tensions become manifest. Many new parents undergo a crucial and stressful time. In the sharing experience provided by the group, they find a container in which they can voice or manifest their tensions and relieve them. Babies benefit enormously from the group as well. In a group, particular vibrations cross the individual boundaries. Playing music or singing in group boosts this phenomenon. It creates a special time for both mothers and babies. In a post-natal class, I often observed babies stop crying as one mother started playing the guitar while others were singing. Babies, in a circle with their mothers, opened their eyes wide and attentively and moved their bodies in rhythm with the song, while their mothers danced in tune with them.

Mother–baby interactions quickly appeared to me as choreographic or musical patterns of communication. Their ability to coordinate their expressions so precisely and easily gave me the impression that the baby was dancing while the mother was speaking or singing. The baby responds to the mother's speech or song with strong bodily movements, especially hand movements.

Colwyn Trevarthen (2002) gives an account of young babies' musical intelligence and social sophistication. In collaboration with a musical acoustic expert, Stephen Mallock, he created a new way of analysing the "musicality" of vocal exchanges between babies and parents, which explains their remarkable ability to dance together. Infants' amazing ability to move in rhythm with music and vocal sounds,and to listen to a narrative, and thus to be "active" participants, suggests that they have a well-organized bodyself. In the mother-and-baby classes, all the babies moved their hands to music, rather like orchestral conductors, and sometimes with the same elegance. Infants' behaviour appears to indicate that their brains are already organized in a highly sophisticated way and that all levels are exquisitely interconnected and integrated. Because the mind and the body are inseparably connected, even more powerfully in a baby, I regard this primary unity as the foundation of a bodyself image.

Parent–baby interactions seem to show an ability to dance that precedes walking. Their bodies are traversed by vibrations and naturally produce movement and vibrations themselves, just like percussion instruments. Playing in a group creates a community environment that the modern nuclear family has missed. In the past, babies grew up in the company of siblings, grandparents, relatives, and friends and they were always in an ocean of vibrations, movement, and interesting things that captured their attention. They used to fall asleep while hearing stories told by their grandfathers in a deep low-pitched voice or while hearing a lullaby, a song produced by a human voice. In the traditional community, there were always rhythmic sounds around. Nowadays, those sounds are often substituted by impersonal inanimate toys. A non-communicative silence reigns in the nuclear family.

Travelling across countries where the lifestyle is more community-based, I found that babies there cried significantly less intensely and less frequently. Mothers too often think that their babies must be ill or in pain when they are crying and become fairly preoccupied. Babies may cry because they lack interesting stimuli. For a busy parent, it is usually difficult to create a special time for her baby. I regularly notice babies stop crying when I make funny sounds, either with my voice or by tapping on the floor. Sometimes it is enough to wave my hands and draw some figures in the air. It is very easy to catch a baby's attention, or at least not as difficult as it may seem to some parents, who get very anxious when their babies are crying.

The resources and strategies depend on the parents. Playing music, singing, and vocalizing together with their children can enhance the parents' ability to play and rediscover primary forms of self-expression. In order for the baby to enjoy playing, it is important that parents rediscover their own enjoyment of play.

I think psychology has neglected primary psychobiological attuned communication as the foundation of child development. Studies on babies' minds have long been dominated by formulations relating to adult problems and thoughts. The emotional dynamics of the mother–infant dyad and their rhythmical non-verbal inter-actions are the foundation of linguistic and cognitive development.

Voice in baby massage: mirroring

When I began to observe women massaging their babies, I paid particular attention to the role of the mother's voice during massage and, no less importantly, of the teacher's voice, in regulat-ing the baby's movements and behaviour. For example, singing a tune that the baby enjoys may reduce her squawk to a gummy smile and encourage her to lift her head and chest off the floor when she lies down for back massage. The link between voice, posture, communication, and bonding soon appeared to me to be rather strong. A pleasant vocal sound tends to relieve muscular tension in the jaw, vocal cords, and whole face, as well as in the neck, shoulders, chest, and abdomen, where it eases breathing. All these elements work together and when they are in a balanced rela-tionship they are reflected in harmonious posture and an integrated body image. I would say that a voice that is truly present is one that comes from a body that is communicating, rather than from a mouth.

The soothing or exciting effect of the mother's voice is depen-dent on her ability to get in tune with the baby's feeling in the "here and now", with her need to be stimulated or left on her own, to be woken up, or to sleep. The mother is like a resonating instrument whose strings are tuned by the baby's sounds, crying, and move-ments to produce the right notes. Their communication becomes ineffective when either mother or baby plays, sings, or dances out of tune. High tension is likely to disrupt the communication. However, this is a necessary path towards improvement. Becoming able to attune is a process of learning and getting to know each other. It implies acceptance, lack of rigid resistance, and creativity in experimenting with new strategies.

If synchronization facilitates attuned communication and inter-actions, misattunement is triggered by a mismatch and relates to stressful desynchronization and destabilization within the dyad. Through learning and reattunement, the mother helps the infant to regulate her emotional state by alleviating distress and reinforcing positive psychobiological states.

As a regulator of the baby's affect and muscle tone, the mother's voice may use varying pitches in tune with the infant's cues to enhance and retain the flexibility of the baby's posture as well as her own. Babies enjoy it when mothers mimic their consonants and vowels. This seems to encourage self-knowledge and the development of a true self, as the mother acts as a mirror. At the same time, the baby through her own responses acts as a mirror for the mother. A beautiful reciprocal mirroring occurs within the dyad.

Once an adult has an integrated self and body image, any imitation is an invasion of that integrity. Conversely, during the early months of life, when the infant's self is incompletely formed, the imitation of her gestures, facial expressions, and vocalizations appears to foster the process of self-discovery and the bodyself image integration. The infant's mirroring in the mother and father is fundamental to her overall development and occurs very early during any contact. Perhaps before coming into the world and being able to see, the foetus is seen, in the sense that she grows in connection with the image that the mother is nurturing in her mind.

Mindful massage provides a special time for the mirroring process, which is never passive or chimp-like. Chatting with the baby and repeating her sounds, as well as smiling at her and laughing, promote eye contact, which is a powerful channel of communication. Mimicking the baby's sounds creates a playtime that is for her the most effective means of learning. Being aware of the power of voice can help mothers to focus on their voice while massaging, as voice can produce a massaging effect itself. As the mother's body is the baby's first environment outside the womb, the more varied her expressions—for instance, different tones, rhythms, and resonators—the better it is for learning.

A pleasant vocal sound comes from a comfortable posture that has an effective point of support in the body. The bodily support enables an individual to release tension, thus, to make better use of her posture, breathing, gestures, voice, and movements. It is dependent on the "body focus", a bodily perceptual reference point that, like a prow, enables us to move in space and works as an organizer of muscle tone and postural attitude. For instance, if we close our eyes and visualize our body in motion, we should see and feel one part (sometimes two or more parts) that moves first: this is our body focus. It is important for a parent to find an effective point of support and body focus to make massage as more enjoyable and beneficial as possible. A baby who develops a flexible confident posture is more likely to find a well-functioning body focus when moving in social and physical space and to have better self-know-ledge. An individual's body focus is unique because it is the result of the earliest experiences recorded in her muscles. Bodily percep-tual focal points are not easily detectable because they operate auto-matically and at an unconscious level. Ruggieri & Katsnelson (1996) demonstrate that if an individual is asked to change the bodily area used as a focus, important changes occur in the subjective feeling of tension, pleasure, and stability. High tension and rigid posture make it difficult to have an effective body focus. With reference to an economic theory of the bodyself (Ruggieri, 1988), I shall now report two cases.

During a baby massage class, two babies were crying persis-tently. I knew that a smell, sound, or high temperature that they dislike can be enough to make a baby cry. Sometimes the baby may not be well or it may simply be that it is not the right time for the baby to be massaged. After a few attempts, there is no need to insist. However, I was amazed when I observed their mothers' posture. One showed high tension in her shoulders, clearly reflected in a rigid chest and closed and raised shoulders. Her neck was pulled down into her shoulders and the tone of her voice was heavy and sharp. She spoke with a remarkably fast rhythm of voice. Her posture did not show any attitude of approach towards the baby. I presumed that her voice was the result of a personal muscu-lar pattern and postural attitude developed throughout her life. When I encouraged the woman to become aware of that link through some postural and breathing exercises, she was able to find a more beneficial point of support in the bodyself and, conse-quently, to relieve the excessive tension. Obviously, this involved a simultaneous and complementary work at an emotional level. With so much stiffness in the upper body, her diaphragm could hardly descend into the abdomen to produce healthy functioning of the breathing, throat, and vocal cords. As a result, she was almost unable to find a comfortable and enjoyable posture. There was no smile on her face. As often happens, the longer the baby cried, the more her tension and stiffness increased, causing a communication breakdown or misattunement between mother and baby in a vicious circle.

A baby's crying often gives rise to a sense of failure in the mother. The mother wonders whether there is something wrong with her, which may only increase her tension and reinforce the circle. Conversely, focusing on her posture and the body points where the tension is concentrated and feeling the chest and abdominal muscles involved in breathing can open up her sensory channels, connecting her with her own self as well as with the baby's. The mother's mind also opens wide and finds new strategies and more fluid gestures for interacting with the baby. An empowered perception of the bodyself allows for a better understanding of the baby's cues and, therefore, for attuned communication. The newborn's and child's biological field is open and extremely responsive to changes of movement, voice, and expression. It is not easy for a mother, who is naturally involved in the relationship with her baby, to put this into action, but her awareness of the links is the first important step in the journey into the baby's experiences.

Sarah, the mother of the other crying baby, Louis, showed rigid arms and hands. I had noticed the same pattern during a breast-feeding class (see also Chapter Three). The shoulder of the side on which she was breastfeeding appeared locked and raised towards the neck. Her facial muscles looked quite tense, producing a preoccupied expression. She handled the baby as though she was something precious and fragile. Her way of touching him was really peculiar: she appeared to be straining every movement in order not to hurt him. From the observational work into the dyadic dynamics, I came to foresee the possible effect of that kind of touch on the child's developing body-self perception and image. The woman was going through severe emotional difficulties. Her husband had abandoned her when she was two months pregnant. During their relationship, physical and psychological violence had been inflicted on her. Sometimes I encouraged her to focus on her posture during baby massage and breastfeeding. Her trust in me soon proved to be the pillar of a positive approach that focused on the unique mother–baby interactions. After a few months, I could see the emotional and psychological benefits through changes in her posture and her way of holding the baby. Her touch became more confident, firm, and fluid, and her shoulders and chest opened wider; her gestures and movements evolved more freely and became more receptive to the world and to the relationship with her baby. The eye contact and reciprocal smiling became more frequent and intense. The woman appeared to be less preoccupied and more present in the baby's experience.

CHAPTER SIX

Movement and communication
The baby massage experience

Mother–baby interactions do not occur in a chain-like sequence;
the behaviour of each triggers several others.
The effects of an interaction
are more like those of a stone dropped into water,
causing a multitude of increasing rings,
than a chain where each link leads to only one other.

I believe that there has been inadequate study of emotional bodily dynamics, or the way in which emotions "move". It seems no coincidence that the word "emotion" derives from "motion" or "movement". Human communication consists of both sound and movement. The five methods of sensory communication—sight, touch, smell, hearing, and taste—comprise a sixth paramount aspect: movement and gesture. While a person is speaking, several parts of the body move in ways that can be either evident or fairly imperceptible; in the same way, the listener's movements can be co-ordinated with the speaker's speech rhythm and her bodily movements. When two people talking to each other are filmed, micro-analysis reveals that both are moving in tune to the words being spoken, thus creating a type of dance in rhythm with the speech patterns. This phenomenon can appear quite clearly in the rhythmic conversation between mother and baby (*proto-conversation*). The mother's voice is already familiar to her newborn—after all, she has had nine months to get used to it in her womb!

Research has shown that unborn babies move in response to noise (Birnholz & Benacerraf, 1983; Fernald, 1992) and, within three days of birth, a baby will turn her head when she hears her mother's voice but will not react in the same way to another woman's voice. Talking to the baby in a rhythmic and even way gives her a vital space in which to respond with vocalizations. Even when she does not appear to do so at first, she responds with her limbs and head, smiling, breathing, and facial expressions, as well as with her gastro-intestinal, autonomic, and motor system. Then she will pout her lips in reply and later will blow bubbles and gurgle. This rhythmic pre-verbal communication through movement builds up the network that is necessary for developing language. The baby often kicks her legs at the sound of her mother's voice or, if she is already kicking, she may go very still when she hears her.

By imitating the baby's cues, the mother establishes the dance between them and facilitates the mirroring process. The baby will hear sounds from two sources: herself and the mother. She will see her gestures reflected on the mother and this process nurtures the representation of self and body. Mirroring is a fundamental part of learning. This is why the infant needs her mother to look at her when she talks to her.

At the beginning of my time in London, when I was first getting accustomed to the English culture and lifestyle and learning collo-quial language, cues from the listener's face and gestures were important for my understanding, as well for reinforcing my confidence. In other words, they acted as a mirror. Language learning, like any cognitive activity, proceeds successfully when we are functioning well emotionally.

When the mother reproduces the baby's cues, for instance, when she pokes her tongue out at the baby, the baby will likely respond with the same gesture. It can be an enjoyable game for both mother and baby, in which the father can also be involved. A baby loves to induce smiles in people and she will smile back with excitement.

She likes to be the initiator, to dictate what is going on. When she looks away, this is a cue that she would like a rest from the game. Her crying may indicate that she is tired and wants to stop. Responding to the infant's feelings and states, and not overwhelming her with stimulation, is the basis for communicating and establishing a bond with her. Her earliest sensory experiences, modulated by the interactions with the caregiver, will teach her about her new world. By understanding the sensory language that the baby is using to experience her new world, parents can tune into her experience and their relationship with her flourishes.

This learning process begins in pre-natal life, when the foetus has already embarked on a sensory adventure, based mainly on hearing, touch, and movement. After birth, from the moment the infant is held close to the mother's body, the bonding process is simply extending. The newborn will feel the closeness of the mother's body, identify her smell, hear the familiar sound of her voice, look into her eyes, and get her first taste of her breast milk.

Baby massage can be seen as a vital part of the bonding process. The physical closeness and skin contact, the massage movements, and the playful time bring warmth and security to parent and baby alike, instilling peace, enjoyment, and a sense of well-being. The reassuring tone of the mother's voice, her smile, and her touch during massage are relaxing and relieve the discomfort of encountering new sensations, feelings, sounds, and sights, the rumbles of her stomach, and the movement of air on her bare skin. She reassures her baby that the world outside the womb is still able to provide, as Leboyer puts it, "the embracing waves" or "the infinite pulse" that conveyed her mother's love (2002, p. 82). The baby's cry at birth may be an expression of an unbearable feeling of emptiness and separation from the womb that held her body and supported her back. The reassuring hands of the mother on the baby's back replace some of that pre-natal sensation.

During massage, mother and baby link the five sensory aspects of communication with a sixth powerful channel of communication that encompasses gesture and movement. Furthermore, the massage movements expand the five sensory channels. During massage, bodily communication is dramatically empowered. This time is equated with breastfeeding, when the mother's face is at exactly the right distance from her for the baby to see her clearly (20–25 cm).

The mother's instinct to gaze down at the baby and look at her face as she feeds is a vital part of the bonding process. The mother is then at just the right distance for the baby to explore her face and to become able to recognize it in few days. I have noticed that a number of mothers, particularly while talking to their baby, tend to keep that optimal distance during massage.

Baby massage can therefore be a fulfilling substitute for the breastfeeding experience when the baby is bottle-fed. Touch is a vital part of the bonding process: nothing is more effective than a familiar touch for comforting a baby. Massage can help mother to modulate touch and become attuned to the baby's sensitivity. Some babies prefer a firm touch, others a gentler one; some prefer fast movement, others slower. Finding the right intensity, quality, and tempo is a learning process and requires becoming attuned to the baby. Baby massage can help make the new mother's confidence flourish.

The use of oil helps massage movements to go smoothly and the mother to modulate her touch according to the baby's need. A study of two groups of three-to-six-week-old infants showed that the infants who received massage with oil showed fewer stress behaviours and head aversions and that their saliva cortisol levels decreased further than in the group without oil (Field, Pelaez-Mogueras, Hossain & Pickens, 1996).

Massage and movement can be done any time and anywhere, provided it is the right time for both mother and baby—for instance, in the morning, while mother is still in bed. After feeding, very gentle abdominal massage can be beneficial if the baby is colicky and needs to bring up wind. It can also help the mother to reduce her anxiety level. Research shows that colic occurs in approximately ten per cent of infants and is exacerbated by parental anxiety (Brazelton, 1990). The mother's tone and rhythm of voice also modulate the baby's movements and synchronize the communication. During massage, the parent's voice and the baby's vocalizations blend with each other's movements, producing a form of dance.

Babies are likely to calm down when they hear a low-pitched voice, probably because every sound they have felt in the womb was low and downward, muffled by the amniotic fluid. When mother communicates with the baby before birth, by breathing deeply and smoothly, she lets the vibrations touch the baby, as deep breathing involves the abdomen. The vibrations produce small waves in the placental fluid, which create massage movements on the baby. Getting in tune or communicating with the baby requires the mother to get in tune with her feelings about her own self and body, in other words, with her awareness of what is happening to her body and of her renewed identity. The mother's thoughts, fantasies, wishes, and expectations reach the baby through her breathing, hormones, bloodstream, and so on.

Babies react to sounds with movement, not only because of their sensitive hearing, but also because their skin is touched by the waves generated by the vibrations. Their muscle system is stimulated by sounds and develops in relation to them. Their body perception and posture begin to organize in relation to sounds. The baby's bodyself image develops in relation to the mother's voice, feelings, and touch. The differences between babies' muscle mass immediately after birth is amazing. They are born with their own genetic make-up but the differences are also the result of their activity in the womb. Some babies are more active than others, presumably also in response to the kind of stimulation they receive from the mother's body.

If we consider the mother's body as an environment that conditions foetal development, we can see a link between the mother's body image and the core of the foetus's body image. The woman's attitude to her bodyself is thus an aspect of the bonding process. Her body image, in close rapport with her emotional life, contributes to creating the uterine environment. Clearly the parents' genetic make-up also plays a part. However, I suggest that what is considered merely "genetic" at birth in some scientific disciplines is already intrinsically environmental, as the baby develops in a micro-environment that is subject to stimuli.

Every child comes into the world with her own character and needs, and she initiates the interactions and responds in her own way. The unborn baby's character seems to affect pregnancy, labour, and the birth process. Some babies appear to be looking forward to leaving the womb and come into the world with open eyes, looking around and exploring with curiosity, as if birth were a game. Others arrive struggling and crying for a relatively long time. The length and difficulty of labour may result partly from a baby's need to stay inside the womb longer. Some babies emerge with closed eyes, quiet, or asleep, without having been disturbed. Every newborn breathes in her unique way. Adults resemble one another more than babies, as they are educated to adapt to society. They learn to control cognitively the naïve feelings with which they are born, which are what make them unique.

The nature of the infant's behaviour at ten days can affect the mother's emotional postpartum state. One study in particular found that irritability with the infant increased the risk that the mother would become depressed (Murray, Stanley, Hooper, King & Fiori-Cowley, 1996). Poor motor behaviour, sluggish behaviour, or tense and jerky movements in the infant can have the same effect, which also affects the mother's perception of her baby.

The difficulty of birth may even be determined by a failure of foresight on the part of the baby in finding the right way to descend. Furthermore, bonding is easier with some babies than others. Some babies are really keen to bond even in the uterus. They kick in response to the mother's or father's voice and then after birth they turn their heads towards their parents in a very alert way. Other babies are sleepier and need more time to bond. It is some-times said that all newborn babies are alike, tiny things with no identity. This is not true. What makes them alike is the mask that adults project on to them. I believe that it is misleading to look at the infant's behaviour from the outside, and from the perspective of adult convenience.

Although they pass through the same stages of development, each baby does it at her own pace. To understand her uniqueness, it is essential to take our mask off and become attentive observers and listeners so as to get rid of our fast rhythms even for brief moments—perhaps just thirty seconds at a time. Interacting with babies allows us adults, especially parents, to be present in their individual experience and to perceive their cues, which consist of movements, gestures, and facial expressions. To do so, we need to travel this pathway and rediscover our own non-verbal language through skin and eye contact, gestures, and our taste for simplicity. Only by understanding infants can we truly understand ourselves and other people. Infants are undoubtedly great teachers.

For a baby it is very important after birth to sense the rhythms of the mother's body, to which she has been accustomed for nine months. It is an experience of continuity. She can be soothed or simply comforted when mother is rocking her with her whole body, by walking, dancing, or simply swinging her pelvis, instead of only her arms. The mother is thereby reproducing the movements that the baby felt in the womb. Even when she was asleep, waves and floating produced by her breathing and heartbeat reached her baby. The foetus receives messages from the mother's movements as she is rocked in the bony cradle of the pelvis. The optimal degree of rocking is likely to correspond to that produced by the mother's pelvis as she walks or dances.

One of the earliest neurological systems to develop in the foetus is the vestibular system, concerned with balance and equilibrium. A baby-carrier can give the baby the stimulation that represents an extension of pre-natal life, thus, a source of security. The baby gets involved in the mother's activities and feels the warmth of her body and its rocking movement. When the mother is walking outside, she can see from the carrier people interacting with each other, diverse facial expressions, and so she can develop very early the capacity to perceive other people's emotional states (empathetic perception) and to feel part of a community. This also enables her to read facial expressions and interpret other people's intentions.

Detailed studies of babies' amazing behavioural capacities have shown that, in an alert state, they see, hear, and move in rhythm with the mother's voice in the first few minutes and hours of life, resulting in a beautiful synchronized "dance" between two companions (Condon & Sander, 1974; Stern, 1977; Trevarthen, 2002). During my observational study, I was often struck by the babies' capacities. While I was holding a baby a few minutes after birth, I said in a calm, slightly high-pitched, and rhythmic voice: "Just a few minutes ago you were in your Mum's belly!" His eyes appeared to follow the rhythm of my voice and his body produced some wriggling movements. Combined with some similar observations this pointed to the voice, together with gestures, facial expressions, and eye contact, as one of the factors that organize the baby's muscle tone and posture.

The newborn has been observed to move in time with adult speech (Trevarthen, 1977). As a speaker pauses for breath or emphasizes a syllable, the baby raises an eyebrow or lowers a foot. During a pre-natal parents' class, I was holding a baby while his mother was telling her birth story. I sat holding the baby in front of her mother. I could feel and see his limbs moving in rhythm with his mother's tone, pitch, and voice frequencies. Sometimes his vocalizing also sounded in rhythm with the mother's voice.

The newborn's amazing capacity to "conduct" the rhythms and melodies of her mother's voice or a piece of music, rather like an orchestral conductor, seems to indicate that the baby is born with a pre-existing mental structure that can create music or rhythm in the body. Many of the baby's actions and movements in the womb are in synchrony with those of the mother: her sleep–wake cycle, her hormonal rhythms, the patterns of the mother's day, her heartbeat, her breathing rhythm, the rhythmic uterine contractions before the onset of labour and up to the time that the baby descends the birth canal. A baby begins to move in the womb very early, from when the embryo becomes a foetus, even if the mother does not feel her movements before she is big enough to stretch the uterine wall. Not only her movements but also her whole communication, consisting of emotions, thoughts, feelings, and imagination can induce movement in the baby. The tiny baby breaks into gentle movements, beginning from the trunk and spreading outwards to the extremities. She may also take pleasure from her own movements and from floating in the amniotic fluid.

A three-dimensional image taken thirty-four weeks after conception with a new ultrasound-scanning machine can capture the unborn baby smiling in the comfort of her mother's womb. Other images show foetuses blinking, sucking their fingers, scratching their noses, hiccupping, and crying. From fifteen weeks, foetuses are seen making complex finger movements, and from twenty weeks they begin to yawn. The unborn baby's smile may reflect inner contentment. It is interesting that a newborn baby does not smile for about six weeks after birth, whereas before birth most babies smile quite frequently. Further research may show that the baby's facial expressions and movements change with external stimuli such as music or the father's voice.

The foetus's boundaries vary as she grows, as does her core perception of the body and of the uterine environment. When the baby develops rapidly at the end of pregnancy, she begins to feel closed in and that her universe is contracting. She begins to feel more confined in the space. When the labour contractions and their propulsion of the baby into the world begin, the experience of confinement through the narrow pelvic canal must be tremendous. It is the mother's body squeezing the baby out that may determine this feeling of confinement. The core perception of a limited space may sow the seeds of a body image, developing in relation with the mother's perception of her own body as confining space.

Given this synchronized development, the disruption of birth seems to upset the baby's earlier rhythms and to lead to a state of imbalance and destabilization. However, the mother's attuned responses help her to reorganize and retain her rhythmic behaviours in order to adjust to the extra-uterine environment

The baby's voice and gestures also affect the mother's way of responding. A newborn baby has an amazing capacity to "conduct" the rhythms of the mother's responses. Research found that fifty-four of sixty-three mothers, after being exposed to the hunger cries of newborns, demonstrated a significant increase in blood flow to their breasts (Lind, Vuorenkoski & Wasz-Hockert, 1973; Ostwald, 1981). The baby's cry causes a physiological change in the mother that is likely to induce her to nurse. The baby can also initiate the secretion of maternal hormones. When the baby licks the mother's nipple, this leads to oxytocin release in the mother, which hastens uterine contractions and reduces bleeding (Widström et al., 1990). The sucking calms the mother and strengthens the bond between mother and baby. These are all aspects of the complex synchronization between two individuals with their own unique character.

Touch during massage has a similar effect to sucking and licking the mother. If breastfeeding problems can occur for psychological reasons—with the breast becoming a barrier rather than an expression of attuned communication—the same can happen with baby massage, when rhythmic communication breaks down. It is possible that the special physical closeness, skin contact, and massage movements during enjoyable playtime increase the maternal prolactin levels, just as licking and sucking instil a sense of well-being in both mother and baby. Thus baby massage could improve breastfeeding, encourage positive affect, and enhance pleasure and motivation in mothering and child-care, promoting a secure attachment. Observational follow-ups are essential for exploring this hypothesis. I have rarely encountered mothers with severe breastfeeding problems in a baby massage class. In birds, prolactin is a

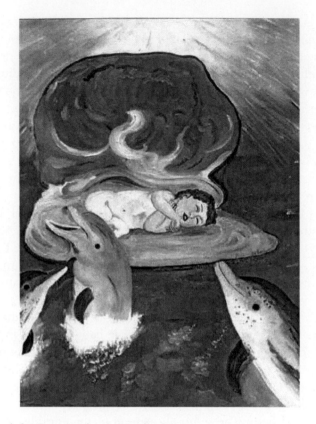

The waterbaby. Painting by Antonella Sansone.

"love hormone": it appears to activate the close attachment between mother and young.

Human babies and mothers are not the only ones to communicate in such subtle ways through touch and cues. The sense of rhythm seems to be shared by various animal species. Communication seems to have survival functions and to be important for social groups. We can observe a wonderful synchronization between mother and baby in many species. Dolphins, of all marine animals, develop complex lifestyles similar to ours. They are playful, intelligent, social creatures and are communicative and co-operative. They communicate with clicking sounds and touching. They gather together and communicate in groups. Baby dolphins are not born with survival skills. They imitate the mother's posture and behaviour. The mother uses sounds that the baby dolphin may not be able to use at first. The basic sounds are used to recognize clicks that are used for echolocation. In the dark, but even in the daylight, as their visibility is restricted, they can distinguish between different kinds of fish through sounds. Their communication through codes and clicks is a prime example of pre-verbal language.

Before a human baby develops use of her tongue, there are coordinated exchanges of sounds, cues, and codes within the mother, father, and baby triad. These codes, containing meanings that parents send to the baby through their responses, are precursors of language. During baby massage, mother–baby communication, governed by cues and codes, is extraordinarily vivid and can impress the most inexpert observer. Because of the baby's nakedness, the relatively long-lasting skin contact and all the sensory aspects of communication and movement are linked and unified, promoting bonding and building the foundations of a unified perception of the bodyself. Moreover, the mother can be rewarded by the closeness with her baby, through which she can pleasurably experience her warm and soft skin.

Massage is a wonderful time for parent and baby to get to know each other. It can be a means of discovering the cause of an illness in the baby. For instance, one mother I met could not understand why her baby had been crying frequently and intensely for a few days. She had started the daily massage routines a couple of weeks earlier, when one day she felt a knot in the baby's stomach while massaging. She ran to the hospital, where a doctor discovered a severe hernia. He said that the baby was just in time to be saved.

Allowing mother and baby to stay close to each other after birth is likely to initiate and enhance sensory, hormone, immune, and behavioural processes that attach the mother and the baby to each other, providing an experience of mutual pleasure. The physical contact promotes more attuned responsiveness. Mother–baby interactions do not occur in a chain-like sequence, but the behaviour of each triggers several others. Thus, the effects of an interaction are more like those of a stone dropped into the water, causing a multitude of increasing rings, than a chain in which each link leads only to one other.

The missing link: community life

During an observational study on the perception of the menstrual pain on a Maldivian island in the Indian Ocean, I was struck by the absence of crying among babies, despite their large number. I made a similar observation in some communities in Southern Italy. In the community, a new mother is never alone. She is surrounded by other women, friends, or relatives, who have had their own babies and from whom she receives emotional and practical support.

During my observations in the post-natal classes at the Birth Unit in London I found that some babies, whose mothers desperately complained about their frequent crying at home, almost never cried during the two-hour session. I would give two explanations. First, the group and sharing experience with other women acted as containment for the new mothers, supporting their feelings, anxieties, and uncertainties. This affected their way of interacting with the baby and, consequently, the baby's behaviour. Besides, the other babies' vocalizing and the mothers' talking produced musical vibrations that either had a soothing effect or were more entertaining than the ordinary solitary tone surrounded by the domestic walls. In addition to this, there are studies (Urwin, 1990) to indicate that babies' interaction with other babies are important for getting to know themselves and others. I consider that pre-verbal interaction between infants very early in life facilitates self-knowledge and bodyself image development through mirroring.

In a traditional society, the social system is an extension of the family group. A first-time mother can rely on the other women's experience. The babies are cared for by other children, other comforting arms, and even other lactating breasts. Many things are taken for granted because they are passed down the generations. The weight of decision for the mother is lighter. A woman starts to learn how to care for babies when she is herself a small child and there are always babies around. In industrial societies, a woman gets information mainly from books or health professionals, which are often contradictory and confusing. Intellectualizing may direct a mother away from her own feelings, intuitions, and personal resources.

I have seen women attending post-natal support classes for over a year, simply because the group met their primal need to share in a community. In a community, by the time a woman has her first

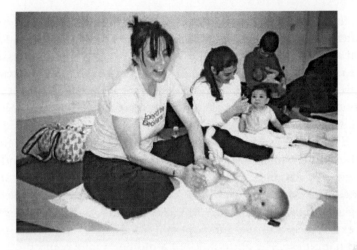

The sense of community provided by the class frees from the isolation that derives from the nuclear family. The group can act as a container for both mother and baby and create a mirroring among mothers as well as among infants.

Photo by Antonella Sansone

baby, she has seen a baby put on the breast many times. I always suggested to pregnant women that they attend a post-natal class at least once to watch what it is like caring for a baby, breastfeeding, massaging, dealing with a crying baby, changing a nappy, and to listen to their feelings. The sense of community provided by the class is a challenge to the isolation that derives from the nuclear family, which is a product of Western societies. In the traditional community, there are fewer questions and doubts. For example, when I questioned the women about labour pain during this study on a Maldivian island, they laughed, as if it were something so natural that it did not need to be talked about and this sounded inappropriate to them.

The community lifestyle, like any kind of society or culture, influences how natural processes such as pregnancy and birth and their outcome are experienced. The baby in traditional societies spends most of the time in touch with the human body and in firm and secure arms. She constantly witnesses the activities of the mother or other community members and is always surrounded by movement and lively situations. She is unlikely to get bored.

Furthermore, adults can get on with their work while babies are watching. Nowadays, computer toys have become substitutes for that natural stimulation when babies are born. The parents' individual instincts and intuitions, the stimulation the baby is provided with by their personalities and creativity, are being replaced by advice from psychologists and paediatricians because they are believed to be the real experts.

Everything seems to contribute to widening the gap between parents and babies and to making parents feel powerless and confused. For instance, thinking as a result of Western medical attitudes that babies cry just from hunger, anger, or pain restricts the opportunities for understanding other needs, thus depriving them of experiences that are fundamental for their healthy development and happiness. The abundance of a mother's love could hinder her ability to meet the baby's actual changing needs. For example, she may enjoy physical contact, but provoke it erratically or in response to her own rather than the baby's needs. The mother who understands the sadness felt by the baby left in her crib without stimulation and intepretation of her bodily cues, enriches the baby's personality by conveying her feelings and discovering a multitude of creative strategies.

Mothers in many cultures, who have to work in the fields, attach the cradleboard to their backs while they get on with tasks such as food preparation or washing clothes at the riverside. Their bending over must also facilitate the right position for the baby at birth. As breech births are on the increase, it seems possible that one important element may be the prolonged sitting position assumed by many women at work, particularly those who make substantial use of the computer. This not only constricts the genital apparatus, with consequences for pregnancy, labour, and birth, but deprives the foetus of movements that are vital for her development. The sedentary work needs to be complemented with enjoyable exercise. I often suggest to pregnant women that they spend some time crawling every day, to prevent the baby from developing in a breech or transversal position. For women whose baby's position has been diagnosed as unfit for a natural birth, this advice can be even more important.

Obviously, we cannot go back to a traditional agrarian society and most of us recognize the benefits of industrial societies.

However, looking back at traditional society can help us to find the missing link and to establish the continuity between past and present that is one of the pillars of a healthy society. Being aware of our past can help us to understand the persistent crying of many babies, for example, by not putting them on to the breast whenever they cry, thinking that the only reason is hunger. If we lose the creativity to think of the variety of the infant's needs and ways of responding to them, we restrict the infant's perception of her own needs and feelings, thus of her bodyself. This results in an impoverishment of her personality development. Many mothers insist on nourishing their baby with food even when they appear not to need it, because this is often the easiest and quickest response.

A baby becomes aware of her own needs by the mother meeting them. The need-satisfaction sequence gives the baby some sense of herself and enables her to recognize her need when, for instance, she is hungry. When a mother holds her baby close to her breast, she will naturally open her mouth and turn towards her. This is known as "rooting" for her nipple, an early, natural reflex that is so strong that she will show "rooting" actions whether she is breast-feeding or bottle-feeding.

A mother instinctively recognizes her baby's cues when she is angry. However, this is not always so obvious. Reading the baby's cues requires observation, which does not fit well with a rushed rhythm of life. Being receptive means being responsive to the baby's feelings and not overwhelming her with something that she does not need at that moment. A baby can quickly become tired: she may well fall asleep or express her mood by crying until her mother responds. I regard the mother's capacity to recognize the baby's cue when she is hungry as a fundamental key to healthy eating behaviour. A failure in the hunger-satisfaction sequence may cause eating disorders. One aspect of anorexia may therefore be the refusal to eat as a means of rebellion against a mother who was not receptive enough to fulfil other needs than hunger. Thus, the eating disorder is not itself the illness but a "symptom", a sign that "stands for" or communicates other needs.

Returning to the subject of community life, in a small rural town in Southern Italy I saw babies being taken on horseback, hung in a cradleboard, or on a basket attached by straps, around the mother's shoulders. In some Indian and American cultures, there is a tradition of giving babies a soothing oil massage. There are always movements and sounds around them, either produced by the human body or by activities; even when the mother is resting, there is movement from her breathing. It is as if when there is close contact, the baby is still an extension of the mother, now outside her body, creating a smooth transition from intra-uterine life. The mother's touch, voice, and breathing reproduce the familiar intra-uterine sounds that give a sense of security and, like regulators, stimulate the baby's breathing rhythm, either when she is awake or when she is sleeping close to the parents. I used to sleep between my parents in their bed during the first few months of life and up to three years in a cradle next to my mother. I have a vivid memory of that time and I still feel a sense of security stored in my body from hearing their movements in bed and touching my mother's hand. This was reliable proof of their presence, a vital resource for developing an internal parental model and for enabling me to tolerate the separation and face the events that were happening to me.

Babies also sleep best when attached to the mother's body in motion, because it gives them security (Cunningham, Anisfeld, Casper & Nozyce, 1987). In Tanzania, when the mother is not working and the baby starts crying, she produces the movements and sounds of grinding maize to soothe him: she bends over forward, straightens up, and bends again. For a baby, it is always a playtime with the mother's body. The mother-and-baby yoga class, in which babies crawl, swing, and jump on their mothers' bodies as they lie on the floor and stretch, recreates an ideal play and community context. I saw how fluently they switched from playing with their mothers' bodies to playing with toys, the latter appearing thus to be an extension of the interactions with their mothers. As a psychologist and infant observer, I had the opportunity to witness the benefits of a mother-and-baby class. While babies were interacting with other babies as well as with their own or other mothers, there was action and movement everywhere and they received visual, auditory, and motor stimulation. When we sang together, the babies danced in rhythm.

In traditional societies, babies spend time with older children and adults. Older children take part in the work, helping to pick the cotton; then they play for a while, swinging the baby. The mother comes over and sits under a tree, breastfeeding. There is always a lively and colourful scene around them. The baby can hear the sounds of the river and see birds flying in the sky and multi-coloured butterflies. I witnessed this lifestyle in parts of Southern Italy and on a few islands of the Indian Ocean and I was struck by the babies' behaviour, which was so different from those of indus-trialized societies.

The participation in working life does not start immediately after birth. In some societies, mother and baby go through a period of isolation in a dark room for a few days, where mother and baby get to know each other through touch, movement, sounds, and smell. It is a successful way of establishing breastfeeding. The seclu-sion provides the baby with an experience of continuity and prepares her for life outside. In Yucatan, the Mayan woman spends the first eight days after birth swinging with her baby in her ham-mock. The cooking is done by the woman's mother and sister-in-law and other family members. Being cared for by other women, she has time to get to know her baby. Not surprisingly, a Western woman who cannot rely on her family's help often feels isolated and distressed.

In some cultures, there are many powerful beliefs around con-ception, fertility, and birth (Moser, 1982). Because contact with nature is very close, human fertility is closely associated with the fertility of animals and the earth. For instance, when a woman gives birth, it is believed that plants grow better, fruits and flowers blossom, rice germinates, and the community grows larger. Child-bearing is thus a sacred event to be celebrated. Within an integrated approach to bodyself image, such beliefs are seen as strengthening the motivation to give birth and can affect the natural processes of pregnancy, birth, and child-care.

When listening to birth stories, I often focused on the attitude to pain and its cultural element. For instance, Japanese women seem to ask for anaesthetic during labour significantly less frequently than Caucasian women. As the midwives confirmed during my study at the Birth Unit, most Japanese women appear to meditate in labour, to be somehow more detached, and to go through the labour process with a fuller acceptance of whatever is going to happen. I think that because Japanese society is mainly conserva-tive, women tend to retain traditional beliefs about birth, which enable them to confront labour and birth as a sacred event. One

Japanese woman, while telling her birth experience, said, "When I have a headache, I take drugs, but birth is something so important, it is my baby coming into the world, so I couldn't ask for an epidural, and give drugs to my baby". Her facial expression, tone of voice, and posture reflected her description of something sacred.

In an industrialized society today, birth has become a medical rather than a natural or religious event (Oakley, 1982). There is no space or time for meditation, feelings, or awareness of the bodily changes and the baby's signals in labour. Birth occurs among strangers rather than familiar figures. My sister-in-law gave birth to her first child lying on her back, facing a dozen nurses and student obstetricians. Clearly, the labour environment has significant effects on the way the woman perceives what is happening to the birthing bodyself and it therefore impinges on the experience of pain.

The feelings of inadequacy and discomfort in some hospitals and the sense of being out of control exacerbate the tension and, consequently, lower the threshold of sensitivity to pain. They inhibit the labour process. Some women may experience such a major life event with a sense of failure and powerlessness. Starting motherhood with reduced confidence and self-esteem, with guilt at not having been able to express their bodyself affects bonding. It restricts the baby's possibility of finding a place in her mother's mind, in the "maternal reverie" as well as in her body language. The woman is likely to respond with fear, confusion, even panic, or ambivalence; all feelings that are manifested through her muscle tension are reflected in her gestures, her way of holding her baby, and her capacity to sense and understand the baby's cues and needs. This impinges on the baby's experience of a maternal presence that contains her physically and emotionally.

Providing a woman with a labour environment in which she can feel free to express her own needs, to let her body dance in rhythm with the labour process and the baby's cues, with supportive and warm midwives, is crucial for starting motherhood with self-confidence and assertiveness. Listening to birth stories from women giving active birth and from women delivering in traditional hospitals, I found remarkable differences between the two groups. Unfortunately, the importance of the period immediately surrounding birth and its influence on the mother–baby relationship and on the child's development is usually overlooked.

In industrialized societies, in contrast with traditional ones, the independence on which they are based is imposed on children too early, even by making them sleep in a separate room immediately after birth. This is not the way to develop independence, since there is much evidence that independence comes from a secure attachment (Winnicott, 1963; Bowlby, 1988). From my own experience, I slept with my parents for the first few months of my life, and when I moved from their bed to the cradle, I needed my mother to hold my hand to fall asleep. Her hand was for me an extension of her. Hearing my parents move in their bed or breathe gave me a sense of security. Nevertheless, I think I grew up as a fairly independent child, with a firm internal parental model and a sense of a united couple. It is very unlikely that I would have done so if a primary attachment had not been cemented.

Acknowledging our past and, most importantly, selecting some elements that can combine with our Western lifestyle, requires strong confidence in our own feelings and beliefs as individuals and considerable determination. A determined woman who decides to breastfeed a child up to the age of one or three years because they both enjoy it, or another who lets her child sleep with her, is likely to receive a lot of criticism from other people in our society. She needs a lot of strength and trust in herself to resist the rigid cultural bonds. However, it relates to a rediscovery of what is already inside her, the primary body language between mother and baby, within the couple, between father and baby, and within the triad. I observe that this is the starting-point for developing new insights and coping with the tensions of Western life. By rediscovering body language, some communicative dysfunctions can be resolved. Parent–child interactions constitute the very first social system, in which society at large is reflected. This is why this book is not aimed at teaching any theories or techniques but simply at shedding some light on our inner world and resources, in the first instance as individuals who have been parented.

Movement and sound

Babies need movement and sounds. They are not used to absolute silence or immobility. In the womb, there are always sounds, with something going in the mother's body even during sleep, or echoes from the external environment. During labour and birth, babies are immersed in noisy sounds and in the powerful stream of the labour contractions. They are often expected to cry or get distressed by hunger, anger, pain, wind, or because they are not being comforted enough. So, when a baby is crying, the mother will be likely to give her the breast, either for feeding or comfort, or as a substitute or dummy. Might she be crying because she is missing the stimulation of the womb? Or because she is suffering from an absence of movement and sounds?

There is a tendency to study psychological development as something that begins at birth and yet an enormous amount takes place before birth and it is vital that we understand the foetal period if we are to understand infant development. A newborn baby is very often seen as a creature with only physiological needs, whereas she is a human being with emotions, feelings, tastes, and interests that need to be satisfied when she is born. Crying is commonly considered a sign that something is wrong with the baby, a sign of illness, or even an unhealthy condition. This is because we adults generally cry when we are in pain, or from grief, so we project our feelings and cultural beliefs on to the baby. If we adults are bored, bothered, or uninterested, we can go for a walk, read, talk about our feelings, and share them with someone. A baby lying alone in a cradle may cry because she is feeling annoyed in a room that is lacking in colours, sounds, and lively scenes. She may be annoyed by a mother who insists on putting her on to her breast because she is worried that she is not feeding enough. The baby can sense the mother's worry through her arms and gestures, thus her way of holding. She may be conveying that she wants to be away from the breast, to change the scene and have a different special time, such as bathing, massage, singing, dancing, and so on.

I have heard mothers express concern about their babies when they make abrupt movements with their legs and arms, as though there were something wrong with them. They appeared to be scared by these powerful movements. These gestures, as well as some kinds of crying, are in fact natural aspects of a strong and healthy baby's communication. Babies have a lot of physical energy that they need to channel through movement, vocalizing, and crying. Giving them a special space and time, where they can be engaged with something, can be a way of making their energy flow. Their bodyself image and postural development will be enriched, since their muscular system as well as their minds will not need to store unexpressed energy.

I followed up some babies whose mothers complained about crying, who during the mother–baby support class did not cry at all but appeared fairly interested in the women's talk and in the other babies' babbling. The babies' bodily signals appeared to be orientated towards the source of the voice: their eyes, head, and hands, sometimes their whole body, looked like the prow of a ship. Very often, their bodies were moving in rhythm with my voice and gestures as I spoke. Two main factors come into play during the class: (1) the mothers' feeling of being contained by the group relieves the tension generated by their loneliness when they are at home, which is inevitably transmitted to their sensitive baby; (2) babies interact with one another and therefore are stimulated and get involved with what is going on.

Babies cry when they are lonely and bored, but enjoy it when there are people around, changing images, and sounds. As they grow, they need a richer and more varied scene. It seems that a receptive group provides the mother, as well as the baby, with an envelope for their feelings. Furthermore, it helps the mother to find the mental space that is necessary for getting in touch with her own feelings and reflecting on her baby's experience and being. This is why the pre-natal support group experience can be extremely important for a pregnant woman and father-to-be to be able to nurture that vital space.

Visual stimulation and movement

Babies like to have a great variety of visual stimuli. Caregivers need to be creative to provide the baby with these. This means that they need to be able to experiment in order to let the baby experiment herself through rich interactions. On the other hand, the baby's own tastes and unique personality also modulate the parent's creativity in responding. For instance, if you have a garden with trees, many natural stimuli will entertain your baby. If you have a bird in a cage, the sound and sight of her jumping and the bird's sound itself may provide interesting or soothing entertainment. Babies like repetitive sounds and movements. They also like, when they are a bit older, looking in the mirror, and even when they are not aware that the image reflected is theirs, they are interested in the image and its movement. They may enjoy watching the play of light and shade on the wall, objects fluttering, and shiny or coloured objects. You can put multicoloured balls and rattles on the crib and make them move with a ventilator on a low setting. They can also practise trying to reach them. You can even colour the walls and ceiling of the baby's room.

The young baby appears to be aware of a world outside the body, and especially a world that offers live companionship soon after birth. I have seen babies looking around with an expression of curiosity as soon as they come out of the mother's body and others involved in communicative games a few days after birth.

In traditional countries, babies can see everything that is going on and be the centre of attention. They are unlikely to get bored. It is not a relative or neighbour who looks after them but an entire village. Nowadays, parents need to create stimulation in the house for them, or to take them outside regularly, possibly in the country-side. Babies need very simple things, but a lot of attention from the caregivers, as the following example shows.

I was testing the response of a newborn infant, a few days old, to a colourful ball, first hanging from the ceiling, and then when being held by me by a thread. In the first instance, the baby made tiny movements with his head, whereas when the ball was held by me, the baby's attention was focused on it and he followed the movement of the ball with his hands, feet, nose, and mouth. As the ball moved around, the baby's whole body moved. In contrast to the previous situation, the baby's interest was not aroused by the ball itself. The ball was being moved because I was interested in the baby and in his response. It was clear that we were playing a game together and the baby had a sense of my inten-tion. I do believe that a very young baby shows attention and awareness of an object outside the body. This weakens common theories about the baby's fusion with the outside world and lack of awareness.

The mother's smell and taste

Babies have a strong sense of smell and can recognize their own mothers' smell even before they recognize their faces. They can distinguish between different smells. Initially they respond to new smells; then they quickly adapt and stop responding once the smell becomes familiar. In the presence of a new smell, they show interest by moving their heads; their heart rate and general activity level change.

A recent study, for example, has shown that babies as young as six days old can recognize the smell of the mother's breast milk and distinguish it from other mothers' milk (Vallardi, Porter & Winberg, 1994). These amazing capacities prepare the baby to interact and communicate with the caregivers and with a larger social system in later life. A mother can recognize her baby among other babies through smell from the first day after birth, after only one hour of contact. Touch and smell are the first and most basic channels by which a mother identifies her infant. A mother recognizes her infant's smell and the feel of her skin even before she remembers the sound of the baby's cry or a photo of her. Thus, not only is the infant's own sensory system particularly strong, but the mother also is programmed with sophisticated sensory capacities. She can recognize her newborn by olfactory cues and by touch (Kaitz, Good, Rokem & Eidelman, 1987; Kaitz, Lapidot, Branner & Eidelman, 1992). This is an adaptive system that enables the mother to communicate with her infant.

The primitive system bypasses the logical and rational mind and allows the mother to adjust to the baby's primitive language. This is why intellectualization may direct mother away from her own feelings and from her natural capacity to be in contact with her senses and rely on them. The mother's awareness that smell is an important part of the baby's life and that her smell can be a powerful source of comfort to her newborn, as it increases her sense of her presence, is not an intellectual form of knowledge. It is dependent on the mother's primitive capacity to be in touch with her senses and body language.

Leaving on the vernix caseosa not only provides an element of protection for the skin, but it also represents an important cue for mother and baby to recognize each other, giving both an element of security. Apart from the physiological benefits of this, described in Chapter Three, there is an important psychological aspect, because the familiar smell (an extension of the mother) strengthens the baby's sense of security.

Babies after birth become attached to a particular comforter because it smells of their mother and, as a baby gets older, she may not want such a comforter washed because it will lose the smell. There are lots of simple strategies for soothing a baby. For example, a mother can cuddle her in a blanket and use the same one to wrap the baby up, providing a comfortable containment. When the mother has to be away for a while, she can leave an item of clothing that she often wears and that smells of her. This helps the baby to cope with the separation.

There is another aspect of the power of smell that I would like to highlight. Smell is the primary sense and it is connected with pheromones. We tend to lose it as we grow up, especially in industrialized societies. Skin contact with a baby stimulates the mother's sense of smell. It is possible to help restore it during pregnancy by aromatherapy, using fragrances and scents. This can help a pregnant woman to focus on this sense and open a powerful channel of communication with her baby. Furthermore, olfactory memory is very different from auditory and visual memory. As, together with taste, it is the most primary sense, it can take a mother back to her earliest relationships, to her primary period of life. This constructive regression can lead to the rediscovery of primitive language that reduces the distance between adult language and baby language and therefore facilitates their communication.

Taste is another primary sense. Our first taste is the neutral flavour of amniotic fluid. Sensitive to the slightest change in its sweetness or in rare cases acidity, by the seventh month the foetus's taste buds are well prepared to savour the first sweet drop of milk after birth. Breast milk is an ideal source for the baby to develop a good sense of taste, as the milk taste changes according to the mother's food. The baby gets used to a variety of tastes very early, so that the introduction of solid food may be easier. By contrast, babies who are bottle-fed get used to the same taste.

Touch

Touch, the primary source of stimulation for the foetus, is perceived very early and enhances pre-natal learning (Brazelton, 1995). Touch not only stimulates growth but is the primary source of communication with the foetus (via sound vibrations and amniotic fluid movements). Touch is also a powerful channel of communication between two individuals who love each other. Touching provides stimulation and can communicate that the world is a safe and trustworthy place. It can affect human functioning at different levels, from the simplest cell to the higher psychological level.

One woman, whose labour contractions were irregular and whose pelvis was not dilating, said during her birth story that she suddenly felt a change in her body: the contractions became very strong and the pelvis started dilating. Two hours later, she gave birth in the water. I asked her what she thought might have caused that sudden change. She said that when her partner began to massage her back, she felt a flow of energy throughout her body. This must have triggered the labour contractions. She described a feeling of containment that, she pointed out, was surprisingly not overwhelming, since she suffered from claustrophobia. Instead, she felt a wide space around her, in which to move freely, and she felt her breath expanding. Her partner's touch changed her perception of her breathing, her whole bodyself, and the labour environment, enhancing her sense of security and self-confidence.

A baby, who is without emotional and muscular defences, is even more responsive to the power of touch. In intensive care units, tiny and sick babies often "forget" to breathe because they are understimulated. Nurses sometimes slap their feet to stimulate them to start breathing again. This hospital routine should be substituted by more caring ways of giving stimulation.

Massage is a time when sensitive touch can reach its most powerful expression. It opens all the sensory channels, strengthens breathing, and lets any tension flow from the body out towards the periphery. When a baby is screaming with colic or another ailment, touching allows the tension concentrated in a specific area to flow throughout the body. When the baby feels pain in one part of the body, she experiences a feeling of fragmentation and all the emotional and muscle tension becomes locked in that part. Gentle stroking can help the tension flow, reconnecting all the parts of the body in union.

This process of "flowing energy" is absolutely mutual. During massage, the parent's back should be relatively straight, with her movements evolving from the lower back functioning as a pivotal "centre". The cross-legged position is ideal, as it facilitates movement, rhythm, and the appropriate distance between parent and baby. The "cradle pose" is best, as it provides a womb-like containment. The mother can sit on the floor with legs stretched out, back supported against furniture. Her knees are bent slightly outwards, and the soles of her feet are in contact with each other's. This position helps the baby to feel more securely positioned and helps to keep her warm.

The skin is a medium for physical and emotional contact, for the comfort of holding and being held, and also for the transmission of smell, touch, taste, and warm sensations that can be a source of pleasure to mother and baby alike (Pines, 1993). A baby's skin is especially sensitive to touch. Through skin contact, a mother conveys non-verbal messages to her baby, who responds with changes in muscle tone, galvanic skin response, breathing, movements of the head, limbs, and of the whole body, eye contact, vocalizations, and sucking. These bodily interactions shape a rhythmic form of communication that is based on shared codes. These daily moments cement the relationship between parent and baby and will shape the child's way of relating to others. Touch is a personal, intimate form of communication between parent and baby. It contains the imprint of their unique relationship. It can even have a healing power, provided that there is sympathetic communication. This is why only a mother can truly know her own baby and why it is important to rely on her feelings and not to let other people tell her how she should respond to her baby. Nor is it worthwhile relying on a book, without a critical approach to it, guided by self-confidence.

For babies born ill or prematurely, touch can be especially powerful. "Kangaroo care" is a practice based on skin contact that allows babies to remain attached to the support machines but also to experience regular contact with the mother's chest. The father's touch is as important as that of the mother. It is vital that the parents feel that the baby belongs to them and not to the hospital, both for them and the baby. The baby feels secure and the healing effect of touch is immediate. Field (1995) describes the development of premature babies who receive "kangaroo care", spending almost all day in close contact with their mother's body. These babies showed less fluctuation in body temperature and heart and respiratory rates and are ready for discharge significantly earlier than control-group babies.

Some babies born by emergency caesarean section in hospitals are whisked away for tests and put in an incubator while their mothers come round from the anaesthetic. They have a picture of their baby but they do not get to see her all day, sometimes for several days, because they have to stay in bed. These babies are deprived of a vital primary experience and can derive enormous benefits from gentle massage.

Baby massage does not involve the same form of manipulation as an adult massage by a professional masseur; there is no vigorous kneading. This massage is a gentle, warm form of communication, as a newborn baby needs a very soft and mindful massage. As the baby grows stronger, so should her mother's touch. A firm touch communicates strength, love, and confidence. Her strokes should be slow, rhythmic, and adjusted to the baby's own threshold of stimulation and pace. The quality of maternal touch reflects the image of the baby in her mind, which is going to affect the baby's personality and self-image. For instance, if a baby is ill and hospitalized for a while just after birth, her mother may subconsciously nurture a picture of her as fragile and weak for a long time, thus handling her with insecure touch.

The mother projects her fears on to her baby via touch, eye contact, vocalization, and tone of voice. Positive visualizations and affirmations can help parents to free themselves from restrictive images of the baby and allow their baby to develop her full potential. Baby massage has the potential to nurture positive imagery as, while massaging, the mother pictures her baby relaxing, enjoying herself, and letting go of tension. This experience enhances the mother's positive self-representation, which will help her baby to develop positive attitudes about herself. For instance, while massaging her stomach, the mother can say, "How nice and soft your tummy is!" This does strengthen the baby's perception and mental representation of that part of her body and its association to relaxation. By sharing a special experience with her baby, the mother communicates—through her vocal tone, touch, and general body language—respect for her, helping her to build the trust and values that will help to ensure a healthy life.

CHAPTER SEVEN

Facial expressions and bodyself image

What a neonate does with her mother in face-to-face interactions
proves that a human being is born with readiness to know
another.

A substantial amount of activity during the first two years of
life
is extraordinarily social and communicative.

O ur posture is moulded by the muscle memory of our early
experiences. In this memory are imprinted our parents'
facial expressions and quality of touch, which play an
important role in the interaction with the baby. They affect the
infant's responses and movements and, therefore, her posture and
body image development.

As soon as the child is born, she uses her maturing sensory
capacities, especially smell, taste, and touch, to interact with the
social environment. However, at two months of age, the organization of the occipital cortex goes through a critical phase (Yamada et
al., 2000). In particular, the mother's emotionally expressive face is

by far the most potent visual stimulus in the infant's environment and the baby's intense interest in it, especially in her eyes, leads to periods of intense mutual gazing. The infant's gaze evokes the mother's gaze, acting as a potent channel for the transmission of mutual cues. The pupil acts as a powerful non-verbal communicative tool and enlarged pupils in the infant release responses in the caregiver (Hess, 1975).

Face-to-face interactions are communicative events that provide the infant with a large amount of cognitive and social information. The rapid co-ordination of mutual responses between mother and baby suggests the existence of unconscious communication. These mutually attuned interactions are fundamental to the infant's emotional development.

A facial expression occurs through a complex co-ordination of tiny muscles, which allows a particular emotion to be expressed and recognized. Muscular tension in the face, but also in the neck, shoulders, and even more distant parts of the body can alter the co-ordination of the muscles involved in the emotion. Therefore, high tension can lock expressions, acting as a barrier to communication, and restrict the child's range of responses and movements. Babies are especially sensitive to a wide range of varied visual stimuli.

Nowadays parents tend to introduce objects prematurely to provide visual excitement. For a newborn, however, much stimulation comes from the caregiver's expressions, voice, movements, and gestures. When there is excessive tension, the variety of expressions in the parents lessens and, as a result of the mirroring process, also in the baby.

Varied facial expressions are a sign of well-being and liveliness. Eye contact and smiling are powerful ways of relieving tension and pain. They are both powerful sources of communication, especially in our primary life. Babies are particularly curious about the human face and its changes of expression. This leads to an imprinting of parental expressions in our facial features. Facial and postural features are acquired not just genetically but are also moulded by the interplay of expressions. The baby's resemblance to her mother or father varies day by day, sometimes moment by moment, according to the expression she adopts. In other words, the definition of our features, as well as posture and body image, is not determined only by genetic heredity, but also by our earliest interactions and their emotional impact. There is a very strong likelihood that smiling children have smiling parents.

The mother and father are like mirrors for their children. Conversely, they can also see their own reflected images in their babies. It can be a wonderful game watching their baby's varied expressions and movements and reproducing them. They will rediscover the primary harmony of their body image. This may be why parents who enjoy the advent of a new baby show a special light in their face. It is the liveliness of the baby's own expressions that is reflected in their face. Playing together at mimicking each other's expressions and vocal sounds is a communicative event that encourages both the baby's and the parent's self-discovery. This is a basic process of getting to know each other. The baby is certainly an amazing teacher.

Babies who are only three days old can imitate the expressions on their mother's faces. In a study of babies' ability to mimic adults' expressions, babies were held face-to-face by someone who adopted a happy, sad, or surprised facial expression and who kept this up until the baby looked away (Harris, 1989). An observer who could see only the baby's face would guess, on the basis of the baby's expression, which expression the adult was modelling. Guesses were correct for a sad expression in fifty-nine per cent of cases, for a happy expression in fifty-eight per cent, and a surprised expression in seventy-six per cent of cases.

Many researchers have shown that when only a few minutes old, a newborn can imitate facial expressions (Meltzoff & Moore, 1977; Harris, 1989). Imitation requires a responsive developed sensory system. The visual system provides one of the most power-ful channels of communication. Mothers have long known that soon after birth their babies could see and respond visually to them. However, doctors were reluctant to believe them and thought for a long time that until the age of about six weeks babies could not see. Infant psychologists now know that within the first few days of life infants can see, possibly in the same way as an adult (Carpenter, 1974; Klaus, Kennell & Klaus, 1996). Researchers have observed that when newborns in the fairly alert state were shown pictures, the infants looked at them and fixed on a photograph (Fantz, 1964). They observed visual preferences and a particular attraction to sharp outlines, as well as to contrasts between light and dark. Both eyes follow the direction of the pattern and the baby pays attention not only by looking but also by lifting the upper eyelid, "brightening" the eye, and ceasing to suck.

Babies can also recognize colours and are especially attracted to the human face. This complex event is missed by anyone not sensitive to the baby's non-verbal language. Newborns' vision is best at a range of 20–25 cm, the same distance from which an infant views her mother's face during breastfeeding. While breastfeeding, the baby studies the mother's face and learns from her expressions. Equally, the mother learns from the baby's expressions and can understand her experience. If objects are moved closer or further away than this optimal distance, they go out of focus and become blurred for the baby.

However, a baby's reaction to facial expressions is far more complex. Her response to these, as to sounds, can be detected in changes of muscular, cardiac, and respiratory activity. It seems to me that rather than simply imitating the facial movements, as recent evidence suggests, newborns feel the emotion in their body and, as a result, reproduce the expression (Tronick, 1989; Bowers, Bauer & Heilman, 1993). They can establish empathy. Two individuals can smile at a baby at the same time while only one may induce the baby's smiling because of the particular empathetic feeling between them. A "clicking" then seems to occur between the two.

The mother's face moves animatedly and is accompanied by talking, touching, and moving. The correspondence between these signals makes an expressive pattern effective; in other words, it makes the pattern communicative. Babies do not understand the words uttered in a conversation, but because of their extraordinary sensory and motor abilities they feel the emotional content of a message and respond in accordance with it. Some research has shown that if the mother's face is accompanied by a voice other than her own, or if her voice is accompanied by another face, this is felt to be incongruous and produces an obvious turning away, a "tuning out" (Tronick, Als, Adamson, Wisu & Brazelton, 1978). The findings suggest that the more "coherent" the messages, the more engrossed the baby's attention is.

In the light of this research and in line with an integrated model, I hold that a persistent turning away by the baby, resulting from the mother's tendency to send ambivalent messages, can shape the baby's muscle responses and posture, thus also her emotional behaviour. This can give rise to confused, ambivalent feelings, altering the perception of the bodyself image. A "turning away" attitude, as a result of contradictory messages and failure to meet the baby's needs, can evolve into defensive reactions to objects and people, with an impact on the child's later relationships and social experiences (Parker, 1995).

Babies and young children feel and learn the correspondence or discrepancy of signals more easily than one signal in isolation, as their muscular systems store the whole emotional experience rather than the single sensory stimulus of a smile, cuddle, kiss, and so on. What is stored is the psychic as well as the bodily experience. I consider that these two kinds of experience are just two facets of the same process. The parent–child relationship takes shape gradually through these exquisitely bodily interactions.

Babies prefer complexity, diversity, movement, change, and multi-coloured scenarios and they have a strong visual as well as muscular memory. All the postural patterns and gestures in response to sensory stimuli are recorded in their muscle memory. Babies can actively use what they have seen from the parent's expressions and what they have felt in response to them.

The baby's feats of visual perception and memory indicate that her visual talent is based not only on reflex eye movement but, more importantly, on higher mental and bodily functions that continuously involve the whole bodyself. This complex talent, appearing soon after birth, draws newborns into eye contact, a vital element in human interaction. In the primary mother–baby gaze, obviously also the father–baby gaze, the first post-natal dialogue begins.

As an example of contradictory messages, when a mother smiles at her baby with tension in her mouth or in her eyes, perhaps being drawn away from her baby's experience by her thoughts and preoccupations, the baby senses the tension more than her smile and receives conflicting signals. If this is not an occasional way of responding, but the mother's attitude or a repeated pattern, it will shape the baby's development and her communicative style. The baby's smile, for instance, will be moulded by the mother's smiling patterns through mirroring, as the baby's mouth and eye muscles will be likely to develop the same pattern.

Empathetic perception

It is well known that babies learn through imitation. I hold that this is far more than mere imitation, as the following case in my observational study will demonstrate. During a mother-and-baby postnatal yoga class, my attention was captured by a one-year-old girl walking on tiptoe in a dance pose. I knew that her mother used to be a dancer, so I asked her if the child had ever seen her walk in that way. She said that she had never tiptoed in front of the child. Then she added that the only relevant thing she remembered was the child watching a dancer on television one day. I do not believe that this episode itself could have been enough for the child to remember and imitate the pose, especially as walking on tiptoe had become a habit. I conclude that the mother's own postural attitude must have been at the basis of this phenomenon, through a multitude of signals that the girl was able to sense, learn, and absorb in her posture. The child had seen the programme before she could walk, so quite a long time before performing the dance pose. Her muscle memory, not just her brain, had stored the visual stimulation and, more importantly, the repertoire of the mother's body language and her implicit emotional involvement in dance.

The input from the outside world, in this case the visual stimulation provided by the dancer on television, matched the input from the baby's own muscle system, creating an empathetic perception. This "empathetic perception" is likely to have its foundation in prenatal life, when the baby absorbs information from the mother's emotional posture. This is not to exclude the genetic contribution. Perceptual information is picked up in emotional and social interaction. Therefore, muscles, movements, and general posture are involved in the process of imitation, which is a mutual mirroring in which emotions and motivations play an important role. In the same way, a baby picks up and records her parents' facial expressions through an empathetic perception of all the signals from their posture. A facial expression is accompanied by postural behaviour, such as a muscle tone variation. When a mother smiles at her baby, she is likely to show a forward-leaning posture (approach attitude), for instance with her shoulders anticipating a holding gesture (broadly containing). The baby senses and simultaneously learns the integrated pattern as a coherent message. This is consistent with

Bowlby's (1969) account of how in intimate settings feelings are detected through facial expressions, gestures, tone of voice or prosody, posture, physiological changes, and tempo of movement.

While observing babies being massaged by their mothers, I have come to see the importance of open shoulders and chest, free of tension, while mother interacts with her baby, smiling, talking, or simply looking at her. Usually the baby responds by wincing, smiling, laughing, and sucking her hands in a signal of enjoyment. It is equally evident how the rigid closed-shoulders-and-chest pattern, associated with constricted breathing, hinders fluid massage movements and facial expressions, as well as rhythmic communication, depriving both mother and baby of the pleasurable massage experience. Fearful or worried expressions induce a defensive reaction of backward closed shoulders and chest (flight attitude), which makes the containing function of massage almost impossible. In this case, a mother massages only with her hands, as her posture acts as a barrier to enjoying being with her baby. Despite my considerable experience as an observer and baby massage teacher, I am repeatedly struck by the importance of the mother's smile during massage as a powerful indicator of enjoyment and, at the same time, a powerful reinforcement of enjoyment for both mother and baby.

Towards language

The mother–baby communications entail implicit rapid cueing and responses that occur too rapidly to be translated verbally at the same time (Lyons-Ruth, 2000). This rhythmic unconscious communication allows for the development of linguistic symbols that represent the meaning of an experience. This process also occurs in successful psychotherapeutic work with parents and infants, in which the process of sensing and communicating emotional states is accompanied by the exploration of meaning.

Facial expressions, an important aspect of interactive communication, are involved in the baby's linguistic development. It is noticeable during infant massage how the mother's smile and eye contact induce vocalizations and babbling in the baby. When the mother reproduces the baby's vocalizations through mirroring, there is a complex interplay of facial muscles while she articulates and scans. The baby, and the young child later on, picks up and records the pattern in her muscles, and reproduces it through mirroring. It is a sort of rhythmic dance between the facial muscles and expressions of baby and mother, in which the face of each acts as a mirror for the other.

To develop language later on, the baby needs space and time to be satisfied with these pre-verbal communications, consisting of eye contact, smiling, touch, attentive hearing, and rhythmic muscular co-ordination. Healthy linguistic development is based on this rhythmic co-ordination. It may be that some speech problems, which are on the increase in children of modern industrial societies, are related to an earlier lack of time and space for parent–baby communication through face-to-face mirroring interactions.

The first smile

With eyes shut and weighing only 5 lb (2.26 kg), the unborn child is captured smiling in the comfort of the mother's womb. It is commonly known that smiling begins in the womb, where it is endogenous and independent of any external stimulus. However, because a foetus is highly responsive to signals from the mother's body, it may well be that the smile or any facial movement actually reflects inner contentment, perhaps elicited by the mother's enjoyment, her reassuring voice, any internal or external stimulus reaching the womb, or a particular position assumed by the mother's body. A confident posture shapes the pelvis in a way that provides the baby with a comfortable place. There is no evidence that the pre-birth smile has no social meaning. Although it is not social in terms of face-to-face interaction, it is environmental if we consider the womb as an environment shaped by the mother's thoughts, feelings, and attitude to her bodyself, via the immune system, bloodstream, breathing, and heart rate.

Statements concerning babies are often formulated from the perspective of adult convenience, as the result of their projections on to the babies. My attempts at inference are aimed at acknowledging the wide range of the foetus's and the baby's amazing capacities, on the basis of the reported experiences of a large number of parents and their babies. I hope to encourage adults and institutions to have great respect for the pre-natal as well as the post-natal baby and to counteract their preconceptions. Babies have extraordinary communicative capacities and much more dignity than they are often credited with. They can experience frustration, pride, and shame very early and, when only a few months old, they can even "show off" when appraised by others. These emotions are of the utmost importance for achieving knowledge and skills, including linguistic skills.

If we conceive the mother's body language as being shaped by her thoughts, emotions, attitudes, bodyself image, and expectations, and as forming the baby's primary environment, there is evidence of a possible social meaning of the baby's smile in the womb. Foetuses may take pleasure from their movements, licking, swallowing, sucking, and floating in the amniotic fluid. It is possible that when they suddenly move and kick in the womb, they are reacting to a state of mutual pleasure in what are communicative events.

The mother's creativity in interpreting these responses on the basis of her sensations and intuitions, beyond what the foetus is actually doing, can be a powerful bridge between her mind and her body, and therefore also between her bodyself and her baby. This exquisitely bodily interpretation can make the communication realistic rather than idealized, as it is likely to happen to a woman whose high expectations and fantasy may nurture an "ideal" baby. My focus is much more on the unique and implicit mother–baby communication than in what the foetus is actually doing. It is in the mother's subjective experience. For instance, the study of movements or heart rate scanned by a machine, regarded as variables for studying the foetus's behaviour is far from reliable if this is done in isolation from the mother's feelings and interpretations concerning those foetal activities.

It is superfluous to postulate a reflex, non-social smile in the pre-natal baby or a few weeks after birth, as the foetus is already able to feel pleasure and contentment. The baby's smile is generally one of the things mother enjoys most about her baby. She, or anybody else, would find it impossible not to respond to her smile. This circularity or mutual pleasure is one of the most important indicators of empathetic parent–infant communication.

Facial games and sounds

Babies are attracted by movements and changing stimuli. The baby massage classes gave me the opportunity to observe the maternal capacity to play with facial expressions and vocal sounds, which is a powerful way of establishing eye contact and entertaining the baby. Eye contact, like touch and smell, is a primary channel of communication. It is also a way of relieving pain or tension. Listening to birth stories from women at the Birth Unit, I found the eye contact between a birthing woman and a communicative midwife to be helpful in relieving the labour pain or anxiety. Communicative eye contact can convey just the fact of being present and available. As a primitive form of body language, it is an important cue in the labour and birth process. Moreover, unlike speech or actions, it does not elicit intellectual processes in the woman, which would interfere with the primitive brain involved in birth. Eye contact can be a cue of quiet presence and trust, which is what a woman needs from a skilled midwife.

Babies learn from other people's, and especially their caregivers', expressions. Imitation of their facial expressions and gestures seems to facilitate the process of self-discovery. It is an important means of learning. Therefore, the wider the range of expressions and the greater the correspondence between facial expression, voice, and posture, the richer the learning is for the baby. For example, when a mother is teaching her child not to touch something hot, it is worth displaying a serious expression and using a firm tone of voice and, simultaneously, indicating the hot object. If instead the mother smiles, the child feels that she is joking and is likely to experience a distorted perception. The child, through mirroring, tends to reproduce the same severe expression and to experience the emotion associated with the dangerous object. The infant learns most effectively when she receives a wide range of interactive cues and when, consequently, she experiences the changes in her own body and feelings, rather than just hearing words.

The mother's vocal tones and facial expressions resonate and amplify both the intensity and the duration of the affective state in both members of the dyad. The mother is then empathetically attuned to the baby's inner state. This means looking at the baby and connecting with her when she is fed, talking and singing to her, or smiling and playing with her while changing her nappy. Using varying tones of voice, facial expressions, and gestures in accordance with the message facilitates communication and promotes the child's overall development. All this is a form of dancing with the baby, which means meeting her needs, getting in tune with her cues and pace, in short, being "receptive".

Lynne Murray pioneered experiments with "still-face" and "double-video". First, mother and baby communicated happy moments with vivid expressions and the baby produced many different expressions in response to the mother and looked very happy. This was then recorded in a one-minute video. The recording is a perfect copy, but it produces only a depressive state in the baby, who looks confused and disturbed. The baby seeks live conversation with co-ordinated and expressive bodily responses that require equally rich and expressive responses from the mother.

Eye contact and body image

The important elements that help establish the bonding between parent and infant include eye contact, skin contact, the parent's voice and baby's response to it, smell, rhythms of communication, activation of maternal hormones by contact with the baby, and temperature regulation.

Eye contact is one of the most powerful channels of communication at our disposal, and it strengthens the connection between parent and infant. The baby's visual system is biologically programmed to seek out the mother's eye and nipple; maternal hormones darken the areola during pregnancy, perhaps to help attract the baby's gaze. Eye contact may be a powerful cue to the infant's physiological system; it sends signals to the brain that allow it to reduce the production of stress hormones initiated during childbirth. During massage, for instance, because the infant is positioned face-to-face, eye contact, as well as the mother's voice, smell, and touch, moulds the quality of interaction between parent and baby.

Researchers examined what happened when a mother was asked to maintain an unchanging, neutral expression and to be unresponsive to her three-month-old baby's signals (Tronick, Als, Adamson, Wisu & Brazelton, 1978). Initially, the baby tried to elicit the mother's attention. After a few minutes, the baby began to fuss and cry and became irritable. If a mother is sad for several days, her baby will become distressed and irritable. This mother transfers her emotion to her baby through a quiet facial expression of sadness and is less sensitive and responsive to her.

One study (Field, 1985) compared early facial interactions of three-month-old infants with cranio-facial abnormalities (cleft lip and palate) and their mothers with those of normal control infant–mother dyads to determine the degree to which early mother–infant interactions were impaired by cranio-facial deformity. This found that although the mothers of these infants looked at them just as much, the infants looked less at these mothers and engaged in less smiling and vocalization. The mothers also smiled and vocalized less, with less imitative behaviour, contingent responsiveness and game playing. Although it is unclear why these mothers were less active, it is suggested that they may view their infants' condition as long-term and become depressed by this reality. The attitude of these mothers presumably reinforces their babies' perception of their abnormalities through a mirroring process, affecting their body image development.

Babies are particularly sensitive to stimuli in movement. The mutual appeal of the mother's and the baby's eyes is facilitated by the richness of their expressions and establishes key patterns of interaction with implications for the development of the bonding process. In comparison with other areas of the body, the eye has a multitude of interesting qualities, such as its shininess, the fact that is mobile while also fixed in space, and the pupil's variations in diameter in response to light but also to emotions, as well as the different effects of variations in width of the eyelid fissure in relation to muscular tension and contractions around the eye. It has been observed that the pupil of the eye acts as a tool of non-verbal communication (Hess, 1975) and that large pupils in the infant release cognitive behaviour.

Eye contact can release strong positive feelings. When the infant looks at her mother, the mother feels much closer to her. In home births and in hospitals where they practise natural childbirth, the mother picks up the baby after birth and holds her in a face-to-face position, speaking to her in a high-pitched voice. The psychoanalyst Fraiberg has described in detail the difficulties that parents of blind infants have in feeling close to them (1974). Without the mutual gazing, parents feel lost and like strangers to their babies until both learn to substitute other means of communication for this.

Newborns tend to scan the outer contours of patterns rather than inner details. When babies look at other human faces, they usually scan the outline and then move to the eyes and mouth (Haith, Bergman & Moore, 1977). They find eyes particularly engrossing. When alert, babies look around curiously. They can recognize depth, show preferences between abstract patterns, and are especially attracted to sharp outlines, as well as light and dark contrasts. Babies are particularly interested in complexity, diversity, and movement, and they have strong visual memory.

I found it remarkable during my observational work how much babies preferred looking at my face to inanimate objects that I showed them. Since smiling is an extremely powerful reinforcement (McFarlane, 1974), the visual interaction is important in fostering the closeness between parent and child. The baby's capacity to establish eye contact and the powerful effects on adults is showed by the following anecdote. Three young researchers were required to assist infants each day. They did not particularly like babies, found newborns unappealing, and planned never to have a baby. As they carried out the assessments, each of the women had her first experience with a baby, following the baby's eyes with her own. Their feelings and attitudes towards the babies changed amazingly. Each wanted to hold the baby and came back later in the day and the next day to visit. She would talk first about this wonderful baby she had tested. In a few weeks, all three had decided they would some day like to have a baby.

The compelling attraction of a baby's eye contact with her parents, or with adults in general, can induce rewarding feelings and even resolve some communication difficulties. Another case shows the power of eye contact in affecting an infant's growth. When I worked at the University Hospital in Rome I saw a four-and-a half-month-old baby who came to hospital because her parents were concerned about her lack of responsiveness, delayed development, and low weight. She also had strabismus. The parents were convinced that her strabismus might result from a brain abnormality. When I observed the mother and the baby interacting, I noticed they never made eye contact. When I asked about this, the mother said, "I don't know which eye she is using, so I have stopped trying to look at her eye-to-eye". After surgery on the deviating eye, when the baby's eyes could move together normally, a remarkable change occurred in the mother–baby interaction, with more smiling and responsiveness. At one year of age, the baby had gained weight and was showing a normal rate of growth.

Parents' ability to share their social life with the baby not only helps the baby to work through the separation from the mother and the transition to the external world; it also provides her with a variety of entertaining scenarios. For instance, using a baby-carrier, not only around the house but when walking or shopping, provides the infant with social stimulation, and she can feel involved in what her parent is doing. In the security of her bodily warmth and movements, the infant can see varied expressions from other people and develop the capacity to get in touch with their emotions. This capacity will strengthen her social skills. She can feel like part of a human community and her sense of belonging will enhance her sense of identity. Every learning step is possible when the infant is in comfortable contact with her mother. The sense of security allows her to be attentive and to explore the surroundings. The same stimulation can turn out to be irritating when the baby lacks eye or skin contact.

The quality of the earliest eye contact between parent and baby affects the baby's capacity to relate to others. While observing the behaviour of children over five months old in mother-and-baby classes, I saw how the mothers' presence and eye contact allowed them to feel secure and explore the space around them, to interact with other children and therefore to experience themselves. In most social settings, babies are abruptly separated from their mothers and, in some cases, the social and physical exploration may be restricted because they are missing the mother's physical presence.

The sense of security and self-confidence enables the baby to attain a level of attentiveness and perceptiveness that enables her to make eye contact with other people, interacting with them, moving around, familiarizing herself with the environment. An environment can be rich in stimulation, but if there is no comfortable contact with the mother, the baby will hardly experience it. A sense of security and cognitive-intellectual development interact continuously, shaping the child's personality.

Movement is, therefore, the essence of life and what babies are most fascinated by. An individual, either as a baby or adult, realizes that she is feeling an emotion because of the changes in her body—through arousal or activation, respiratory or cardiac changes, temperature and muscle tone variations, or changes in facial expression. On the other hand, we can see as well as feel an individual's emotion through her body and postural signals: changes in tone of voice and facial expression, tempo of movement, variations in the brightness of the eyes, variations of pupil diameter, change in posture, and so on. Obviously, we are not aware of all the cues that we perceive while interacting with another individual. Babies are particularly sensitive to bodily changes, and are able to detect feelings through body language.

The capacity to feel and share emotion is called "empathy". For instance, the eyes of an individual who is in love are particularly bright, wet, and show a dilated pupil. This is an example of a coherent message. If we are told that we are loved without this expression and an attuned voice, designed to establish eye contact, we are unlikely to feel loved. Our daily life is full of incoherent messages, mainly for conventional reasons, and because of the constraints that are put on our authentic feelings by various kinds of authority. We learn to be polite and well-mannered and to control cognitively the emotions with which we are born. For example, under some circumstances such as at work, we cannot expose our true self and often need to summon conventional images of ourselves. However, some families use a kind of communication based on ambivalent messages. These messages will affect the child's development, sometimes with severe consequences.

It is interesting that the word "person" derives from the Latin for the mask an actor wears and the part that he plays, and the word "persona" means the image of ourselves that we project in the society to which we belong. Various brochures, handbooks, and adverts highlight the importance of considering a baby as a person. However, she is the opposite of a person. Adults project their language and preconceptions on to the baby. A baby is just her own experiencing being. At first, she has no cognitive or linguistic means of processing and accepting a lack of eye contact or warmth of voice; she can only feel confused and lost. For a baby, eye contact is not something an adult may overlook; it is experience itself.

Interactions with the baby that lack eye contact can impinge on the development of the child's bodyself image, through the deprivation of the mirroring process. Meeting the baby's feelings and needs implies getting rid of the mask while interacting with her and being less of a "person".

In some individuals, inability to establish eye contact or locked facial expressions may be the result of long-standing emotional inhibition related to their earliest experiences. We can see some individuals with a persistent sulky expression, as though they are using facial muscle tightening to inhibit crying. This is a pattern built up gradually through their primary life rather than an expression elicited by a particular occurrence. I refer to "patterns", repeated gestures, and locked expressions that have an emotional content. Very often we find similar patterns in the parents of these individuals. I would say that we look like our parents more in expressions and posture than in features. Our heredity encompasses our early relationships, perhaps also our pre-natal life.

A mother's rigid facial expressions can act as a barrier to communication and thus to mirroring with the baby, as can tense shoulders, neck, chest, or voice during breastfeeding or baby massage. The baby's facial muscles, through a back-and-forth process, are stimulated by a variety of expressions and emotions, which establishes a fertile foundation for language. The key factor is attuned contact. The mother's variety of expressions and her muscular articulations while talking to the baby mould the baby's use of facial expressions, posture, and body language in general. Depressed mothers usually show a persistent sulky, angry, or sad expression. Their babies may internalize that parental portrait, with effects on their personality.

Children whose parents use varied and lively expressions are likely to be more communicative, as they learn to use a wide repertoire of cues. Facial expressions, as well as tone of voice and touch, are modulators of the baby's emotions and muscles, thus of the way in which she perceives her bodyself image. As they induce muscular micro-responses, they can enhance the flexibility of the baby's posture and body image. This also has effects on the mother's perception of her bodyself. The baby can see the movements caused by the mother's changes of expression and perceive the movements of her own face in response. She is very interested in movements generated by her own as well. This mutual mimicry enhances the parent's communication skills. The games in early life during parent–baby interactions, which would appear as insignificant moments to an insensitive adult, are vital experiences for both parent and baby. Through eye contact, vocalizing, mimicking, touching, sniffing, and so on, parents and baby strengthen their communicative abilities and reciprocal knowledge.

Supportive or therapeutic work with parents and infants cannot overlook ongoing parent–baby interactions, made up of those vital games. Any kind of work that overlooks the concrete relationship pushes a parent further away from the baby's experience. Psychological development, the most complex level of human functioning, begins in very early life through an evolving relationship with these bodily rhythms of communication.

Mirroring and the sense of boundaries

Babies are particularly interested in faces. They have an extraordinary capacity to imitate their parents' facial expressions. If the mother sticks out her tongue, the newborn will tense her body slightly and begin to push her tongue out. Nevertheless, this is something more than simple passive imitation. The baby must have a sense of relationship between the mother's face and a part of her own body and, furthermore, a sense of having a tongue and of it being part of her own body.

The mirroring process is complex and mysterious. The shared games affect the behaviour of both mother and baby remarkably. One mother described how her baby's vocalizing inspired her to make nightingale sounds. The baby responded by producing a similar sound and the game continued like a dance until they both fell asleep.

The mother's body language and body image regulate this rhythmic mirroring in a complex almost indescribable way. The mother's body image is a mirror for the baby's body image. The father's bodyself image plays a complementary part, and his different body language is a valuable enrichment for the child's development. The father provides a model of identification that is distinguished from the mother. The two "others", instead of the one

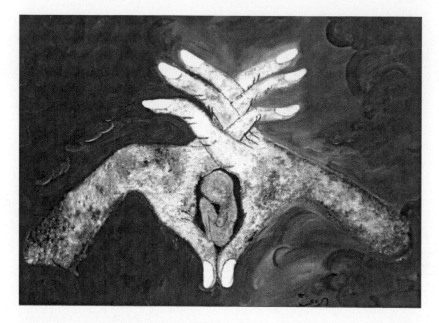

Attunement. Painting by Antonella Sansone.

"other", are a vital source for the formation of the infant's gender identity and bodyself. The baby, with her expressions and body language, on the other hand, is a mirror for the mother and modulates the mother's perception of her bodyself image. In an exquisitely different way, the infant is a mirror for the father as well. I shall be dealing with this issue further in Chapter Eleven.

I suggest that the baby, when she looks at the mother's face, sees and feels her bodyself through the mother's responses. Babies like to dictate and induce responses. These back-and-forth responses impinge on the infant's process of discovering her own being and boundaries. The mother's reproduction of the baby's facial expressions, sounds, and gestures, encourages self-discovery even more than her stimulation and guidance. In other terms, the baby sees her self and body image reflected in the mother's body language.

The mother's use of body language is closely related to how she perceives her bodyself image and regulates her muscular system and emotions. I hope the link is now emerging more clearly between the mother's body image and the development of the baby's body image, and between their sense of boundaries.

Winnicott observed (1960, 1987, 1991) that mothers are mirrors for their babies and spend a lot of time imitating their babies. Through the mutual mirroring, infants learn about themselves and their bodies. They also learn about their parents. A wide range of expressions and body language used by the parents enhances, through mirroring, the baby's ability to use more varied interactive cues, increasing her communication skills later on.

The mirroring process is not a deliberate, self-conscious activity but a powerful unconscious process that will be imprinted in the child's muscle and sensory systems. By interacting with the baby and getting to know her, parents learn how to modify their own boundaries in relation to the infant. It is a matter of flexibility in the use of their body language while, for instance, talking to their baby, touching, smelling, massaging, bathing, playing with her, and so on. It therefore also concerns the perception of their bodyself. Lack of confidence, incapacity to listen to their own feelings and rely on them, or feelings of guilt or fear, hinder the fluctuation of the parents' body images and, consequently, the flexibility of their boundaries.

The baby's needs become manifest through bodily signals that she sends out and that are interpreted by her mother. An appro priate response from the mother, which fulfils the baby's needs, enhances the baby's contact with her own needs and, therefore, strengthens her sense of self and the link between her needs and the communicative function of her body language. These powerful inborn pre-verbal systems for communicating, nurturing, and surviving are the basic network from which verbal communication is built up.

Parents' ways of managing their own boundaries in relation to the baby's vital space mould the baby's perception of her own boundaries and being. If, for instance, the mother is anxious about her baby's health or development, or if she does not feel supported by her partner, this affects the way she feels about both herself and her baby. Her body language and way of holding her baby will reflect her internal state and affect the baby's feeling about herself and her developing bodyself image. For instance, if a mother feels disappointed and sad because of surgery or illness at birth, she may not be able to hold her baby immediately. She needs to believe that there is a lot to do after this critical phase, to safeguard the relationship and thus the child's healthy development. However, what seems to be missing in the first hours or days of life can be repaired, as babies have an extraordinary capacity to adjust.

For parents who missed the earliest bonding experience, believing that all is lost for the future relationship with their child can deprive the relationship of further important resources. In this case, sharing experiences with other parents and receiving support can help work through the difficulties. Both parents and their babies can get to know each other, although the bonding process may require more time. Feeling supported helps parents to acknowledge their feelings and those of the baby, otherwise confused in a critical phase. The parent's capacity to distinguish between her own needs and those of the baby is a crucial step to setting clear boundaries. Excessive fear, confusion, low self-confidence, and guilt feelings make this distinction difficult.

At the Birth Unit, consistently with the natural birth philosophy, the space of the couple and the baby are respected from conception onwards. The hospital's approach to birth contributes to the development of parent–baby boundaries, which is based on respect of this mutual space that can be either strengthened or impaired by the medical attitude towards parents before and after birth. In active or natural birth, infant, mother, and father are allowed to be together from the earliest moments of the baby's life in a space that respects their own pace and where there is no rushing or excessive medical control. This physical and emotional space provides more opportunities for parents to meet each other's eyes, to learn about their baby, to ask questions of the caregivers, who are always available, and thus to establish the bonding. A cascade of sensory, hormonal, and emotional events can flow freely without the risk of being hindered by institutional financial considerations.

A concept of coherence

Gestures are motor patterns with a cultural, social, and psychological matrix. A gesture evolves in a flexible and dynamic interplay of different parts of the body. While some muscles contract, others relax in a time sequence. Nevertheless, when a muscle or group of muscles breaks the harmonious sequence, as a result of prolonged contraction or concentration of excessive tension, the evolution of the movement, gesture, or facial expression is inhibited. This condition can be produced by emotional tension and linked with personality features.

An adult's posture is the history of contracted gestures that were originally complete and expanded. An adult tends to lose the infant's flexibility, emotional fluctuations, facial expressions, and gestures, in response to environmental demands. Therefore, an individual can use rigid muscular patterns as defensive mechanisms to withhold emotions. A balanced and smooth posture, related to an adjustable body image, is related to a rhythmic sequence of contracting and relaxing muscles, which is connected with our emotional and psychic rhythms. Psychosomatic disturbances are characterized by a break in this rhythm. We normally use only a small percentage of our potential, as we get accustomed to an uncomfortable posture and we may not be aware of this. Our posture impinges on our self-representation and the ability to find the strategies for making better use of our posture, or of our bodyself image, affects our posture.

Posture, like a facial expression, has communicative power. The correspondence between a gesture or facial expression and its emotional content is fundamental for healthy communication between parents and child. When emotions are inhibited because they encounter an obstacle in posture and body language, communication is altered. The coherence makes a message ring true and enables a child to trust her parents and grow with clear reference to models of identification and a sense of security. The possibility of relying on her parents will enable the baby to rely on herself and to move towards independence. Contradictory messages during an interaction—for instance, between a facial expression, tone of voice and forward- or backward-leaning shoulders—are likely to cause confusion in the child. Conflicting messages used by some parents may be at the basis of a child's psychological disturbances and learning difficulties.

Through honesty with their own feelings, parents can show the child how to be true to her own feelings and her bodyself. This requires an experienced self-knowledge and leads to a valuable use of communication skills. To be consistent, it is important for a parent to "acknowledge" and to reflect upon her own primary language, posture, and needs. Parents' own self-discoveries foster the knowledge of their child's own needs and boundaries. The child's self-esteem is significantly nurtured by coherent communication.

Examples of ambivalent messages are when a parent cuddles her baby with stiff hands, embracing her only with her arms and not with a containing chest; or says, "I love you" in a sharp tone of voice or with a blank facial expression; or teaches her not to touch a hot surface while smiling, and so on. These conflicting messages, while harmless on an occasional basis, tend to jeopardize communication when they become habitual patterns.

When there is anger, it is better not to try to hide it, as this could send conflicting messages that the sensitive infant is able to pick up. It can be better to do something to relieve the anger and than to pretend to communicate when the melody is missing. Or, with an older child, it can be helpful to express the anger and subsequently talk to her honestly, apologize, and give her love in another instance. In daily life, we adults receive and send a multitude of contradictory messages, but we have the logical reasoning to process them. For a baby or young child, who senses and feels enormously and who enters a world in which conflicting and inconsistent messages, prevail, these may have remarkable effects.

My impression is that a happy baby receives coherent communication, as it results from my observations of children's pride and confident posture and personality while interacting with their mothers. To take an everyday example, a baby's enjoyment in being massaged is closely related to the mother's pleasure in massaging. It is like a dance that can be enjoyed by each as long as the partner is also enjoying it. I consider baby massage to be a therapeutic setting because of its potential to open all the sensory channels of communication, which forms the basis of early mother–baby dialogue. During massage, mother and baby can rehearse their rhythmic interactions, enhancing their communication skills and capacity to exchange attuned messages.

The importance of coherent messages also concerns the period of pregnancy. The uterine environment is created by the mother's bodyself by the mediation of hormones, emotions, mental representations, expectations, thoughts, beliefs, and so on. When the pregnant woman is happy, all these factors work harmoniously, influencing the foetus's development. Imagination is a mental and physiological process that can induce bodily changes and, in turn, be influenced by them. Research and observation show that when individuals are asked to visualize, changes occur in muscle tone and posture, body temperature, tone of voice, and feelings (Fisher, 1970; Lang, 1977; Ruggieri & Moria, 1994; Zikmund, 1972). This is why visualizations or daydreams can facilitate bonding, allowing the mother's body to create a hospitable environment in the womb. In the womb there are many channels that the mother can activate with her baby to make the communication effective. The rhythms of her heart rate and breathing and the melody of her voice provide a welcoming mental space for her baby. Touching the abdominal wall and gently swinging the pelvis exert a rocking effect on the baby and singing a melody, playing music or an instrument, practising yoga, or floating in the water enable her to share the same environment with the baby. All this provides the pre-natal baby with a massage experience in which attuned communication reaches its maximum expression. The mother thus delves into the primary period. Her deep and rhythmic breathing, combined with a feeling of enjoyment, unfolds. Her diaphragm gains access to the abdomen, producing pelvic flexibility and a smooth rocking movement.

The baby develops in a watery environment and every stimulus from the mother's body and ripple from her mind generates small waves that touch and massage her. Immersed in a sea of buzzing, the baby will feel the connection with maternal energy if the mother is able to listen to the new creature and to all the bodily and emotional changes fostered by her development. In this way, pregnancy promotes self-understanding, as the major changes can bring a renewed identity and mould a new space in the woman's bodyself image.

True communication with the unborn and the newborn baby depends on the mother's capacity to connect with what is happening to her body and self and to reflect on her experience. Rhythmic mother–infant interactions occur at a subconscious,level but the mother's capacity to give meaning to those attuned exchanges gives her and the baby a crucial opportunity for integrated self-discovery and knowledge. This forms the basis of cultural acquisition. Mindful baby massage and many other creative forms of contact can be seen as an extension of the pre-natal bond. Traces of pregnancy and birth are everywhere: on the skin, in the bones, stomach, back, gestures and body image, our happiness, grief, and attitude to pain. Memory is not confined to the brain, as it is not just a mental process; it is in our muscle systems and gestures, our breathing and posture.

CHAPTER EIGHT

From communication to speech

The infant's innate capacity to develop language
is already the fruit of a relationship.
Mother and baby begin interacting during pregnancy
through a variety of mediators: hormones, breathing, and
heart rhythms,
maternal expectations, thoughts, and postural attitudes.
The mother's body is also the expression of her culture
and her closest relationships.
The father contributes to shaping the womb environment
by touching the abdominal wall and talking to the baby,
as well as by supporting the mother.
The tiny baby thus has her earliest learning experience.

Pre-verbal communication: the primary bodyself-image

Before 1970, there was little curiosity about young infants'
interactions with their parents. Psychoanalysts had a theoretical interest in the development of the infant's ego. The
problem of how linguistic communication began led to observation

of how mothers and fathers communicated with infants before speech. It was found that the primary communication starts from face-to-face contact, more specifically eye contact. This opened up a whole new field of investigation.

My observations concern two powerful primitive non-verbal tools: touch and voice. I have concluded that every aspect of infant development is so closely related to the actual relationship with her mother, father, or other caregivers that any study that is done in isolation from this relationship is somewhat artificial.

Recent studies clear up two points (Stern, 2000; Trevarthen, 2001a). The infant is capable of differentiating herself from the world, things from people and her mother from other people and reacts differently to each. The orientational behaviour of neonates shows that they possess an organized motor system, an ability to perceive objects as separate from the body, and a sense of their form and position.

I shall give an account of the different conversations that the three-month-old Yusuke established with me as an observer and with his mother. While we were facing each other, he made single vocalizations accompanied by mouth and tongue movements and hand-waving. After a while, I observed the mother–baby conversation. He turned away from me and gazed at his mother. She smiled broadly at Yusuke. He smiled back, giggled, and wriggled. Then she waved her head and moved her lips silently. Yusuke babbled for a while and it really sounded as if he was telling her something. Despite the lack of words, the fluency and frequency resembled those of two adults in conversation. His mother smiled at him more broadly and he repeated the same flow of sounds, this time for even longer, in a further attempt to be understood.

I observed the difference between the two conversations. Whereas he made single vocalizations to me, for his mother he produced a flow of cooing that sounded more intentional and emotional in content. It sounded like a melody with a variety of alternating pitches and pauses. In terms of tone and rhythm, this flow sounded like a sentence or speech, despite the absence of words.

What is interesting about proto-conversation between mother and baby is rhythm and musicality. First of all, there are graceful fluctuations between the baby's cooing, "Ah" and the mother's saying a long "Aaaah" with falling pitch and then, "ch ch ch . . .

ch ch", which create a melody. They really get into a sort of duet or dance. The baby's cooing to her mother is more melodious than the sounds he makes to me.

Accurate observations are an invaluable resource in conjunction with theory and illustrate, for example, how skilled and powerful infants are as active contributors in a relationship. Babies' ability to relate to the mother and objects around them, which is obvious to those who have observed a newborn soon after birth, may indicate that they have some representations of the mother, their bodyself, and objects, although their co-ordination and prehensile actions are still ineffective. The baby has an innate predisposition to use the mother and objects around her to satisfy her need to explore and perceive. The baby's brain, as studies on foetuses and newborns show (Yamada et al., 2000; Trevarthen, 2001a, 2001b), is organized in a way that makes her prone to relating to objects and perceiving them. However, to develop this predisposition, the infant needs a relationship, the mother's body, which provides an environment for her earliest experiences.

Klein (1921) describes the infant's innate curiosity to explore the mother's body, the instinct for knowledge. Bion (1962) highlights the baby's need for interaction with the mother to experience herself. Stern (2000) refers to a core self or an innate core self-image. It seems likely that the baby is born with a prior image of the mother's existence, developed during intra-uterine life through the mother's feelings and thoughts about her. Before she can see, the baby is seen and felt and may feel the image of her mother's bodyself as well as of her own bodyself.

The fact that very young babies sometimes imitate others' gestures accurately, even when to do so they move a part of their body that they cannot see, has always intrigued me. This is certainly a learning process, but it also seems to point to a prior image that takes shape before birth. Even in the first month of life, a baby may imitate a mouth movement by her mother. To do so, the baby must have an image of the mother's face in her brain that fits the motor system of her face and allows her to identify with her. This system would be that of the muscle memory, where all primary sensations and perceptions are recorded.

Movements of the head and hands, as well as the face, may thus elicit imitation. The baby must have identificatory models of these as well. For her part, the mother's imitation of the infant's gestures plays an important role in encouraging this prior image to function. This is one crucial dimension that is missing from studies on infant development that overlook the early relational dynamics.

The baby therefore has an innate capacity to learn, but if she had no mediator or partner from whom to learn, this capacity would be lost. Anatomical studies (Nelson & Bosquet, 2000) of the foetal brain indicate highly complex functions. These structures require inter-action and communication following birth for connections and functions to be established, as well as exploratory experiences. Language is certainly a product of cultural history but its acquisition requires the infant's brain to develop highly specific structures. Appropriate stimulation and experiences gained by the infant at her own pace bring her body and self to their full point of development.

The pre-natal as well as the post-natal baby's brain has a net-work that needs loving interactions, physical, and social stimulation to be nurtured and, therefore, to function by forming connections between the different parts and becoming specialized. It seems likely that this network is partly organized during pregnancy, since the womb is the earliest environment that shapes the foetus's development. This ambience is formed by the mother's hormones, blood, breathing, and heart rhythms, sleep–wake cycles, thoughts, emotions, and other factors that are not easily detectable.

I have noticed in mother-and-baby classes that when the mother speaks sympathetically and expressively to her baby (proto-conversation), the baby tends to move her right arm more than her left. The same reaction occurs when rhymes are sung in a mother-and-baby music class. The baby waves her right hand with the melody and moves her mouth in rhythm with the mother's singing. Babies can be extremely talented in feeling the vibrations of a song in their body. They can "conduct" the rhythms and melodies of their mother's song with their hands, especially the right This asymmetry of gesture corresponds to the cerebral asymmetry of language and is already present at birth. In toddlers, the left cerebral cortex, which controls the right side of the body, begins to develop in relation to speech and language acquisition. According to Trevarthen (1999), this communicative use of the right hand in very young infants is more subcortical. This primitive bodily communication, already asymmetrical and involving the deep brain (the site of emotional and motivational systems), is therefore the precursor of the development of asymmetry in the cerebral cortex, which is associated with language.

The baby is a co-ordinated and sentient subject who is motivated to act with intentions in relation to the world around her. She needs to retain her co-ordination, flexibility, and harmony through a play space in which she can practise her skills. Baby massage and mother-and-baby classes are a good place for the baby to satisfy her motivations to explore, because of the freedom with which she can interact with other babies in her mother's presence. The mother provides the baby with the security necessary to separate from her and co-operate with others.

Attachment and trust nurture the pre-verbal network that is fundamental for developing verbal utterances. To be able to name an object, to think and talk about an experience, the child needs to have had that experience, to have related to the object. The quality of the primary (pre-verbal) relationship, whose foundations lie in the infant's trust in her parents, shapes the fluency of the child's speech in the same way as it shapes the flexibility of her posture and the co-ordination of her gestures and movements.

The baby's innate capacity to perceive (and represent) her own bodily activities, as well as objects and the environment, is related to images developing through the interconnections of nerve cells, which form pathways between the brain and the peripheral organs. These images may begin to absorb information from the foetus's own movements and activities in intra-uterine life and they become more specialized through learning experiences. On this view, the baby has an innate core image of her own movements and postural changes. This has similarities with Stern's idea of a core self that is present from birth (Stern, 2000).

As the body plays a crucial part in the development of ego and self, I suggest that the baby has already a core body image at birth, formed from the very beginning of pre-natal life. Any movement she makes in the womb sends information to the brain, feeding a core image, thus a perception, which is more complex than a sensation. The core images of the baby's movements, respiratory, and cardiac activities, postural changes, sensations, and feelings act as a sort of mirror in the baby's brain or, say, in her mind. It is as though the newborn, while producing a gesture, facial expression, or other bodily utterances, simultaneously switches on a corresponding image of them in her brain. The mother, by mimicking the baby's sounds, gestures and expressions, sustains these images. All these perceptual images of gestures, sounds, breathing, and postural changes gradually combine and integrate to give shape to a united perceptual image of a bodyself. In a similar line of thinking, Meltzoff & Moore (1995) argue that the infant's imitation is not confined to body perception but appears instead to be mediated by a representation of herself and other people. Imitation thus forms a bridge between self and other.

The primary bodyself image becomes more articulated and integrated through experience. Mental representations and bodily displays, such as pre-speech mouth and tongue movements, cooing, vocalizations, and gestures develop simultaneously in a feedback relationship. There is no linear causal relationship. Language, as a symbolic or representational process, develops in close connection with the bodyself image.

The mouth-tongue-chest-hands system

What infants do at a few days old in face-to-face interactions with their mothers demonstrates that the baby is born ready to interact with another human being. They show signs of intentions to speak and appear to have well-organized, sometimes even witty or humorous, exchanges with mothers. They appear, even as neonates, to have motives and feelings, and to behave in adjustment to the mother's movements and gestures. There are communicative bodily cues and movements, facial expressions related to emotions, and mouth and tongue movements that are evidently precursors of verbal expression.

As a baby massage setting offered me such a rich pre-verbal scenario, I came to the conclusion that it may facilitate the communication between mother and baby through different channels: touch, hearing, smell, eye contact, and movement. For example, a six-week-old girl first smiled at her mother's face, then responded to gentle baby talk with cooing vocalizations and a conspicuous hand movement. Such gestures above the shoulders are significantly correlated with "pre-verbal" mouth and tongue movements. The mother imitates the preceding vocalizations of her baby.

This is a further example of how the infant actively adjusts to what the mother does: the baby watches the mother with an intensely focused gaze and an attentive expression. The mother notices this and responds with talking, touching, and changed expression. The infant then responds excitedly, smiling, vocalizing, and gesturing.

Eyes-head-arms-hands and legs and feet are connected in a single system with a signalling function. A four-month-old infant may tend to break visual contact with the mother and to set out to explore her surroundings. This does not mean that the relationship becomes weaker, but it does mean that the baby is signalling, by avoiding eye contact, her will to deal with other objects. She is able to terminate the "conversation" by abruptly turning away. The mother would be wrong if she felt rejected by this.

The mother's eye contact continues to be a source of security, pleasure, and vitality, especially in an unfamiliar environment. I have observed children at the onset of their interactions with peers in the presence of their mother: they crawl or walk back to her just for eye contact, then, reassured, they go back to play.

The fact that infants perceive a human face as having special relationship to themselves is supported by many experimental studies (Halliday, 1979; Brazelton, 1983; Lester, Hoffman & Brazelton, 1985; Thoman, Ingersoll & Acebo, 1991; Trevarthen, 1999). They appear to be capable of specific imitation of mouth movements, tongue protrusions, vocalizations, and hand movements. The infant's cyclic responses to the mother's expressions establish the relationship. On the other hand, her expressions are frequently and unconsciously mimicked by the mother to strengthen the interactions. All this occurs within a mirroring process.

The infant's motor responses contribute to organizing her muscle tone, posture, and breathing, which will be importantly involved in language. Here the relationship between posture, breathing, and language is developing. Face-to-face and body-to-body interactions between mother and infant may resemble postural attitudes, facial expressions, and gestures that occur between adults in conversation. This observation would support my idea that these primary bodily interactions mould our postural attitudes, body language, and communication skills. Furthermore, these primary non-verbal interactions are recorded in the muscle memory, as well as in the brain, presumably in pre-natal life.

Bateson (1971), an anthropologist and a linguist, calls these pre-natal interactions "proto-conversation", which prepare the infant for the "proto-language" phase, when she begins to vocalize. She also studied mother–infant conversation by filming their inter-actions. She concluded that these delicate interactions were the foundation for the development of speech and language, but also for emotional attunement.

I suggest that the way the baby uses body language and its range of expressions may be related to pre-natal interactions. The baby thus comes into the world with a core personality that affects the mother's responses, which affect the baby's behaviour in turn. Two siblings may experience the mother differently and the mother may have a different perception of them, according to their differ-ent make-up.

Some of the adaptations in the mother's behaviour are partly organized and voluntary; others are shaped by the mother's uncon-scious primitive bodily expressions. She behaves differently from the way she would towards an adult. Her elementary utterances are instrumental in synchronizing with the infant's needs and sus-taining her own language. Nevertheless, the mother's instinctive behaviour benefits from experience with her own baby. Rather than delaying acquisition of speech, as many psychologists have believed, baby talk seems to promote infant development. Similarly, when the mother kneels, crawls, lies down or assumes child-like positions in a yoga class, the child's interactions appear to increase.

Much of the baby's behaviour, expressing excitement or an urge to act, is followed closely by the mother, whose skill and under-standing of what the baby is doing enable her to establish syn-chrony, or empathy, so the two behave as if dancing together. However, before attaining this synchrony the caregiver needs to watch the infant's bodily cues and adjust her own bodily and postural displays accordingly, for instance, by crawling with her, thus facilitating playing with her. This dance is important for the development of conversational exchanges about individual experi-ences in speech.

It is striking how tiny infants may get attuned through orienta-tion of eyes, ears, hands, and feet to adult speech in rhythms that are early attempts at speech. This capacity to attune is the necessary framework for linguistic development and stems from innate "images" of co-operation and interaction that predispose the infant to co-ordinate her expression with adults, especially her mother.

One research project on the parts of the infant's body involved in interaction (Condon & Sander, 1974) found that as someone approaches the infant, interacting gently with her, the two instinctively establish a rhythmic co-ordination of looking, listening, smiling, vocalizing, and reaching to touch. This attuned communication between a newborn and an adult, especially the mother, is instrumental in establishing an effective relationship of care.

Deficiency of expressions or responsiveness, or lack of creative play, may have long-lasting effects on the mother–infant relationship. Tension, preoccupations, or fears, displaying themselves through tight muscles and postural language, restrict the repertoire of expressions and may provide a poor physical and emotional holding experience for the baby.

The infant projects her rich repertoire of body expressions on to her mother, inducing her to respond with a similar rich repertoire. The mother herself mirrors because she is intensively identifying with the primitive personality of the infant. Her rudimentary tone of voice, while talking to the baby, is a powerful modulator of their interactions, enabling them to dance. Her smile and way of touching and holding are other regulators. If she exerts rigid resistances to letting primitive language unfold, for instance because of excessive intellectualization or unconscious fears, she will deprive the baby and herself of the "regulators" of communication..

It is the mother's primary body language that expresses her true motivation in interacting with the baby. This motivation may support or fail to support the infant's body language, actions, and feelings. In fact, the infant's facial expressions, oral movements, postural and breathing changes signal feelings of enjoyment, curiosity, puzzlement, annoyance, sadness, fear, and an effort to "say" or to "show" something. This amazingly specialized set of utterances aimed at signalling the baby's feelings must have an innate core bodyself image. For her part, the mother's bodily or primitive language signals emotions, sensations, thoughts, and her whole inner world, through which the baby connects with her inner space. It is a primary mother–baby connection that arises during pregnancy.

Pre-verbal mouth and tongue movements, cooing vocalizations, gestures, and postural and facial displays are precursors of verbal language. There may be a pre-verbal imprinting during intra-uterine life from the melodic quality of sounds to which the baby is subjected and by the mother's use of her body and verbal language in communicating with her.

Infants below six or seven months of age like games that allow them to explore the face, hair, eyes, tongue, hands and various postural, facial, and vocal expressions. After six months, play medi-ated by an object—with the other person making it roll, bounce, rattle, jingle, appear, and disappear—gives more enjoyment. The mouth and tongue movements, usually in rhythm with the surrounding sounds and movements, are a rudimentary form of speech. These movements are often made soundlessly but at other times young babies are highly vocal, making a variety of cooing sounds as they move mouth and tongue. A specific pattern of breathing through the chest's rhythmic movement can also be observed.

However, pre-verbal mouth and tongue movements and changes in breathing are different from those infants make to objects they intend to explore with mouth and tongue. These move-ments are combined with a variety of body language, including hand waving, which is different from the pattern of reaching to things, eye contact, facial expression changes and they generally produce a more fluent, emotionally intense cooing and babbling.

Observing infants during massage offers the opportunity to witness the "mouth-tongue-chest-hands system" involved in the interactions with parents. "Hand-waving" movements are often related to adults' gesticulations in "eager" and "graphic" conversa-tion. The importance of this system as a pre-verbal framework for developing language suggests that when the mother is gently massaging the muscle around the mouth, chest and hands, she induces stimulation that will allow the baby to practise movements in those areas in a playful and humorous situation. As a regular practice, this establishes co-ordination that is fundamental for developing fluent speech. Moreover, when the mother mimics her baby's cues while massaging, she acts as a mirror. She thereby rein-forces the baby's perception of the mouth-chest-hands system and its communicative and social meaning. This has effects on the development of her bodyself image. The baby imitates the mother's expressions, tone, and rhythm of voice. However, she never imitates passively, like an echo; she is constantly actively involved.

The mother's eye contact, which can reach its apex during baby massage, helps to develop a harmonious functioning of the "mouth-chest-hands system". It has a powerful reassuring or soothing effect on both baby and mother, letting the energy flow throughout the body, spreading evenly through the muscle tone. However, even if the baby spends the entire massage looking and smiling at other babies and never makes eye contact with the mother, the connection is there, involving other channels. Moreover, the "mouth-chest-hands system" is stimulated by other babies' cooing or vocalizing.

A three-year-old boy I observed for a year once a week at his home had difficulty in articulating words. After a few observations, I noticed that he was reluctant to establish eye contact while I was talking to him. His father, an apparently loving single parent since the mother left when the child was a newborn, in one observation described the child as unable to look into his eyes while talking with him. Further observations reinforced the idea that the eye contact might somehow be evoking in the child something that had been missing in the pre-verbal phase, when the mutual attuned interactions between parent and baby are crucial. I also noticed that when the child began to make eye contact with me later on during the observational period, looking at the movements of my mouth while speaking, his pronunciation improved significantly.

Observations such as these and other research (Bruner, 1983; Trevarthen, 1999; Trevarthen 2002) point to the conclusion that the foundation for interpersonal communication, verbal, gestural, and postural, is present at birth and likely to be present before birth. It consists in the games that mother and baby play with their body language.

Music and dance as pre-verbal communication

I have mentioned above that what is interesting about pro-conversation is *rhythm* and *musicality*. During my observational work in mother-and-baby classes, I focused attention on how the infant

Dancing to speak a language. Painting by Antonella Sansone.

perceives emotion through the mother's tone of voice and its musical qualities. Mother–baby interactions appear to form musical patterns of communication. Their ability to co-ordinate their expressions so precisely gave me the impression that the baby dances while the mother is speaking or singing.

I shall also endeavour to consider the gestation period in relation to early communicative development. Many of the cerebral structures that are important in early communication are functional during the first two months of the embryo's life, long before the cerebral cortex is even beginning to develop. The pre-natal baby is in fact amazingly sensitive and responsive to musical vibrations.

This explains why mother–baby interactive games are greatly enriched by song and dance. Infants clearly enjoy musical forms of expression. Music is a powerful medium between the baby's innate mirroring images and other human beings. It enhances the enjoyment of movements and vocalizations with others, promoting the sharing experience. It increases the co-ordination of the mouth-chest-hands system, which enhances breathing and communication skills. Music is structure and communication.

Babies have a tremendous ability to move in rhythm with music. They move their hands elegantly to music like orchestral conductors. By singing rhythms and rhymes and dancing with the baby, the mother can rediscover her own primitive language, the continuity between present and past, facilitating the baby's transition from the womb to birth and from birth onwards. This discovery helps the mother's transition as well, because it makes a shared language possible. Music and dance can thus nurture the infant's pre-verbal phase.

In our industrial societies, the enjoyment of singing and dancing as practised in some traditional cultures in labour and early child-care, has been lost. Winnicott considers play as the infant's primary cultural experience, provided that it is carefully adjusted to the infant's state of curiosity and satisfaction (Winnicott, 1991, pp 99–100). Singing and dancing make play rhythmic and communicative, as they enhance the infant's co-ordination of movements and gestures and help her to find her own pace. In the same way, belly-dancing, for instance, the traditional Egyptian dance used for preparing for labour, can enhance perception and awareness of uterine rhythms. Stimulating the foetal vestibular system through rocking pelvic movements, helps the foetus to learn how to make movements that are in tune with the mother's dance. This may entail a core sense of rhythm that is the foundation of communication.

Singing, dancing, or simply listening to music from the very beginning of pregnancy can help mother to get in tune with the baby's pace, to find a space for observation, thinking, and feeling, as music expands the internal space in both mother and baby. It may help the mother to detect the baby's temperament in the womb, as given pieces of music induce different responses. This strengthens the mother's perception and awareness of the baby. In a study on a baby's behaviour in the womb, it was found that during an opera by Verdi the baby kicked a lot, while with another kind of music he stopped kicking (Hepper, 1991).

There is an extensive literature describing foetal heart-rate changes in relation to external sources of auditory stimulation.

Research into heart-rate changes in near-term foetuses (Lecanuet, Granier-Deferre, Jacquet, Capponi & Ledru, 1993) shows that they perceive differences in vocal characteristics of two speakers most clearly when there is most contrast between their sound frequency and timbre. This suggests that the foetus shows preferences and a specific responsiveness to sounds. The hearing area of the foetus's brain is activated very early by sounds. Lecanuet, Granier-Deferre and Busuel (1991) investigated whether the mother's naturally occurring speech would elicit foetal response. Forty-five healthy women with normal pregnancies at thirty-six–forty weeks' gestation participated in this study. Heart rate data were collected using a commercial heart-rate monitor. Mothers were asked to repeat a rehearsed phrase of adult-directed speech at least six times. In different conditions, mothers whispered the same phrases. Foetuses consistently responded with a heart-rate decrease during maternal speech. During whispering, in which foetuses received similar vestibular and tactile stimulation from maternal respiratory movements, no response was detected. Lecanuet believes that this early experience shapes the developing auditory system and later newborn preferences.

In another study, both the heart rate and the respiratory activity of the foetus proved to be an effective psychophysiological measure for understanding the effect of the mother's voice on the developing foetus (Masakowski & Fifer, 1994). DeCasper and Fifer (1980) showed that newborns under three days old would change the pattern and timing of their sucking patterns in order to hear recordings of their mothers' voices over other female voices.

A further study (Moon, Cooper & Fifer, 1993) examined what aspects of the voice the newborn was remembering. Sixteen newborns were presented with female voices either conversing in the language that they heard in the womb or another language. The results showed that newborns responded to the language that they heard in the womb. That is, the infant may be showing a preference for an intonation pattern characteristic of their mother's native language.

As further proof of the baby's responsiveness to sounds, it has been found that the newborn is pacified by the music played or sung when she was in the womb. At as early as five weeks, a foetus will react to loud sounds originating outside and inside the mother's body; however, it is widely felt that the inner and outer ear are not properly developed until around the twenty-eighth week, after which the foetus is probably better able to hear reliably.

The theory as to why music improves brain function derives from recent brain-scanning research, which has found that music is a stimulus unique in its ability to bring different parts of the brain into co-ordination with each other. In research, the thirty-eight-week-old foetuses of four pregnant women were brain-scanned while a musical nursery rhyme was played via a loudspeaker directed at the mother's abdomen. Significant changes in the babies' brain temporal lobe activity were picked up by the brain-scanner in response to the nursery rhyme. Indeed, in one case the baby moved so much in response to the music that it was impossible to obtain a proper image of the brain.

The cortex starts growing when the foetus is three months old. It is strongly involved in language. If pre-verbal communication is an organization of sounds and rhythms, the earliest relationship to sounds is established in the womb, where the foetus is immersed in an ocean of sounds. The melody of sounds by which the foetus is surrounded may shape her future linguistic development in the same way as it may mould her future motor behaviour and posture by activating or pacifying her muscular system.

Playing music, singing, or dancing during pregnancy can affect the foetus's growth through the effects it has on the mother. It can bring vital energy to the mother's emotional and physical state, especially if she is depressed. Observations have found that pre-birth depression may affect the baby's growth and temperament. Babies of mothers who were severely depressed during pregnancy seem to tend to cry more. Music thus may prevent a crying temperament in the baby by mastering the mother's depression and strengthening the connection with her.

It is, in fact, this degree of inner relaxation that is most beneficial. It calms the nervous system, clears the mind, and facilitates understanding of the pregnancy, birth process, and the baby's rhythms. Music appears to work mainly because of the mother's state of relaxation as a result of listening to the music, rather than any direct effect on the foetus. Moreover, the mother's relaxed state increases the flow of blood to the placenta. The choice of music has to fit the mother's tastes for the music to be communicative.

Rhythms that have the most positive effects on the foetus's development seem to be those that do not deviate from the rate variability of the human heart, which lies in a range from 60 to 150 beats per minute. Rhythm in all societies—from primitive drumbeats to the patterns in Mozart symphonies—tends never to deviate from the rate variability of the human heart. As the first and most dominant sound the foetus hears, the heartbeat is a sound of the utmost importance. Picking up and cuddling a distressed baby may produce a calming effect mainly because her ear is pressed against the adult's chest so that she hears the reassuring heartbeat that she was used to during intra-uterine life. Fears that playing music too close to the mother's abdomen could damage a baby's hearing can be banished by the fact that external sounds at the skin surface are reduced by fifty decibels when they reach the uterus. This means that most sounds are heard at half-volume. While studies have found significantly accelerated mental development in babies who had been exposed to classical music, shown for instance in a greater ability to stay seated upright and an awareness that hidden objects still exist in some aspects of sensory-motor co-ordination (Lafuente et al., 1997), studies of the effects on linguistic development are needed.

To give a vivid description of the effect of playing music during pregnancy and labour on baby's pre-verbal development, I shall report a case from my own observation, mentioned in the introduction. When I entered the hospital room to listen to Clare's birth story, she was playing the same piece of Balinese music that she had played regularly during pregnancy and labour. The baby stopped breastfeeding and started crying. I thought he might have been disturbed by my unfamiliar voice or by the door opening. Then he stopped crying. As the mother began talking, the baby started crying again. When she stopped, he calmed down. The sequence continued for a while. During the pause, he decreased his movements and looked around as if he were searching for the source of music, which he really appeared to enjoy. Then he made tiny movements with his mouth and head, which appeared to relate to the melody. These were evidently pre-verbal movements, induced by familiar music. His mother went on telling her birth story quite loudly and instantly the baby went back to whimpering. He was clearly telling his mother that he wanted to listen to his familiar music.

Singing or playing music enhances communication with the pre-natal baby, because she feels the vibrations and rhythms of the mother's body amplified. At the same time, through her responses, the mother can feel the baby's rhythms amplified and the interplay of crescendo and decrescendo movements. These mutual rhythmic games lay the foundations of a synchronized communication and the child's later language.

In pre-natal communication, the father can get involved by hearing the baby's motor responses to music through speakers or by touching the mother's abdomen. His talking to the baby is also a powerful way for the baby to get to know her father's voice. A Japanese woman gave me a vivid report of father–foetus interactions, "In my pregnancy I had a strange experience. I was living in Tokyo and my husband in London. We were living apart but we talked on the phone every day. When I moved to London and we lived together, we used to sit and watch television. When my husband was talking to my baby through my abdomen, I felt the foetus actively moving towards him". The fascinating debate about the relative importance of genetic and environmental factors is relevant here. Genetic inheritance and the environment work together in the womb to shape the baby's personality, and her body and verbal language.

Learning, use of bodily expressions, and language acquisition all occur when the infant is interested and participates. The baby, especially at around eight months, takes the initiative in a joint interaction when she actively invites the mother by looking, smiling and gesturing, and the mother can amplify these intended actions. Smiling, apart from being a vital expression of pleasure, is one sign of a complex repertoire that shows that babies are innately prepared to signal their intentions and interests.

Each of the baby's bodily cues has a communicative function from the first few minutes after birth, even when she kicks in the womb. The earliest eye contact proves the baby's need to establish an interaction. If birth institutions do not provide mother, father, and baby with a place in which to meet each other's eyes, a vital step into the relationship is obstructed. Human intelligence develops from the very beginning of life, probably pre-natally, as an interpersonal process. Rudimentary pre-verbal and later verbal communication are the paramount means of individual mental growth and essential components of civilized society. The primary rehearsal ground is the infant's play, both with her own body and self and with other children.

The infant's play experience is an important learning process. There is no fixed phase when the infant starts to play. For instance, while breastfeeding, the baby plays with the breast as well as feeding. When her mother talks to her while feeding, attention to the mother's mouth leads a baby to imitate some of her speaking movements. These mutual patterns prepare for the emergence of language.

The development of controlled voluntary reaching for objects and manipulating and sucking them at around four months means that a conversation can become about what the infant has looked at, reached, done, as a communication about experiences. Thus, interactions play a key role in fostering exploration of the world. They go to constitute the infant's individual differences.

Variety of interactions for linguistic development

Adults behave in widely different ways with infants, some being shy and fearful, and fathers differ in important ways from mothers. For instance, there is evidence that some fathers play more boisterously with them than mothers. They seem to excite infants more to calling and laughter and to vigorous body movements. It has also been found that some fathers tend to touch and talk more gently to baby girls than boys, with whom they would be more vigorous (Eidelman, Hovars & Kaitz, 1994). These differences impinge on the infant's bodyself image and sexual identity. Their gestures and quality of touch are also affected by the cultural gender stereotypes and the way in which they were parented, which they tend to project.

During one observation, I studied the different repertoire of language used by a father and a mother with their one-year-old daughter. The father was using a more explicit and word-based language, more like adult-to-adult. The mother was using more bodily cues and mutual codes, with a less explicit language based on an intimate understanding that contained symbols and meanings. Then I considered the language the child was using towards her mother and father. When speaking to the mother, the girl used more gestures and bodily signals, while when speaking with her father her language was more verbal. The psychophysiological experience of pregnancy establishes an intimate bodily communication that forms a different repertoire of language used by mothers from that used by fathers.

How a gesture evolves

I am trying out the gesture the infant makes of raising her arms when she wants to be picked up to see how she organizes a gesture as a communicative event through interactions with the mother and understand how, on a more complex level, her posture and body language are the result of co-ordinated and integrated small gestures. These gestures develop through interactions and acquire increasing communicative functionality. Therefore, an effective use of posture, bodily, and verbal utterances in later life depends on a rudimentary effective communication that is rhythmic or attuned.

How does an infant learn to raise her arms to signal to her mother that she wants to be picked up? She certainly could not do so if there were no caregiver who regularly put her hands under her armpits: the first few times she shows no adjustment to her behaviour. The child soon becomes familiar with being picked up and starts to show anticipation of her action: she raises her arms herself and contributes to the mother's action, reducing the effort required. Her muscle tone, in accordance with her need, for instance, to be comforted and the mother's response shape her own gesture and posture. It is difficult to describe how this happens. An accurate observational study of mother–baby interactions (Sansone, 2002) has suggested to me that the infant's posture, breathing, and body language in general begin to organize in relation to the primary caregivers' body language. An entire world of vibrations conditions the baby's muscular tone and internal world, as well as those of the caregiver, and sows the seeds of language. There is no boundary between the emotional and the muscular or general physical levels.

At first, the baby responds to the physical stimulation of her mother's hands: as the mother touches her, the baby adjusts her position and the mother then accommodates her gestures to the child's position. Bodily signals are transmitted from one to another. The quality of touch induces a feeling and modulates the child's postural response. The child thus has a complete experience. An interchange of muscular tone information gives rise to mutual postural adjustments. Physical or emotional tension weaken the capacities of mother and infant for rhythmic adjustment, making mutual understanding more difficult.

The mother's gesture of picking the baby up and holding her is internalized—recorded in the infant's muscle memory and repre-sented mentally—as consequence of the regular daily holding. It is not the physical stimulation itself that is recorded, but the child's emotional experience while being held. The quality of holding combined with the child's own personality provides an experience of fulfilment. As the child grows, she can anticipate the mother's behaviour, raising her arms to signal her wish to be lifted.

Infants are picked up to be fed, washed, bathed, massaged, and comforted; and the preparations for these activities occupy a large part of her day. Food is prepared, baths are run, massage involves undressing, using oil and towels, and so on. The child now begins to move her arms not in response to her mother's actions but to the sights, smells, and sounds of these events. She is learning how to deal with the world.

I often observe this early capacity to anticipate just through smells, sounds, and sights in babies who are a few days old. For instance, after three to four massage classes, the mother's gesture of laying the baby down, undressing her, and opening the oil bottle is enough to induce great excitement, wriggling movements, and cooing or babbling. The baby is evidently anticipating the massage routines, as she has stored the routines and the associated feelings in her muscle memory.

To give an example of cues being exchanged, Louis, aged ten months, crawls to his mother and scratches her leg while she is bending over in a yoga position. His mother asks, "What do you want?" Louis raises his arms. The mother says, "Wait a minute, then I'll pick you up. The meaning conveyed by arm-raising is important. The child is making a request.

In another instance, while a mother is talking to me, both of us standing, her child crawls to her and scratches and pulls her leg while fussing around. The mother comments, "she wants us to kneel down so that we are talking at the same level as her, and she can feel involved in the conversation". She interprets the child's need on the basis of her gesture and consequently adjusts her posture by kneeling down.

The child's gestures are often accompanied by crying. Crying is a powerful unspoken language. It does not necessarily mean that anything is wrong with the child. Adults very often project on to the child the reasons that usually make them cry. But the infant's cry is primarily a communication. Such projections may make meeting the child's actual needs a difficult task. When the crying baby runs to her mother with outstretched arms, she conveys a specific message to her through the combination of these different gestures: to do so she needs to have mastered one of the fundamental skills of language.

Sentences convey specific messages through combinations of different components. The child becomes able to combine gestures in three phases: one in which single gestures are developed; a second in which single gestures occur in sequences—the child cries and then points or raises her arms or makes intense eye contact— and a third period in which two or more gestures occur together —the child cries and points at the same time. A similar sequence is found in linguistic development: the period of one word at a time, the occurrence of two words in sequence and that of multi-word utterances. The processes—of language (when, for example, the child says "Mummy up") and gesture—are very similar.

Any study of linguistic development that neglects the communicative function of the body and how the use of body language progresses is lacking. Primary unspoken communication plays a major part in linguistic development. This may explain the increasing incidence of delayed speech in young children nowadays. Working parents do not spend the necessary time interacting with their baby. Regular mutual interactions are important for the infant to mirror gesture combinations, postural attitudes, and breathing rhythms that shape the chest, shoulder, throat and mouth articulation, which are all fully involved in the later verbal phase.

Crying attracts the mother's attention and conveys information. In a similar way, pointing both attracts that attention and indicates an object. There is very little difference between this communication and the subsequent speaking of the object's name with a whining intonation while pointing at it. The difference lies in the acquired capacity to symbolize, so that a word can stand for an idea and, thus, an object or event experienced, which cannot yet be separated from primary gestural communication. With the ability to name objects, the child's language becomes more explicit. The early words seem to be used only for the fun of it, in games with the mother, as a rehearsal of the child's mouth and lip movements, and for the plea-sure of making newly discovered sounds. With practice, the child becomes increasingly able to use them in co-ordination with the primary gestural ability.

Rhythm and communication

The transition from primary to symbolic and verbal language unfolds through sounds associated to the caregivers and surround-ing objects that vibrate and resonate in the baby's body, organizing her muscle tone and bodyself-perception. Verbal language is, there-fore, a projection of sounds internalized during regular interactions with the caregivers. Considering the pre-natal baby immersed in a concert of sounds, it seems likely that an important network for linguistic development forms in the womb. The mother's capacity to feel and attune to her bodyself rhythms and to primary language enables her to attune to her baby's needs, sustain them, and so respond properly to them. The communication then becomes a melody.

Articulated gestures and confident posture, related to the child's trust in the mother's or father's reliability, shape the chest and throat movements and breathing and they are involved in vocalizing, babbling, and later speaking. This trust builds up through the trian-gular mother–baby-father interactions and grows in co-operative interactions with other children and shared experiences. Indeed, speech is the expression of these early internalized bodily commu-nications. Deficiencies in this early internalization process are likely to impair the fluency of language and speech.

To be able to articulate words, a child first needs a companion who spends time vocalizing with her and waiting for the repetition, inducing a mirroring. The partner will scan the words and sentences just for the fun of it, making entertaining sounds and pauses at the child's own pace. These rhythmic conversations, made of sounds, cues and codes, are already meaningful. By the time the child produces words, she has long been using meanings.

Lack of rhythm impinges not only on the emotional level, but also on the harmony of the vocal cords, breathing, and all the muscles involved in speaking. It may even affect muscle tone regulation throughout the body. As a result, a fragmented or inarticulate speech may develop along with an non-integrated bodyself image.

Excessive tension, as a result of emotional and psychological difficulties or general stress, may alter the rhythm because it acts as a barrier to absorbing and internalizing sounds. Sounds occupy an internal space. This could explain why maternal intonation is an important element in the conversation with the baby, acting as a mediator between her resonating body and the foetus's muscle tone. Singing and playing music can help to establish the rhythm, as they relieve tension in the voice and body. Moreover, they create a play-time for both baby and parent that enhances the communication.

If from the beginning of life the infant moves in precise, shared rhythm with the organization of the speech structure of her culture, with the intonations of the mother's, father's, and sibling's voices, then she actively participates through complex social-biological processes in a multitude of communicative forms. While the infant moves in rhythm with her mother's voice and gestures and thus is affected by her, her own movements may in turn reward the mother and stimulate her to continue. Their dialogue is thus interactive and self-sustaining.

Newborns move in rhythm with the structure of adult speech. When the infant is already moving, changes in the configuration of her moving body parts become co-ordinated with changes in the sound pattern characterizing speech. The baby is certainly an amazing dancer. So the mother's alternating pauses or syllable stresses, with crescendo and decrescendo, affect the baby's bodily and emotional responses, thus the organization of her posture, as well as her language. These communicative, relational, and social functions of posture and body image are very seldom considered.

Posture is studied mainly by physiologists, physiotherapists, and orthopaedists, who usually overlook its meanings and its effects on relationships. Some postural and body image imbalances or long-term misuse of the body have their roots in the transitional period from the pre-linguistic to the verbal phase.

As an adult speaker pauses for breath or stresses a syllable, the infant may almost imperceptibly raise an eyebrow, lower a foot, or expand her chest. Baby-talk is highly effective in training infant movement. Neither tapping noises nor unconnected vowel sounds without emotional content, nor adult speech show the same degree of correspondence with the new-born's synchronous movements as rhythmical pre-verbal or verbal patterns. Observational evidence shows that during their first encounters, parents receive signals, such as body and eye movements and sounds from their infant, and also send signals to the baby in turn (Brazelton, 1983). Both the parents and the baby are equally actively involved.

Given that many of the foetus's activities and rhythms are attuned to those of the mother, it seems that a pre-linguistic network is already organized at birth. This is due to a variety of rhythmic influences: the mother's sleep–wake cycles, daily hormonal fluctuations, ordinary daily patterns, regular heartbeat and breathing rhythm, and the rhythmic uterine contractions that precede the onset of labour and continue until the baby emerges from the birth canal. These pre-natal influences probably establish a sense of rhythmic interaction and may increase the likelihood of the newborn's responsiveness to the mother's presence, voice, actions, and gestures. They may therefore form innate pre-natal images. Characteristics that are termed genetic or innate at birth have long been primarily environmental.

The sucking gesture

I shall now consider another rudimentary gesture to see how the infant actively organizes it through interactions with her mother. The non-nutritive sucking should also elucidate how the baby is always active in converting what she experiences with her bodily faculties into meanings.

Like other mammals, the human infant is equipped with psychobiological processes to ensure initial feeding, attachment to a caregiver, and sensory contact with the world. Non-nutritive sucking, a buffering mechanism, has the effect of relaxing large muscle groups, stilling stomach movements, reducing the number of eye movements in response to excessive input from visual fields and ensuring the maintenance of a moderate level of arousal for a demanding environment. Such sucking can also be used as a means of self-regulation, when for instance the baby's arousal level is too high. In this instance, the baby sucks eagerly to reduce her increasing tension. Stern (2000) states that the mother tends to overstimulate the baby to keep her alive and active. Sometimes, when for instance she is not fully in touch with her need to be left on her own, she may find it difficult to reduce her arousal. The baby then has to do it by eagerly using the mother's nipple or any other substitute.

Non-nutritive sucking thus soon comes under the child's own control. Babies are soon capable of sucking on a pacifier nipple. Sucking and looking are co-ordinated to ensure a good view. The optimal distance for the baby to focus is that from the nipple to the mother's face, which allows the baby to explore the mother's face from birth. She also explores the mother's body by touching, smelling, and sensing the vibrations running along her body. She sucks as she looks and when she stops, she soon learns to look away. All these gestures show that babies have an extraordinary capacity for co-ordination of actions from the very beginning of life. They appear to search for rhythm soon after birth, perhaps from early intra-uterine life.

The following is a description of four-day-old baby Yusuke, struggling to find a sucking rhythm. His mother moved his head from side to side, up and down, around the nipple, which he failed to grasp. From time to time, his hands came across his mouth as if, searching for the nipple, he made a mistake. Then Yusuke's face plunged into the breast and eventually, after a few attempts, his mouth began feeding. He laid one of his tiny hands on the breast and, triumphant at reaching the nipple, finally appeared peaceful and happy. The mother lowered her shoulder and arm, which had been pressing and squeezing the nipple and, with her body adjusted, she could now feel and enjoy the breastfeeding rhythm.

Usually the sucking rhythm was accompanied by tiny movements of other parts of the baby's body. On another day, Yusuke's mother was firmly holding his entire head with the palm of one hand while firmly squeezing the areola with the other. Trying to find the baby's rhythm, her hands appeared slightly tense. Then

Yusuke, triumphant at possessing the nipple, seemed to suck more eagerly at the other breast, as I could see from the rhythmic movements of his head. His hand lay on the breast, skin to skin, and made tiny movements. It sank into the breast and pushed and released alternately. There was a rhythm of movements and pauses. Yusuke derived visible pleasure from the contact between his hands and the warm breast and, at the same time, from being attuned to the sucking. It looked like a dance. When his head stopped moving, so did his hand. His mother's shoulders and hands now appeared relaxed and her breathing unfolded smoothly. She told me later about the cues that she received from Yusuke's hand movements. "He clutches his hands when he is hungry and in need of the nipple, while he releases his fingers when he is relaxed".

Babies are equipped to respond to human voices, faces, actions, and gestures. Their capacity for co-ordination, however, is mediated by the adults with whom they interact. For example, there is a beautiful synchrony between the baby's sucking on the nipple and the breast muscle so that, by contracting and relaxing alternately in rhythm with the sucking, the milk can be expelled. The mother's balanced muscular tone and her smooth caring movements, linked to enjoyment, her ability to sense the baby with awareness and reflect upon her, are crucial factors in facilitating the "rhythm" and thus boosting the connection with the baby.

The baby's primary tool for achieving her ends is another familiar human being. The baby's sensory and motor activity during the first 18 months of life is extraordinarily relational, interactive, and communicative. Stern (1977, 2000) underlines how early infants are stimulated by the adults with whom they interact. There is good evidence that withholding a social response to the child's initiatives may alter the development of her bodyself perception, thus of her body image (Stern, 2000). A receptive response is the most powerful reinforcement of harmonious co-ordination of the infant's whole being. I often observe how intense expressions from the mother's face during feeding and vivid eye contact elicit the baby's attention and enhance the synchrony of sucking in almost every interaction. It seems likely that the child's later eating behaviour is, to some extent, shaped by these primary bodily rhythmic interactions. Repeated poor rhythm may set the pattern for eating behaviour dysfunctions such as anorexia.

If during play the mother assumes a sober, immobile expression, the infant tends to smile less and turn her head away from the mother more frequently than when the mother responds with a wide range of facial expressions and gestures. These initial social responses, elicited by the mother's bodily cues, are at the basis of self-development and cultural acquisition.

From the start, the child becomes readily attuned to "making a lot out of a little" by forming combinations. She works at varying a small set of elements to create a wide range of possibilities. Pre-linguistic and linguistic communications interact continuously and the child's actual speech unfolds in relation to ongoing actions and other contextual elements. The fluent co-ordination of all these elements makes a communication effective. The baby's perceptual world, far from being a buzzing confusion, is organized by rules. Language will serve to specify and explain what is already present in the baby's primary meaningful experience.

Language requires a unique sensitivity to a patterned sound system that is present in vocalization interactions between parent and baby and between babies. This is why parent-and-baby support classes promote the infant's linguistic development. Other babies' vocalizations act as a mirror or sounding-board for the baby. The child organizes knowledge and language according to what she can do with her body, with things and others surrounding her. She builds up knowledge of the world through her own sensory and motor experiences. Play is a vital foundation for these experiences. Parents play a very active role in negotiating with the child and through negotiation she learns to carry out her intentions. In learning to speak, the child learns not just the grammar of that particular language, but also how to fulfil her intentions by the appropriate use of that grammar.

The adult's capacity to communicate at a level at which the child can comprehend, using sensory and child-like cues more than verbal ones, is crucial. Although the mother's ability to use a primitive language with her baby is expected to be instinctive, some mothers tend to talk to their babies in a fairly complex manner. They may sound like a monologue and it is noticeable that very few signals of active interaction appear in the child's body language, particularly in their facial expressions. Our speaking ability and linguistic games as adults store the imprints of our primary interactions and relationships. Before a mother tongue, there is a "child tongue". A mother tongue is a resource for meanings of simple signs, which are indeed the baby's own. I shall give an example.

Steven's eyes (at eight months old) are on his mother, who is holding an object, not on the object itself. He may be expressing his intention towards the object. Here the meaning may be not just "I want you to give me that" but "me and you, me and the world beyond", and the expressions are the baby's own inventions. This also shows the child's increasing self-awareness and awareness of an object outside the bodyself. These early meanings will be encoded as speech sounds.

Another example of the extension from sensory experience to verbal development is the way in which we learn the meaning of names given to the sensation of pain. Words are first connected with the primary and natural expression of the sensation. For instance, a child cries because she has hurt herself; then adults talk to her and teach her exclamations, and later, sentences that belong to their cultural experience. They teach the child a new pain-behaviour.

The interactions between the mother's tongue and the baby's own tongue, whose codes are usually fully understood only by them, are remarkable phenomena, taking place mainly below the level of conscious awareness and at a level of rapid cueing and response that occurs too rapidly to be translated verbally at the same time; it is difficult even for the mother to describe what is going on between them. It is fascinating in its indefinability. If the mother is asked what the child has been saying, she is likely to say that she was not saying anything at all, since she cannot talk. Yet, although she is not speaking the mother's tongue, she is using her own tongue. The mother's prompt response to her language, as well as to her smiles and gurgles in earliest infancy, is difficult to explain.

The receptive mother talks to her baby so that she can receive the message in accordance with her developmental pace. It is a message that is not understood literally, but in the context of that unique mother–baby relationship. Rather than imitation, this is a kind of tracking that shapes mutual understanding and linguistic skills. A baby starts to exchange meanings and to set up a code system from birth, perhaps from intra-uterine life, through the interplay of mutual gestures, movements, respiratory, and cardiac rhythms, and feelings. Speech occurs through the co-ordination of the vocal cords, which function in rhythm with breathing. Breathing both organizes and reflects our emotional life. In the mother–baby interactions, breathing fills their languages with emotional content and synchronizes their communication. Smooth breathing connects their mutual perceptions and their bodyself images flow through each other in a mirroring process. It makes their interactions resemble dance steps and their communication a melody. Freedom from tension and smooth breathing, as reflections of a fulfilled emotional space, sow the seeds of a fluent co-ordinated language.

Emotion and the emergence of language

The flow of reciprocal interactions between adult and infant is fostered by emotions. While an infant is communicating with someone, the perception of the person is affected by the repertoire of their facial expressions and postural changes, which signal the quality of emotions. The richness of adult facial and bodily expressions during interaction with the infant thus sustain the infant's language and the flow of communication. If someone conversing with a two-month-old intentionally withholds all responses and just makes a blank face, the same transformation of the baby to puzzlement is observed.

During baby massage, the lively interplay between the mother's facial expressions and those of the baby reinforces their communications. The baby needs the interacting person to communicate something with an emotional content, someone to become attached to, in order to mirror her gestures, intentions, feelings, breathing, and posture. She can thus nurture the core image of her bodyself, which is of the utmost importance for fluent linguistic and communicative skills.

Development of speech obviously involves maturation of the mechanisms for auditory perception and oral production. In the first year of life, complex neural mechanisms elaborate and integrate articulate movements of lips and tongue that occur in rhythm with breathing. This can be seen in the rudimentary pre-verbal activity of newborns in co-ordination of chest and throat activities. The pulmonary-laryngeal system is essential for producing controlled utterances. Although even six-week-olds may make disyllabic utterances, clearly differentiated vocalizations co-ordinated with mouth and tongue movements begin in the second trimester after birth, when the infant starts to babble. This bodily aspect of speech production constitutes a fundamental framework for verbal development.

These processes are far from purely mechanistic. The co-ordination of the baby's bodily utterances, a precursor of verbal language, occurs in relationship with her emotional experiences and the possibility of finding a reliable and receptive caregiver. These are the foundations of the infant's self-esteem and trust in her own capacities and in the world. Comfortable posture, an integrated body image, and communication skills organize in close connection with the infant's experience of physically and emotional support from a receptive parent. Such support allows the baby to relieve any tension and fear through mindful holding, thus to grow up self-confident. Fluent speech is boosted by this feeling of being supported, which allows the infant to grow co-ordinated. Posture, emotions, and language are intimately related. Posture has a relational, emotional, and communicative function, as well as a physical one.

Perceptions and thoughts are monitored by and also affect breathing, which plays a major part in speaking, and the emergence of language is linked with emotions. Before she is able to control mental representations of ideas that may be expressed to others by language (symbolic capacity), the baby needs a balanced control of her own bodily skills and language. She will have discovered a self-support, a support in her own body through the initial support provided by her primary caregiver. This effective self-control gives rise to an awareness of bodyself-image and posture.

During the mother-and-baby yoga class, this self-support can be visible in the baby's self-controlled upright sitting, smooth and balanced walking, and flexible bouncing when falling down. On the basis of such postural achievements, the infant develops the motivation and interest in sharing initiatives and experiences with other children, which is an important leap towards speaking. Before they begin to acquire and use words deliberately to tell other adults or children what they feel, intend to do, or have done, infants need to have this vital motivation and to be provided with a playground in which to nurture this motivation. The path leading to this motivation is the pre-verbal cooing and babbling of mutual interaction. Through them, the infant acquires a sense of rhythm, an alternation between pauses and sounds that is the precondition of language.

Stretching in a yoga class, retaining flexibility, staying with a position at their own pace without an imposed timetable in their mother's presence is a playful time with important effects on development. It seems to enhance the capacity to co-operate constructively with other children and learn from them. The meaning of the world can only be understood in communication and co-operation with other people, which leads to pleasure, achievement, and pride.

Over eighteen months of weekly observations in baby massage and mother-and-baby yoga classes, I have seen many babies growing up happily, showing their confident posture, and bright curiosity to explore and interact with other children. It may be difficult to see an adult's sadness or happiness clearly, but the child's emotions, mental state, and health are clearly apparent in her walking, breathing, and body language. An unhappy baby will behave in an emotionally and physically unco-ordinated way, and suffer extremes of emotions that are hard to control. Where I have observed healthy development through a secure posture and ability to interact, this means that those classes met some of the child's vital needs. However, these classes need to be run by someone truly interested in infant development and able to provide emotional containment to parent and baby. Even the infant's first articulated words arise naturally from a co-ordinated posture, no matter at what age. What does really matter is that everything happens in the class at the child's own pace. This corresponds to the aim of this book not to refer to rigidly defined stages.

Babies with special needs can draw invaluable benefits from the interactions with other children, and from yoga or other exercise. Such benefits will be good for society as a whole. In fact, a well-functioning society depends on its capacity to provide its children, particularly those with special needs, with a space in which to practise their individual skills and to transmit knowledge through institutions that are designed for this. The success of this transmission relies on the caregiver's capacity to acknowledge and meet the child's own interests, motivations, and needs. This implies the capacity to observe what is going on in the child's actual experience.

Rigid institutions that do not consider a child an attentive participant and contributor to the learning process contribute to major problems in society. Children cannot be compelled to achieve a set level of performance at a given age. This applies particularly to nursery schools and to every out-of-school setting.

Mother-and-baby yoga and baby massage classes are potential arenas for physical, emotional, and cognitive or linguistic development, as the child is allowed to progress at her own pace, through the transitional area occupied by the parent, as well as by other children and adults and an observant teacher. The child finds here a place in which to nurture her innate capacity to interact and explore her emotional, communicative, and postural skills. In such a valuable playground, she strengthens her motivation towards the co-operative understanding that governs the principles of human society. In the class, infants interact with other parents, children, the teacher and sometimes the observer, a variety of human beings who are free from defences against becoming too close or too attached and who are free of a judgemental attitude.

Professionals who believe that infants do not speak a language, think, or make any original contribution to society and that they are passive biological organisms to be shaped into a human condition betray the children's true nature. Infants possess a powerful rudimentary communicative repertoire that allows the infant–caregiver relationship to be established. This relationship is related to family and society like the seed of a fruit that grows into a whole plant. The primary relationship is first cultural and later becomes social. The infant's imitations of gestures and postural attitudes are never passive but empathetically motivated attempts to communicate that function as signals. The caregiver's interpretation of them in pre-verbal communication and her mimicking of the infant's repertoire lead the infant to use them with increasing awareness and to reflect on them. This is essential to social life.

Babies can experience emotions such as frustration, pride, and shame, and this is strongly evident in their body language. I am frequently impressed by very young babies' "show-off" posture when they are confident. These feelings are fundamental in developing human relationships and self-confidence and in acquiring knowledge. We have only to pay sensitive and sympathetic attention to their everyday expressions of pleasure and displeasure, curiosity and uncertainty, confidence and mistrust.

To understand how infants contribute to social life and to the growth of culture we need to "observe" these creatures, who are too young to speak but amazingly capable of understanding our feelings and psychophysiological states. They communicate their wishes, intentions, and needs according to what another may do for them from the very beginning of life. They are capable of a shared understanding and they develop in direct response to the quality of this understanding. The following is an account from ten-month-old baby Yusuke's everyday life, from two of my weekly observations in his home.

Yusuke's mother placed a toy in the middle of the room, trying to draw his attention. It was a spiral with a hole on the top, in which a ball is supposed to be inserted to travel down through the spiral. His mother showed him how to do it, starting with the first ball. Yusuke, seated on the floor between me and the toy, put the ball in the middle of the spiral rather than on top. "Here .... look, do it for me", his mother tried to correct him. Yusuke put it below the top again. He then picked up a red ball and handed it to me; "Thank you, Yusuke", I said, persuaded by his smile and gesture. I felt he was requesting me to put it in for him. I put it into the top hole. He then stretched his arms out and handed me another ball. I was torn between his mother's instruction and Yusuke's intention. I felt empathetic and decided to put it in halfway. He looked straight into my eyes and clapped his hands. I was struck by how much understanding there could be with such a young child.

On another occasion, Yusuke crawled straight over to me and stretched his arms towards me in a picking-up gesture. I lifted him up and placed him on my thighs in an upright position. While I was releasing him, he seemed to share my intention. I got the feeling that he wanted to be picked up just to be "high up" and see all around him. After a while, he returned to me and expressed the same request accompanied by a few sounds, "Ah, ah .... ah". I responded to him and we did it a third and last time. When I placed him on the floor, I said, "You want to be high up to see around, don't you?" He stared at me immobile and enchanted, and I wondered whether he was interested in the tone of my voice or had a sense of what I had said. Then he smiled and giggled with pride.

An infant's behaviour is so individually adapted to her unconscious and conscious sensitivity and her understanding of the adults who share her life that it is difficult to categorize. If we consider that the caregivers, for their part, belong to a specific culture that has shaped their behaviour since their primary experiences, any definition becomes even less useful.

Baby massage and baby talk

The richness of mother–baby interaction during baby massage classes has led me to believe that it has the potential to foster linguistic development and prevent speech difficulties. As the foundation for the complex patterns of movements, vocalizing, and babbling that the infant brain can regulate, infant massage can provide an ideal transitional zone between pre-verbal and verbal development.

In our industrialized societies, where this form of contact has almost been lost, baby massage can be a powerful tool for reinforcing the communication between parent and baby. It can therefore be a helpful practice for parents and babies with special needs. Because babies are very sensitive to touch, sounds, and smells, their development needs to incorporate proper stimulation of sensory channels. Baby massage nurtures the flow of communication by activating those channels.

Infants under seven months old like games that allow them to explore the parents' faces, hair, tongues, hands, and all their postural, facial, and vocal responses or initiations. Baby massage promotes the physical and emotional closeness and playfulness needed to practise these games. For a tiny baby, this is an important form of learning.

Before language acquisition, there is regular practice of these pre-verbal games. The early dialogue between mother and baby consists of touch, eye contact, a variety of facial expressions, movements, cooing vocalization, and reciprocal imitations. Playful time spent exchanging baby talk cements the pillars of linguistic development. The mouth-chest-hands system, which is particularly involved in cooing and breathing, as well as in later verbal language, is visibly activated by the containing massage routines. Most importantly, mouth, chest, and hands move in co-ordination, making the infant's bodily communication valuable and attractive to her mother.

The mother's repertoire of body language can be modified and enriched by baby talk and skin contact. The baby's lively movements—cooing, vocalizing, and babbling while being massaged—can be an amusing picture. The mother's mimicking and the baby's sounds influence each other, resonating and expanding their communication, so that they really appear to be dancing.

Smiling is a vital expression of enjoyment and one of the most powerful means of communication. It is a vital reinforcement of language. Baby massage seems to make smiling and laughter special features of the baby's face and personality, as well as of the mother's. It can thus prevent childhood depression and treat maternal post-natal depression. The infant's smile can have an amazing healing impact on an adult.

The shared experience with other babies—hearing babies of different ages talking, thus a wide variety of cooing and babbling—provides the baby with a stimulating foundation for development. This also acts as a mirroring process, promoting self-discovery. Babies in fact tend to imitate each other more than adults, particularly when the latter speak an elaborate adult language with them.

Babies respond remarkably well to gentle touching, with cooing and conspicuous hand movements. These are visible signals that they need touch. Such mouth gestures or hand gestures above the shoulders in general are significantly correlated with pre-verbal mouth and tongue movements and the hand gesture below the shoulders with movements of chest, therefore, with breathing. They all occur in a beautiful co-ordination.

During massage, the baby usually watches the mother with an intensely focused gaze and an attentive expression. The mother sees this and responds with a changed facial expression and attuned massaging. The baby may then be stimulated to smile and vocalize. What is going on is not a simple imitation, but a cyclical and complementary reaction by the infant to the mother's gestures and, in turn, the mother mimics the infant's movements and vocalizations in a sympathetic communication.

Gestures recorded in face-to-face interactions between mother and infant, remarkably concentrated during massage, may resemble postural attitudes, facial expressions, and gestures between conversing adults. In the richness of body language that baby massage promotes lies an essential foundation of our adult communication skills. I am referring to both body language and linguistic skills and their complementariness. Our communication skills, the capacity to get in touch with people and learn from others, is substantially based on the repertoire of body language that was used with us by our primary caregivers and that we used in our primary life. Comfortable posture, balanced muscle tone, and fluent breathing, corresponding to an integrated identity and bodyself image, enrich the repertoire of body and verbal language and make the bodyself communicative and full of emotional and creative life. On the contrary, rigid posture, excessive muscular tension, and locked breathing restrict communication skills and may encourage an escape into intellectualized or elaborate verbal speech.

Just as baby massage helps retain the infant's flexibility and smoothness of movement, promotes co-ordination, regulates the rhythm of breathing, and strengthens perceptual self-awareness, it seems likely that it can also retain the communicative function of the body in adulthood. No studies have yet been carried out on this, as baby massage is a recent practice in the Western world, although it is one of the ancient healing techniques and is still used in many non-industrialized societies. Such an investigation would require a longitudinal study. Nevertheless, there is enough evidence that touch is the most highly developed of the senses at birth and the primary means of communication, playing a significant role in the parent–child relationship.

The emotional dynamics of the mother–infant dyad and their rhythmic interactions are certainly fundamental to linguistic and cognitive development. The evidence that there is continuity between bodily and sensory rhythmic communication and verbal language gives me confidence that baby massage has the potential to strengthen this bridge and smooth the transition. It would be interesting to explore this connection with further research.

CHAPTER 9

The baby's cry

When a baby draws a dog with five legs
We would do better not to intervene to correct the number
of legs;
We can wonder whether the child is drawing a dog in
motion,
perhaps very fast.
Doing so, we can understand what she is communicating.

A three-year-old child draws a human being
with an enormous chest and arms and small legs.
I ask him who it is.
He says that it's Mum when hugging him.
He painted his stored sensations of being held by a loving
mother.
If I had corrected the disproportion
I would have missed the richness of his communication.

A crying baby may have effects on the parents' bodyself perception and on their entire view of the world and other people. People often say that they feel hurt or angry when their baby is crying. Getting in touch with their own needs, feelings, and inner resources is an important path to discovering effective ways of handling their baby and meeting her needs. By opening the sensory channels, the caregivers enhance their perception and understanding of the baby's cues and hence the communication, resulting in less crying.

Many of us have mixed feelings about crying. We get anxious, tense up, and want the crying to stop right away. It arouses fear and may remind us of anguish we felt when crying alone in a crib with no response. Therefore, we project our inner infant and our impulse is to stop that baby crying.

A baby crying may make a parent distressed. Any parent with a crying baby is at risk of being violent to that baby. They should not be judged negatively for this, as both parents and babies become part of a vicious circle. The increasing tension or frustration that is usually caused by a crying baby, displaying itself in increasing muscular tension, tightened gestures and thus the way of holding the baby, acts as a barrier to communication and understanding. It restricts the possibilities for discovering ways of holding or responding to the baby, which are unique for that individual baby.

There are many cultural beliefs around crying, and the parents' response to the baby is affected by the meaning that they attribute to it. Many parents have hostile and violent thoughts about their babies and their crying and some may lose control and physically assault them.

Mental representations or beliefs shape behaviour and use of body language and gestures. Between the two levels is the muscle tone, which acts as a modulator. However, adults' beliefs about a baby's crying usually have nothing to do with the cry itself, which is primarily an expression of her own language and a form of communication. A mother's belief that she may have caused the baby's crying and the associated sense of guilt may only lead to two individuals crying, because she may feel as if it is she herself crying. This happens when the mother's and baby's needs are merged and there is no boundary. Becoming aware of this is the key to getting rid of tension and listening to her feelings. Acknowledging the boundary is the way to encounter the baby's individual feelings.

For a healthy baby, crying can be the only way of releasing all the power inside her small body, which cannot yet be channelled through walking, running, or speaking. It may be for a vast range of reasons—hunger, anger, pain, sorrow, fear, an uncomfortable position, being wet, being overheated, an unpleasant smell, needing to be left alone, boredom, simply wanting comfort, and so on. Unfortunately, we have lost our capacity to intuit their feelings. There is a lot that is "unspoken" in a baby's crying, which needs to understood by listening. This requires empathy, genuine love, and respect for the infant's experience. No professional book or formula can provide the solution for stopping a baby crying, but only the parent's capacity to listen to her own inner infant, then to the baby. She needs to summon her inner strategies for responding appropriately. Moreover, while being listened to, the baby learns the capacity to listen to others and will be likely to follow the model she has been given.

Responding to a baby's cry is like interpreting a piece of music with her. The baby's cry is distinctively associated with a respiratory pattern. Wolff (1969) studied the baby's cry by analysis of the sounds emitted and identified a basic pattern characterized by exhalation-pause-hiss with inhalation-pause. This basic pattern, or cry for hunger, begins slowly and rhythmically and gradually becomes intense and arrhythmic. Variations on this basic pattern are related to different kinds of crying and different effects on the infant's caregivers. The cry of pain is very intense and arrhythmic from the beginning. It starts with a scream, followed by a pause associated with alternating breathlessness and hiccoughing. The cry of pain induces an instant response in the mother, whereas she can delay the cry of hunger, which starts slowly and with low intensity (Bowlby, 1979).

I remember holding a baby who had been crying for a long time in his mother's arms. After making sure that the mother was happy with this, I demonstrated a position for the baby. The post-natal support class was nearly full. I tried different positions with my arms to provide the baby with a comfortable place, while I was walking him towards the door. Then I stood by the door holding him in the "tiger position", a technique recommended by Peter Walker (1995). I cradled his head and neck in the crook of my left arm and let him wrap his arms and legs around my arms, facing outwards. After a while, he stopped crying. He may have been upset by the noise and the lack of air. The mother explained to me that he often screamed and yelled because of colic and it seemed

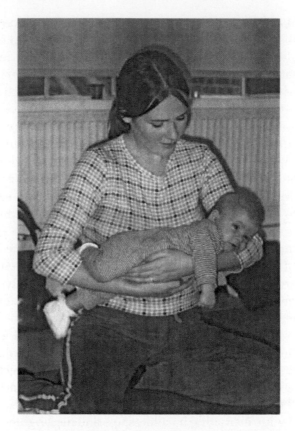

The "tiger" position. In this powerful soothing position, mother cradles the baby's head and neck in the crook of her left arm and lets him wrap his arms and legs around her arms, facing outwards. With her left hand, mother can softly massage the baby's belly.

Photo by Antonella Sansone.

that she could do nothing. I only knew that at that time he might be crying simply because he was not breathing enough air in.

The baby's response is unique. In a baby's cry, there is no future or past, only the present. Responding appropriately requires an absence of anxiety or guilt, of traditional beliefs, or intellectual interpretations. It implies the parent being present with her own feelings and intuitions, which enable her to attune to what is going on with her baby. It is a process of learning about herself, as well as about her baby, and of continuously gaining new insights through experience.

I have previously stressed the importance of "being present", a condition that corresponds to open sensory channels and an aware perception of the environment. In relationships, this facilitates rhythmic communication. Physiologically, this condition of being present is associated with a muscle tone that is evenly distributed throughout the body, perhaps with comfortable posture and rhythmic breathing. There is evidence of a relationship between emotions, respiratory activity, and muscular tension, as well as between anxiety and hyperventilation (Suess, Alexander, Smith, Sweney & Marion, 1980; Ruggieri, Amoroso, Balbi & Borso, 1986; Ruggieri & Giustini, 1991). This healthy condition, which is about balance and adaptability to environmental changes, allows the parent's bodyself image to adapt to the physical and emotional changes brought about first by pregnancy and then by the arrival of a baby. The impact of a baby crying may be even more dramatic. By responding in a way that creatively adapts to the baby's changing needs, the parent teaches the baby, through mirroring, to adapt to the environment and grow in harmony with it.

To make the appropriate response to the baby's cry, the parent needs to acknowledge the anger or fear induced by it. A parent may feel threatened by her baby's cry. A baby, who needs vital stimuli to develop and loving arms to hold her, does not know anything about the parent's fear of losing control, need to establish a routine, lack of confidence, sense of guilt, or conflicts (Gray, 1987). However, the baby senses her gestures, the quality of eye contact and facial expressions, and her muscle tone, which are all direct expressions of her feelings and mental state. The sensory information may be converted either into a global, unified experience of secure containment or fear of threats, according to the quality of response.

Considering the baby's cry as a primitive signal that is part of the complex repertoire of gestural language, a piece of music or song can induce the mother to "dance" or synchronize with her. This means moving both emotionally and physically while handling the baby. Information about emotions is given by every bodily movement, overall posture, and way of walking. Babies are accustomed to a pre-natal environment that is constantly in motion, and they therefore need movement as well as emotions. Detailed analysis of vocalizations in early life may shed light on the effects of non-verbal communication. Rhythmic and musical elements of infant behaviour, such as crying, seem to contribute to what has been called "postural conformity" in the infant–mother relationship, which is an important component of attachment behaviour and the infant's emotional behaviour (Ostwald, 1981).

When a mother gives her breast to her baby who is crying from hunger, and the baby magically stops crying, she is "dancing" with her, as she has wonderfully met her need. When the baby is crying because of an ailment and the mother finds a comfortable position for her, holding her with loving soothing arms and gently massaging her tummy, she is dancing with her baby.

However, if she insists on offering her breast, thinking she is hungry, although she does not stop crying, or keeps massaging her when she is crying, she is not dancing. The baby feels that the mother is not in tune and keeps crying because she has no other means to convey "I am not hungry" or "I do not want to be massaged", or, maybe, that she does not even want the breast for comfort at that time.

There is no judgement attached to these unsuccessful attempts, as becoming able to dance is partly a learning process. There are mothers who are more intuitive, more predisposed to motherhood, but they can all learn through their own experience. Being self-judgemental is not at all constructive. No learning process is easy. There is no need to develop a sense of guilt because of failure in the early stages. The baby is a unique individual with her own needs and language that need to be discovered. Learning the differences between a cry for food, a cry of pain, anger, or longing to be cuddled will help her baby to feel happy and secure.

A mother runs no risk of spoiling her baby if she is present in responding whenever the baby needs her. The word "spoiling" is an adult invention. Parents often label children in this way, thus reinforcing such behaviour. By doing this, parents teach children what they expect from them. Responding to the baby's cry by meeting her actual needs helps her to acknowledge them and reflect on them, rather than build up defences. This leads to a sense of fulfilment and independence.

When the baby is crying simply because she wants comfort or an interesting stimulus and the mother wonders whether the baby is sick or there is something wrong with her, she is nurturing negative thoughts and increasing her muscular tension (Fridja, Manstead &

Bem, 2000). The mother is then conveying her fear and alarm to her baby by the way in which she holds, looks at, and talks to her, thus, through her bodyself image. The baby's experience then becomes even more threatening.

Practical tips

Listening to a baby crying means trying to understand the specific need that has made her cry. This process requires a mental state that equates physiologically with deep and smooth breathing and balanced muscle tone throughout the body, which enables the parent to listen to her inner infant. The second important step is making eye contact and observing the infant's cues: bodily movements, especially of her mouth, head, and arms.

If mother creates a pleasurable and playful situation by producing, for instance, some primitive sounds or singing a theme tune, this will probably draw the baby's attention and keep her engaged. The mother–baby dance can then start. As a baby is very sensitive to sounds, the mother and baby establish a rhythmic communication. If the baby is frightened, she needs the comfort of rocking, walking, and cuddling to reassure her.

Music produces vibrations that rebound on the baby's muscular system, modulating her muscular tone and breathing, with either a rocking-soothing or an activating effect. The melody of a piece of music can tone down the sounds of crying, helping the caregiver to cope with it. Singing a tune that the baby enjoys may lessen her squawk to a gummy grin and even encourage some positions such as lifting her head and shoulder off the floor while lying on her stomach, and looking around in an exploratory attitude. Musical vibrations can therefore strengthen the baby's muscular system and posture. One woman who had just started attending a baby massage class said that nothing seemed to soothe her baby with colic. He screamed and yelled and whimpered at night. She cuddled and tried to soothe him. Only by singing and dancing around the house could she reduce his screaming. After a few weeks, she also saw the healing effects of massage on the baby.

High-pitched sounds can also keep a baby awake or divert his excitement. The shared pleasure reduces the tension in both mother and baby. Mother can dance with the music or crying sounds, or just by gliding about with her baby in her arms. Some Indian music contains deep primitive sounds that seem to have a soothing effect on a crying baby. It may also helpful to induce the baby to sleep and establish routines if it is regularly played in the background.

A baby is soothed by deep sounds possibly because they recall and arouse the sensations of low sounds reaching the womb, the most familiar of which is the maternal heartbeat. The intra-uterine sounds are deepened and softened by the amniotic fluid and the vibrations from the mother's vocal cords that spread through her chest and abdomen in rhythm with her breathing. Sounds recorded in the amniotic fluid can have a healing or soothing effect because they provide an experience of continuity with intra-uterine life. Moon and Fifer (1990) demonstrated the newborn's memory and apparent preference for *in utero* experience. Newborn infants were presented with a recording of their mothers' voice engaged in adult conversation and the same recording filtered so as to mimic a womb-like version, and chose to suck more often to the latter sound.

Dolphin sounds seem to have a soothing effect on the crying baby, as do sounds of nature, such as birds, waterfalls and the waves on the shore. Sounds produced by primitive instruments seem to attune to the baby's cry. Everyday sounds, such as the loo flushing, a hairdryer, vacuum cleaner, dishwasher, or washing machine may have a soothing effect on the crying baby if she has become familiar to them during intra-uterine life.

Having a bath, or massaging the baby regularly, for instance, before going to bed, can calm the baby down and help to establish sleep routines, provided it is not done to a rigid timetable or as a chore. The key thing is to create a playful time for parent and baby.

Crying and cultural meaning

We are biologically programmed to respond to a baby's cry. How-ever, this does not mean that is always comes naturally. The baby learns the social meaning of crying from the parent's response, so if the baby's cry relates mainly to the present, the parents' response points to the future. By absorbing the social and cultural meanings, the baby learns how to control her body and its language, how to master her needs and feelings and to cope with pain.

When the mother assumes a worried facial expression because of her baby's cry and tightens her posture, through a mirroring process the baby is likely to be learning the meaning of crying, for example, that it is something wrong that adults do not do. Although the mother's worry is a natural and unavoidable response, awareness of the mirroring process, through which the baby records observed expressions in her own facial muscles and posture, helps her to control it and play with a variety of expressions. Through mirroring, the baby also learns how to use the recorded gesture. This perceptual awareness in the mother enables her to get in touch with her true emotions induced by the baby's crying and screams. It helps her to find the problem-solving strategies in her own bodyself. Babies are amused by a wide variety of expressions and games. For instance, particularly if she is crying because a lack of interesting stimuli, making a cheeky expression or using a funny tone of voice, or providing an unusual position or gently massaging and rubbing her can create a special time and get her involved. The mother will hear her infant's squawks turn into happy gurgling.

Babies have their own way of perceiving the space around them. Some babies feel uncomfortable in a pram because they need a wider space to stretch in. Others may need a containing space in which they can curl up to sleep. They may begin to show their temperament in relation to the space in the womb. Some babies may hasten the labour process because they are longing to leave the restricted space of the womb. Others may come to the world lazily and slowly, still willing to curl up in the womb.

In my study on a fishing island in the Indian Ocean in 1995 (see Chapter Six), I was struck by the silence, despite the large number of babies. A very common scene was that of a pregnant woman holding a young baby. I had read about the lower frequency of crying among babies in tribal or peasant communities. More research is needed into how parents' cultural beliefs and expectations about their baby's crying mould the baby's response and the quality of her crying.

The key to the lower frequency of crying among tribal babies may be the richness of natural and social stimuli and the low incidence of distress or isolation among parents. A further explanation could be the everyday child-care practices. Many tribal and non-industrialized societies, for instance, practise regular massage on their babies, with a soothing effect.

During a post-natal class, I was holding a baby who had been whimpering probably because he was teething. He was sucking one of his hands and his whimpering sounded like a mixture of comfort from sucking and soreness. After a while, I started reproducing his sounds. His whimpering gradually broke down and turned into an increasingly cheerful cooing. We were then in "conversation". A mutual playful situation gradually replaced the solitary whimpering. The baby got somehow engaged with the amusing sounds and the pain apparently subsided.

Playing with a baby's crying or whimper implies having the self-confidence necessary to feel that nothing is really wrong with the baby's cry, that she is not necessarily ill, distressed, or in pain, that her screaming may be a sign of temper, a whim, or the first display of willfulness and eagerness. This confidence will help a mother not to build up tension and passively wait for it to subside, but to use positive strategies to capture the baby's attention.

Babies have many ways of communicating. They engage in early pre-verbal conversations; they turn their heads away when they are sleepy and become relaxed and floppy. The baby has a great deal of body language, which needs to be sensed first, through close physical contact. There are many messages passing from one body to another: body temperature, smell, muscle tone, breathing, vocal vibrations, and so on. When one partner is in tune with the other and dancing, we can see in the baby a contented comfortable Buddha-like posture corresponding to balanced muscular tone. Any movement and expression is a form of language for the baby.

Crying is not the only way of communicating, although it is a very powerful one. Responding and giving love only when the baby is crying may teach the baby to use crying to draw the parent's attention. In the same way, she can use illness to signal her need for attention. But when love is given regularly, or any time the baby signals her need, she will not need to cry or fall sick to attract the parent's attention.

It may be enough to enhance observational skills to become able to interpret the rich repertoire of the baby's language. There is no point in wondering whether the baby's crying is caused by the mother's anxiety about mothering. The result would be the mother's feeling guilty, which makes things even worse. Crying is a rich, complex language that can indeed make a parent anxious.

The mother–baby relationship forms a circle. Both contribute with the same intensity and in a way that is exquisitely unique. Neither causes behaviour in the other. When locked by excessive tension, the circle can be made smoother by reducing the tension in the bodyself, modulating the holding and vocal intonation. This can only occur through perceptual awareness of the bodyself. The mother needs to rediscover her own insights and abilities in dealing with the baby's cry.

Playful massage to turn a screaming baby into a laughing baby

Massage can help parents to cope with some of the everyday problems of childhood. It can alleviate some of the discomforts caused by wind, constipation, and colic, as well as relieve congestion and thus help the baby to get a better night's sleep. Many paediatricians now refer parents of gassy or colicky babies to infant massage as a way of addressing the problem without drugs. Melissa, mother of three-week-old Martin, joined the baby massage class when it seemed that nothing could calm her colicky baby down. Two weeks after she began massaging him, the episode started to subside. "Within a few weeks his colic disappeared completely. He trusts me and I have become much more relaxed and confident", Melissa said. When I first met Melissa and Martin, they were both so stressed by the colic that they had difficulty in interacting with each other. Within two weeks, the change was remarkable. They were looking at each other, playing together, and vocalizing and Martin began to fully enjoy the massage.

Regular massage has the power to induce a particular state of mind in the mother. This was one of the main aspects of infant massage that captured my interest when I first saw the video-tape of an Indian mother massaging her baby. Cindy, mother of twelve-month-old Mike, said, "Being able to massage my baby has given me peace of mind". Massage can be a way to help a baby and thus to enhance the parent's confidence and self-esteem.

Mothers often ascribe their baby's distress and crying to digestive disorders, such as wind or colic. The needs to be held, nurtured, and played with are overlooked when wind and colic are convenient explanations. Most mothers, as a result of their anxiety about their babies' immaturity, do sometimes experience wind and colic, and traditional methods of winding their babies bring relief. Within the mother–baby dyad, it is difficult to establish what belongs to the mother and what to the baby; the boundaries are often unclear.

However, the very young child may ingest an uncomfortable amount of air into the stomach while feeding and, because of the immaturity of the baby's digestive system, air in the intestines can sometimes result in an uncomfortable pocket of gas and persistent crying. Wind, colic, and constipation can be alleviated through the regular practice of Peter Walker's technique described above. If walking with the baby in the "tiger position" does not pacify her, the mother can also gently pat or massage his tummy with her right arm, while walking and talking to him in low tones, but generally, walking the baby in the "tiger position" will be enough.

Regular and mindful massage, with particular attention to the tummy, can not only give pain relief but also cure the baby. Laying the baby on her stomach will also help to stretch and relax this area, but this should not be done immediately after a feed, as the advice is that babies should not sleep in this position.

Baby massage was initially used to treat special-needs infants but is now widely used as a soothing treatment. One of the most important points is to keep the massage playful, and to keep the baby engaged by smiling and talking. The mother should stop and comfort her baby if she starts to cry. Massage is an art; therefore, no movement should be forced. The healing power comes not just from the technique itself, but also from the attuned and multiple interactions between mother and baby. Massage is an art of communication and its power is enhanced by the containment of the group. This is clearly demonstrated by the following successful handling of a crying baby.

His mother ascribed David's screaming, yelling, and whimpering at night to colic. Nothing she did seemed to calm his rage. She cuddled and rubbed him; she even danced around the house to attempt to distract his attention from his rage. It seemed that she could do nothing until she joined a baby massage class, as described below.

> On the day I went, fifteen women sat quietly with their naked babies in front of them, kicking their plump legs in the air. My son David gazed around as I undressed him, looking at the blue-eyed girl lying next to him. With well-oiled hands, I rubbed David's tummy from side to side, taking care not to press down and using only the weight of my relaxed hands. Then I slowly worked upwards in a clockwise motion towards his chest, then out over his shoulders, gently pulling both arms downwards through my palms.

Some babies, like David, object when they are laid on their stomachs. But it is important to do this for short, regular periods as it reverses the foetal position to which they have been confined in the womb and strengthens the back muscles. It is common in a baby massage class to see babies elegantly lifting their heads and shoulders off the floor, as a reflex induced by lying on their tummies. In this position, their chests open, allowing in more oxygen to fight disease and foster development. The position is also stimulated by the sight and vocalizations of the other babies settled around in a circle. With shoulders and heads lifted off the floor, while their backs are being massaged, their necks move side-to-side as they gaze around.

His mother said: "David, meanwhile, had his nose on the mat, and was disliking it intensely. It was only my singing a tune that reduced his screaming to laughter and encouraged him to lift his head off the floor, before he crashed it down again and started to cry. But after a little rub, he was happily gurgling again ... Since then we have been a few times and I now massage David at home once or twice a week. He is getting used to lying on his tummy every day, and he can now easily hold his head. I have to sing the usual tune more often, but even that is a pleasure".

Babies are extremely sensitive to vocal vibrations and sounds in general. It is common to see changes in their posture in response to sounds. Mothers need to play creatively with synchronizing touch and sounds to get their baby engaged or soothe them.

CHAPTER 10

Breastfeeding

In most traditional cultures, breastfeeding is part of the close, intimate contact between mother and baby and is done naturally and with confidence. The mother recognizes the baby's body language when she nuzzles up to the breast and is fed. It is not restricted to any feeding time, number or length of intervals, and babies are not weighed too often. In many cultures, the baby is attached to the mother's body, always in contact with the smell of milk, and ready to be fed whenever she needs it. For example, in Southern India the baby is kept under the mother's sari next to her skin.

Even when she is not being fed, the sucking, or just the smell of milk is enough to comfort her.

The mother's clothing is well adapted to having a baby at the breast. In our industrialized societies, there is a great deal of inhibition about breastfeeding in public places. Some places do not even allow it. However, a minority of self-confident women use well-adapted clothes and breastfeed whenever the baby needs to be fed.

The time spent feeding constitutes the most absorbing and important time of the baby's early life. One of the central aspects of the parent's role is feeding the baby and, through this, giving not just food but the comfort, warmth, and love for which she yearns. Feeding her baby provides the mother with a unique opportunity to focus on her own feelings, get to know them, and attune to the baby. It is a powerful time of communication, as it unfolds through different channels—touch, smell, warmth, feelings, and vocal tones. Fathers can be involved in this special time through bottle-feeding, when it is introduced.

Breastfeeding is a physiological, psychological, and sensual experience. When the mother can integrate these dimensions, breastfeeding is fulfilling for her as well as for the baby. Every mother-and-baby dyad establishes a unique partnership. There is no optimum time to stop breastfeeding. However long the mother breastfeeds, she will have given her baby a very good start in life. She can herself be given powerful physical and emotional rewards.

Like a receptor, the mother senses all the hormonal and emotional changes induced by the contact with the baby, by her early sucking and touching of the nipple (Widström et al., 1990). She also senses the baby's cues. However, this is not enough. She also transmits her own sensual experience enriched with meanings to the baby. In some mothers, this sensual experience may arouse uneasy or difficult emotions, with the risk of their unconscious projection on to the baby. However, if in the mother there is a balanced connection between mind and body or between her psychological, sensual, and physiological dimensions, she can project her feelings on to the baby. This condition corresponds to an integrated and adaptable bodyself image.

The baby can thus internalize a fulfilling experience and project her positive feelings back on to her mother, providing her with a far more rewarding experience. When this circular process unfolds—a two-way identification and projection in which mother and baby identify with each other and project into each other—the mother provides and thus receives a perceptual and containing experience. Eating disorders, such as anorexia or bulimia, may be linked to deficiencies in this primary feeding experience. The baby's vital needs for comfort, support, and nourishment are primarily satisfied during feeding time, providing a security that can deeply affect her sense of security in later life. Emotional development is closely related to eating behaviour.

Breastfeeding, as an experience involving the woman's whole bodyself, arouses the emotional and instinctual unconscious side of the mother's personality, hence it can help her to get in touch with the deepest aspects of her body image. If the mother focuses on her experience, her body and self-image can be enriched and, through mirroring, the baby is enabled to develop a fulfilling integrated body and self-image.

Body image and eating behaviours evolve along parallel lines. Women who have suffered from body image and eating disorders such as anorexia or bulimia may benefit from nurturing their babies with their own bodies. This can strengthen the acceptance of their body and self-image. If they feel that their body will not be able to give milk, it is important to receive support during pregnancy focused on a listening and bodyself image approach.

If the mother's emotions are so overwhelming as to induce feeding difficulties, there is nothing worse than keeping struggling to breastfeed. The baby will sense the tension and this will deprive her of a fulfilling experience and potentially sow the seeds of eating and body image problems. Of course, it is not advisable to give in at the first difficulties; for some first-time mothers, it is natural to find an unknown experience uncomfortable. However, if breast-feeding becomes extremely demanding, it can be advantageous to switch to bottle feeding and be able to enjoy nurturing the baby through touch, soft words, and skin contact with the breast. She will receive the smell and warmth of the breast, making formula milk a perfect substitute. While doing so, rather than leaving the difficult emotions unresolved, it is helpful to receive emotional support from someone who is able to adopt a listening approach.

The sucking rhythm

The baby's sense of taste becomes stronger during breastfeeding, as the mother's milk changes to meet her baby's changing nutritional needs and provides easily digestible proteins that rarely upset a baby's sensitive tummy, whereas a bottle-fed baby gets used to the same taste of food. This exquisite physiological synchrony is facili-tated by the mother's enjoyment and sense of fulfilment during feeding. The mother creates the ingredients her baby needs for growing not just with the nutrients but also with her feelings. The success of feeding and the quality of milk are influenced by the mother's emotional balance.

When there is no excessive tension from struggling, the rhythm between the baby's sucking and the muscle in the breast unfolds smoothly and the mother can produce an amount of milk that varies according to the needs of her baby. This means that the sucking and milk expulsion rhythms become attuned to the baby's needs. The baby can therefore monitor her needs, and this also protects her from being overweight.

The "let-down reflex" (when the milk comes to the nipple) is linked with the mother's emotional state and enhanced by her self-trust, which is reflected in balanced muscular tone and a fluctuating or integrated body image. When this unity of mind and body exists, with the mother giving her containing feelings, the let-down reflex occurs smoothly. Resistance to letting herself give to the baby can tighten the breast and nipple and cause engorgement. Oxytocin stimulates milk flow and produces the "let-down reflex". This hormone, like others, is closely linked with the mother's emotional state. The baby's cry or just the physical contact with the mother stimulates the oxytocin release and the "let-down reflex" (Lind, Vuorenkoski & Wasz-Hockert, 1973). This demonstrates the psychobiological synchrony between mother and baby, a fundamental process that mediates attachment formation.

The baby's sucking also stimulates other functions of the mother's body. It stimulates hormones that make her uterus contract and return to its pre-pregnant state. As a result of this physiological, sensory, and emotional connection between mother and baby, breastfeeding can help mother to strengthen a perceptual awareness of her bodyself.

Breast milk strengthens the baby's immune system, as infections and gastro-intestinal illness are less frequent (McKenna, 1986). A bottle-fed baby who is genetically prone to allergies will become allergic six months earlier than her solely breast-fed siblings. Moreover, respiratory illnesses are thirty per cent lower.

One important aspect is the close contact with the mother's chest. Her breathing rhythm and her heartbeat can regulate the baby's own breathing rhythm and, at the same time, act as a reassuring factor. In fact, it is one of the most familiar rhythms of the womb. To let the sucking and feeding dance unfold, rather than struggling with establishing feeding patterns, it is more beneficial to feed the baby on demand. Breast milk is rapidly digested, so breastfed babies require frequent feeding. This helps mother to attune to her needs, to understand her pre-verbal communication and to get to know her personality.

There is sometimes a cultural belief that breastfeeding can make a baby "clingy" and dependent. Independence actually comes from secure attachment. Moreover, babies who are fed when they are hungry are usually more able to acknowledge their primary need for feeding and distinguish it from the wide range of others.

The baby's need for food is the prior need and the fulfilment provided impinges on the way of mastering other needs. In the womb, there is no digestion, no hunger, fullness, emptiness, or frustration. When the baby's first demanding need takes over soon after birth, a primary sense of separation from the mother arises. The mother's capacity to adjust her boundaries to her baby's primary needs is fundamental for the baby to set well-defined and flexible boundaries in accordance with changing needs and circumstances.

Sleeping with the baby or next to her cradle makes feeding easier. In the calm of the night, with nothing to distract the mother from breastfeeding, it can be easier to recognize the baby's need as she sniffs and snuggles up (Buranasin, 1991). She does not need to get out of bed for each feed. In a wake-sleep state, when the rational side of her personality is dozing off and thoughts are banished from her mind, the breast milk can flow undisturbed and her sensory experience can be more intense.

Breastfeeding in public makes it possible to combine social life with child-care and may even make it more enjoyable, provided that it does not occur in a smoky or excessively noisy place. Avoiding breastfeeding in public when the baby needs it could alter her feeding synchrony, particularly in very early life. Feeding in public should not be a reason for feeling ashamed but rather for feeling proud. People's embarrassment does not need to affect the mother. If the mother herself feels embarrassed about feeding in public, she can use feeding tops or side slits that help to maintain modesty. At other people's homes, the mother can ask to use a quiet room. The needs of mother and baby should always take priority.

There are various ways for a woman to be fully present in the breastfeeding and mothering experience in general and none of them should be overlooked: eating well, exercising in accordance with the rhythm of her bodyself, for instance, doing yoga, swimming, dancing, or playing music. Attending classes or one-to-one sessions, aimed at mother–baby attunement through work focused on emotional and physical support, can help the mother to integrate her body and self-image and increase her sense of being present. In case of breastfeeding difficulties or problems with the interactions with the baby, a receptive supporter can be very helpful. Mothers of premature infants can often produce more breast milk by using relaxation and visualization techniques, which also induce feelings of calm, comfort, and confidence (Feher, Berger, Johnson & Wilde, 1989).

Hunger is the most common cause of crying in a newborn baby. Wondering whether a baby is getting enough food is a common anxiety. However, it may not always be appropriate to respond to a cry with feeding. This may divert the baby's ability to get in touch with other needs than hunger. She may also learn to use food to satisfy her feelings.

The emotional urge

The success of breastfeeding or bottle-feeding is partly dependent on the way in which a woman copes with the emotional surge aroused during her transition to motherhood. The way in which a mother was nurtured as a child through touch, warmth, and holding influences the way in which she touches, holds, and cares for her own baby (Hopkins, 1990). This emerges noticeably from the case of Andrea, described in Chapter Three, who got mastitis a few days after birth.

During the same visit, it came up that what Andrea remembered as a child about her mother was going out shopping with a friend of hers. She spent very little time with her at home. A midwife told me that when Andrea's mother came to visit the baby after birth she did not touch the baby at all but just repeated: "Sweetie! Sweetie!"

Andrea's memory of her father was no more positive. He was addicted to alcohol and went out with other women. Her parents divorced when she was three years old. Andrea remembered him saying that she was not a good daughter. She did not even want to go to his funeral.

She said that when she went back home after the delivery, she breastfed on a "Victorian bed", in a ballerina pose and surrounded by lots of cushions, and then there were. "Lots of problems". An image of her mother and of repeated patterns took shape from her gestures and words. I made a link with her posture while breast-feeding a few days after birth before getting mastitis: her arms and shoulders looked immobile and stiff and her posture resembled a ballerina pose.

Then I noticed that her baby looked underweight, sad, and distressed. Hopkins (1990) stressed that as a response to inadequate holding, the baby sometimes develops a slumped and resigned state. I felt she needed to be encouraged to hold her baby, to make as much contact as possible with her, especially at this early stage of development, in order to break the repeating pattern and trigger the virtuous circle between mother and baby. Work on mindful body contact (skin and eye contact, cuddling, and massage) and on the present interactions was undertaken to help the mother to get through the crisis. This was intended to enable Andrea to sense and reflect on the baby's experience and eventually to meet her needs. My first aim was to help her become aware that mastitis was not the core problem, and thus to connect with her true feelings.

After a few weeks, the interaction between Andrea and her baby had increased noticeably. She learned to accept bottle-feeding rather than waste time struggling with herself for not being able to give the baby her milk. Baby massage classes proved to be a complementary therapy that provided the containment needed for mother and baby to attune and get to know each other.

The mother's emotional and mental state influences the produc-tion of hormones that stimulate milk flow. Depression and lack of confidence may inhibit the milk flow and affect the quality of milk and feeding. Excessive tension may cause milk-duct blockage and mastitis. Sometimes family support is not the most beneficial. The mother's mother, for instance, may believe in the importance of routines and hold that feeding on demand spoils the baby. If the mother lacks confidence, she can be affected by a judgemental attitude.

Neutral support from a non-judgemental group or one-to-one support may better meet the mother's and baby's individual needs. The sharing experience with other women facilitates self-awareness during the emotional transition and learning from others' experiences. It is as if the woman mirrors herself in the group. The group also provides containment for the mother, which is vital for providing the baby with a containing and fulfilling experience.

As Winnicott notes (1988, p. 78), the mother's milk does not simply flow out like an excretion. It is a response to a variety of stimuli: the sight, smell, and feel of her baby and the sound of the baby's cry that indicates need. The periodic feeding develops as a communication between mother and baby, based on a rhythmic exchange of cues in which the infant's needs to be fed and comforted are met. This encounter is strongly dependent on the mother's perception of her psychobiological synchrony and its symbiotic bond with the baby's needs. This requires the mother to be able to feel and trust her body and focus on what is going on. The following account shows how the mother's confidence in her bodyself and her determination are crucial elements to turn the initial pain of early breastfeeding difficulties into enjoyment.

'The early breastfeeding days with my son, Sam, were a nightmare. The pain of latching on was considerable and Sam showed great reluctance to co-operate. Each feed took ages, he drank very little, cried a lot, and rapidly lost weight. Every time I sat down to feed him, I became very tense as I anticipated the pain of latching on and the frustration of not getting him settled. The midwives kept suggesting that some babies just refused to breastfeed but having gone through labour without any pain relief I was not going to be defeated by a three-day-old baby, so I battled on and within a week became a much more experienced breastfeeder! I was very proud of my achievements and enjoyed disproving everyone's theories. The joy of feeding was thus threefold: the closeness I shared with Sam and the knowledge that I was giving him the best start in life, along with my strength and determination against all odds. I continued to feed him until his first birthday!'

The baby's introduction to feeding patterns is also related to the mother's own attitude to food and, thus, to the way in which she was fed by her mother. Feeding and emotional nourishment contribute together to shaping the mother–infant relationship, as the baby does not initially experience the breast as part of the mother but as the entire mother with all her attentive care.

If the primary nourishing object and its relationship, for instance the breast, is internalized, it takes root in the ego with relative security and becomes the basis for a balanced development (Klein, 1957). The breast is instinctively felt to be the source of nourishment and therefore, in a deeper sense, of life itself. The feeding experience can help the baby to go through the transition, as it partly restores the pre-natal feeling of security.

The release of milk may be altered by the mother's emotions and how she relates to her bodyself image, whether she is comfortable with her physical and emotional changes or is struggling. Emotions display themselves through muscular tone and gestures and can affect milk release not only at a cerebral level (hypothalamus) but also at a peripheral level, by interfering with the muscular canal inside the breast. This muscle needs to be working in rhythm with the baby's sucking, and also in harmony with the mother's shoulders and chest muscles, her breathing, and her whole posture. It is like a dance of muscles. In other words, the communication, whether at bodily or verbal level, is characterized by rhythmic exchanges.

Breast milk production may be lessened by worries about the infant's health or milk intake, obsession with routines, conflicts in personal relationships, or failure to get helpful advice to work out feeding problems. This latter anxiety is nowadays on the increase, as the majority of advice comes from professionals who have an impersonal relationship with the mother. In traditional societies, however, most help and encouragement come from an experienced supporter, relative, friend, or mother, who is able to give emotional support rather than technical advice.

Motherhood is a fundamental experience that brings up deep-seated insecurities and long-buried emotions, which may be so devastating that they can undermine the mother's bodyself language. This primary language needs to be revitalized during the interactions with the baby. All the intricate interactions involving the baby's sucking, which affect the mother's hormones, activate a milk response, enhance maternal feelings, free her body language, deepen receptiveness, perpetuate and shape an age-old human cycle. Brazelton and Cramer (1990) sees the axiety that is characteristic of a pregnant woman as something that mobilizes the energy necessary for the vast work ahead and the development of attachment.

The infant's fulfilment and gratification during feeding may also be a first template for rewarding social and intimate relationships in later life. In this sense of fulfilment, the core of the child's, and later the adult's, eating behaviour may reside. Eating behaviour disturbances may derive from a lack of primary rhythmic communication between parent and baby, not just during feeding, but during any interaction between them.

The attuned rhythm of sucking rewards the mother, modulating her perception of her bodyself, and strengthening her self-confidence, which makes breastfeeding enjoyable. Through the interactions, the mother comes to feel grateful to her baby for the unique experience, as she gives her milk and her attention, while drawing from the baby unique sensations. On a wider lever, this enhances her enjoyment of giving in personal and social relationships and her sense of gratitude to life.

Breastfeeding and body image

The breast gives comfort, not only milk. To feel safe, the baby needs this physical contact. The breast is the baby's own world. However, if she is bottle-feeding, the mother's arms, skin, tummy, voice, and eye contact can replace it effectively. The mouth is particularly sensitive; she sucks for comfort when she is not hungry. Through the mouth, the baby explores the breast, the mother's body, and a variety of sensations. Soon after birth, the newborn finds the nipple by smell (Vallardi, Porter & Wimberg, 1994). If the right breast is washed with soap and water, the infant will crawl to the left breast. Through her sensory channels, the baby makes her primary discoveries. When the baby stops sucking as hunger is satisfied, she may become interested in the mother's hair, eyes, nose, mouth, or smile and then start sucking again. All this forms the baby's immediate primary environment, which enables the baby to explore with her limited vision. Later on, she will become increasingly interested in what happens around her. She then begins perceiving an increasingly wide space and nurturing a mental representation of it.

Babies also like to play with the breast when their hunger is satisfied: grab the nipple with their mouths, lick it, touch the breast with their hands, sniff and, when they grow older, bite. The baby establishes a relationship with the breast, which represents the relationship with her mother. I do not consider it likely that the baby is ever entirely fused with the breast. Her own sensations, feelings, and motives give her a core sense of separation and self. This is consistent with Stern's view (2000) that the newborn baby already has a core sense of self.

I suggest that the baby has a core ego or identity, on the basis of which she soon develops a core self, since "self" implies a capacity to reflect on her sensations, feelings, movements, and actions. This self-reflective capacity is shaped by the mother's capacity to reflect on the baby's activities and cues. During their interactions, the baby moves her face, lips and tongue, arms, hands, and whole body in movements that are directed towards her mother, who acts as a mirror image: the mother is, thus, "receiving her". At the same time, the mother is addressing her with her own sounds and gestures and the baby is receiving her.

There is a sense of identity between their actions, a real conversation on the basis of which language will develop. Neither is passively imitating the other; the child often initiates or dictates the conversation. She often leads the dance and the mother dances with her. The child is practising moving her tongue, lips, jaw, and speech organs. She is also learning how to draw attention to something and to associate a meaning with it through the mother's responses and suggestions.

Enjoying and being present during feeding is reflected in a balanced and harmonious posture, smooth and deep breathing, and an integrated body image. Uncomfortable positioning during feeding entails high muscular tension and unpleasant feelings that can interfere with the baby's sucking and the milk secretion, reducing the supply. The mother's feelings flow along with her milk and contribute to forming its flavour. One woman wrote as feedback on my presentation on the body image at the Birth Unit, "It is true that if there are obstacles in the mind/body image it becomes increasingly difficult to have the fluid bodily movements and the psychological harmony necessary to enjoy breastfeeding". The dramatic role of body image in breastfeeding, usually overlooked by research and psychotherapeutic work, emerges from another woman's account written for me during my observational study, "I can feel my body image every day while breastfeeding him, massaging him, and playing with him. It is very interesting that you are addressing this complicated subject".

If the mother is excessively tense or upset, the milk may not flow smoothly and the "milk ejection reflex" may not be triggered. This may cause sore or bleeding nipples, or breast inflammations such as mastitis. I wonder how many women are told by the doctor that they have lost their milk and must give up breastfeeding because of initial difficulties. This may increase their original anxiety and engender guilt feelings. Without professional support from someone who is sensitive and sensible in helping them to elaborate their feelings, relieve their sense of guilt and anxiety, and gain in self-trust, those hidden feelings will tighten their muscular tone, breathing, and the way of holding their baby. In short, the maternal body language sensed by the baby will be affected and then mould the parent–baby relationship.

High anxiety, causing physical tension, can not only inhibit the milk-ejection reflex but also the sensations as the milk flows to the nipples. The hungry baby consequently becomes rigid and frustrated. Excessive anxiety that not enough milk is flowing and the baby is not feeding may hinder the milk ejection reflex in a circular process. At a postural level, the tension may show, for instance, in tense, closed shoulders and chest, which interferes with the breast muscle involved in sucking and milk expulsion. The pain will then prevent the mother and thus the baby from enjoying breastfeeding.

During my observational study at the Birth Unit and in breastfeeding support groups, I formed the hypothesis that the attuned rhythm between the muscle inside the breast and the baby's sucking is the key to successful breastfeeding. It is a deep-level form of communication between mother and baby. This muscle does not function independently of the mother's feelings, expectations, and cultural beliefs. To make this rhythm attuned, it is fundamental for the mother to feel what is going on in her bodyself, which enables her to sense the baby and give meaning to her experience and to her own. The mother needs to perceive and listen to her bodyself to be able to identify her baby's needs. This dimension is made possible by balanced emotional and muscular tone and an integrated body image.

The breast is the baby's earliest "other": through it she learns to relate to the "other", to establish a rhythm, and thus to develop effective communication and relationships in later life. There are rhythmic exchanges during feeding between the baby's bodily cues and the mother's interpretations that establish the foundations of pre-verbal communication and then language.

The is a beautiful connection between mother and baby during feeding takes the form of a dance. It manifests itself at various levels: hormonal, muscular, sensory, emotional, and psychological. The baby initiates the secretion of maternal hormones. This is one reason why it is important to begin breastfeeding as soon as possible. When offered the breast, the baby often does not suck at first but licks it instead. Righard and Blade (1990) have shown that if a mother has not had pain relief during labour and her infant has not been taken away in the first few hours after birth for baths but placed on her abdomen, the baby often crawls up to her breast and begins to suck. When the baby licks the mother's nipple, the release of oxytocin, which stimulates milk production, hastens uterine contraction, reduces bleeding, and calms the mother. The rhythmic sucking induces satisfaction and fulfilment in both mother and baby and strengthens their bond. Touch can have the same psychological and physiological effects as sucking and licking the mother, enhancing her well-being. The baby elicits behaviours from the mother—touching, eye contact, smile—that are satisfying to her, and vice versa, with touching, sucking, and so on.

For these reciprocal body communications to flow between mother and baby, it is essential that the mother is relaxed enough to feel her own and the baby's bodily signals. This is possible when the mother's bodyself image is integrated and adapted to the baby's needs and personality. It is like a couple dancing the tango, a dance that deeply involves feelings: if a dancer is tense, this tightness acts as a barrier to being in rhythm with the partner and hinders the performance. The two dancers need to trust each other in order to let themselves be led. The mother needs to allow herself to be led by the baby's sucking for the milk to flow. Her response to the baby's sucking involves a "giving" feeling. Tense and closed shoulders and chest, usually a sign of fear, worry, or resistance, and constricted breathing obstruct the sensory channels and reduce the sensory exchange between mother and baby and, thus, the mother's ability to attune to her.

Baby massage, water, and music for the sucking rhythm

I shall now describe two situations drawn from a breastfeeding group and baby massage class.

1. Sarah was attending one of her first breastfeeding sessions. The shoulder of the feeding breast looked locked in and the neck was pulled down into the shoulders. Her face appeared quite tense and preoccupied, giving me the impression that she was somehow far away from the baby and absorbed in emotional difficulties. There was no smile on her face and she made no eye contact with her baby.

On another day, I observed her in a baby massage class. Sarah held her little boy as though he were something precious and fragile. I noticed that every movement occurred in slow motion and disjointedly. She appeared shy and embarrassed. She looked at me, as often in the breastfeeding class, uncertain what to do. I made encouraging eye contact. Then she started to undress her baby. The way in which she laid her baby on the floor and touched her appeared really peculiar. She seemed to be straining every movement in order not to hurt him. Her arms looked quite stiff, her chest closed and her shoulders raised, as though she needed to protect herself. The baby was still and his eyes were fixed in the air. He did not kick or stretch his legs as babies usually do during massage or even a few minutes before, as a sign of anticipation of its playfulness, nor make any sound. Sarah did not talk to her baby or make eye contact. She used her fingers rather than the palms of her hands to massage as though she was afraid of damaging his skin.

I learnt later in a one-to-one meeting that she was struggling to protect herself from painful emotions. She had been abandoned during pregnancy by her husband and had not seen him since. Her superficial touch during breastfeeding and massage may have contributed to the baby's stillness, as though the mother's fear was being absorbed by him.

The first time she came to the yoga class, her seven-month-old child appeared timorous and unconfident. He would not interact with other children for the first few weeks and clung to his mother throughout. Sarah's child is now eighteen months old and his developmental changes are quite remarkable. He is a sociable and talkative child and his mother now appears receptive and more confident. The group experience has proved to be an important containment of her emotions, from which her child has enormously benefited.

2. I followed up Yvette, an underweight baby, in the days immediately after birth. She was remarkably underweight and appeared to be disturbed by any sound. Her mother Samantha was having breastfeeding problems and struggling to give her the breast milk, which was not flowing freely. She had a breast inflammation, for which she was receiving medical treatment. She complained at times that her baby cried continuously and would only calm down if she was picked up, held and rocked. I had the feeling that the pattern of picking the baby up whenever she cried was related to her own need to be contained and her fear of separation from the baby. I thought that her problems were primarily emotional and that a baby massage class could create a special form of containment for both mother and baby and resolve the crying–pick up pattern.

It is important to combine the medical treatment with a sensitive and creative programme based on caring touch and a holding experience for both mother and baby. There is evidence that babies who are touched more cry less, gain weight faster, and exhibit better motor, emotional, and behavioural development, and that a care programme aimed at bonding the baby to the mother's breast like a baby kangaroo in a poncho can save many very underweight babies (Scafidi, Field, Schanberg & Bauer, 1990; Field, 1990; Anderson, 1991). The caring touch of massage throughout the body, by stimulating the nerve endings in the skin, can bring even greater benefits, providing an experience of integration of the parts of the baby's bodyself.

When I spoke to Samantha and explained all the benefits of joining a baby massage class, at first she seemed to have some reservations, and then she said she was afraid she would not have time to join the group. A few days later I saw her in the baby massage class.

I tried to encourage her to focus on gentle and smooth touching. The tiny baby soon appeared to enjoy this and after a few weeks she was noticeably gaining weight. Samantha was still quite apprehensive with her baby but I noticed that she was no longer complaining about the cry–pick up pattern. The special contact during massage has contributed to increasing both the mother's and the baby's confidence, promoting security and separation.

At the age of eight months, Yvette has recently started to attend the mother-and-baby yoga sessions. She still appears a bit anxious and is sometimes irritable when she interacts with other children. Nevertheless, the group experience is helping mother and baby go through the transitional period of separation. The mother's touch, caring massage, and the group itself have proved to be a powerful substitute for the inadequate milk supply.

Although every woman is naturally able to breastfeed and provide the "giving feeling" alongside the benefits of the breast milk, some may find it difficult and feel disempowered and humiliated. There is no need for any sense of guilt or failure, or for anyone to struggle to give breast milk. This kind of worry will direct the mother away from the baby and consequently deprive her of a form of nourishment that is more important and vital than the mother's own milk—attentive touch, eye contact, deep breathing, and the "giving feeling".

Every mother, however, can search for a way of enjoying either breastfeeding or bottle-feeding. Bathing together or listening to an enjoyable piece of music, for instance, creates a resting-place. Musical vibrations have powerful muscular and emotional effects. It can relieve excessive tension and pain and regulate the rhythm of sucking and other interactions, enhancing the dance with the baby. Water as well as music can enhance the sensations of the milk-ejection reflex. They can contain mother and baby together. If a mother is bottle-feeding, she can expose the breast to maintain the baby's contact with it. The mother has many creative resources. The baby still receives the warmth from the breast when she is bottle-feeding. Babies, particularly premature babies, need to be kept cosily warm at all times. If they get cold, they lose the energy they need for feeding. Bodily heat is much more effective than warm clothes and maintaining contact with the breast can be vital for a bottle-fed or a premature baby. Touching, talking to, looking at and reflecting on the baby enhance closeness and relieve any sense of guilt.

The mother's clothes, particularly in winter, may act as a barrier for the baby. At least at home, in winter, the mother needs loose clothing that opens at the front. She can wear a baby-carrier next to her skin under her clothes and put the baby, naked, except for a nappy, into it, so that she is in contact with her breast, and can easily reach the nipple whenever she wants (kangaroo-style). If she is breastfeeding, the breast and chest space is especially warm and is a special source of heat for the baby.

Light clothes will help the mother to sense and understand the tiny movements the baby makes to signal her need to feed or for security. The mother's voice, smell, warmth, and the rocking from her body movements will provide her with an experience of continuity from intra-uterine life. The mother may also be rewarded by her body language in response, and rediscover an extension of her own primary life. She can be grateful to her baby for experiencing a rebirth. If she is bottle-feeding because of initial breastfeeding problems, she can benefit from this experience and the milk may even flow more abundantly.

With regard to the breastfeeding position, there is no standard position to assume. The best position is the one that is attuned to the individual mother and baby. It needs to be found creatively through the way in which the mother's posture adjusts to the baby's needs and feelings and therefore to her posture. The appropriate position depends on the continuous adjustments of two postures, which I call "postural attunement". The key may be in the mother's exploration of her feelings and search for positions that feel right.

Some babies are forced on to the breast in a way that they may associate with discomfort and unpleasantness. They go rigid and their sucking rhythm is affected. For instance, it may be useful for some mothers to lean over the baby who is lying on his back on the bed or on the floor, so that the breast hangs down. This position, with different variations, can help to solve engorgement problems because gravity can help the nipple to be at the right angle and the weight of the breast pulls the nipple away. Other positions can be discovered with the invaluable help of music or water.

Any position needs to be found in accordance with the mother's feeling and not under specialist prescription. In breastfeeding, it can be really helpful to invent new positions to eventually get in tune with the baby. When the baby is not in the correct position, she may get only the nipple in her mouth and be unable to stimulate milk production. The baby then has to work hard to get milk and never gets a satisfying meal.

The correct position, when the baby has the nipple and the surrounding tissues (areola) inside her mouth, is a natural process but at the same time a voyage of discovery for both mother and baby. A supportive environment can play a paramount part in this process. Breastfeeding needs a protected and creative environment, a special space between mother and baby. It does not require an isolated space, since the most important protected environment is provided by the mother's body, as an expression of her emotions, motivations, expectations, and cultural beliefs. There are women who feel comfortable with breastfeeding in a restaurant; others need a private and familiar space. This is related to their cultural background.

Sometimes there is too much worry about establishing feeding rhythms or rigid routines. If the baby is crying, some mothers tend to show the breast to feed and get worried if she does not feed. Sometimes the baby is naturally discontented and insecure and wants to suck or stay at the breast for comfort or for reasons connected with the baby's partly unknown and unique world or to undiscovered aspects of her personality. There may be also too much worry about establishing sleep routines. It can be more helpful not to pay attention to the clock, and breastfeed whenever it is needed, without social or cultural inhibitions.

The weaning experience

The mother will understand when her baby is getting increasingly hungry and yearning for more than milk. It is then time to embark on the next stage of her baby's development. Every mother and baby is a unique partnership. There is no optimal time to stop breastfeeding. However long the mother breastfeeds, she will have given her baby a very good start in life. Continuing to breastfeed for the first year, while introducing solid food at four to six months, ensures a good source of nutrients and security.

Food needs to be introduced gradually, with a tiny bit of pureed food, as a supplement to the usual milk feeds. The baby then learns to take and enjoy food with a different taste and texture, use his mouth in a new way, and to swallow and digest something that is not liquid. The proper use of every part of her mouth impinges on an integrated bodyself perception. This is a gradual process.

Some babies enjoy food from the very first spoonful but others take a long time to accept it. Every baby has her own pace, and this needs to be met in order to develop a healthy attitude to nutrition. Continuing to give milk and loving interactions helps the baby to go through the transition and separation from the breast. The mother needs to trust her feelings about introducing food. She will also soon find which feeding time suits her baby best. Over time, the mother will increase the variety of foods and increase the thickness to help her improve her swallowing reflex. Her development will benefit from everything being done at her own pace. This helps self-perception and self-knowledge. This transition, eased by the mother's confidence, is a crucial time for the development of healthy eating behaviour.

There are so many cultural beliefs and opinions about what to give the baby or when to give it. This is often a source of conflicts. A confident mother, who relies on her attuning feeling, soon learns that nothing can be forced and it is the baby who teaches the way, rather than the other way round.

From six to nine months, the mother can move on from purees to mashed or minced food. New sensations arise in the mouth—new movements and co-ordination of the jaws, new sensations from the swallowing—but also new sensations of taking in and fullness in the stomach. A new perception of the inside space takes shape, not just through the new foods, but, more importantly, through the mother's attuned love in introducing it. In any activity or function, the baby needs to progress slowly to nurture an integrated self-perception.

Starting with one type of food and keeping to it for three to four days helps the baby to get used to the texture and a new taste, and allows time for the parents to see if allergies develop. Allergies may be induced not just by the new food itself, but also by the baby's emotional experience of weaning from the breast. The baby's body is far more dramatically involved in emotions and mental states than the adult's. Keeping to the same food for a few days may help the baby to accept the transition.

Separation for weaning is also a major issue for the mother. It may be hard to accept her baby's leap to a new stage of independence, especially if she enjoys solid food from the beginning and is not entirely reliant on her any longer. However, there are so many other rewarding times of close contact. For instance, baby massage is an effective tool for facilitating weaning.

It is important that feeding be fun for parent and baby, in order to develop a tension-free attitude to food. When new food is introduced, the baby tends to touch it, sink her hands into it, spill it out, throw her spoon around, and so on. The baby is exploring her tactile and taste sensations, and what her mouth is able to do. She is also testing her ability to produce an effect and exploring the inside space—taking in—and the space around her—spitting it out and throwing the spoon around. Eating becomes a big game for the baby and sometimes for the parents. It is important that the baby is allowed to develop this enjoyable attitude.

The mother's facial expressions while feeding the baby are important mirror images, facilitating the baby's approach to nutrition. Singing, laughing, and playing music makes feeding a pleasurable time. Preparing different combinations of food with creativity gets the baby used to different tastes and if the baby doesn't like some of them or she is too messy, there is no need to become anxious. This reflects a mental state that corresponds to the baby's health and enjoyment of the mothering experience. By contrast, high anxiety is expressed in muscular tension and rigid facial expressions, and can be transmitted to the sensitive baby. She may then later use altered "eating patterns" as a means of controlling the mother's emotional behaviour and dealing with her own emotions.

Separation

The baby experiences a major separation and sense of loss at weaning, which follows on from the separation from the womb at birth. The breast and the milk represent love, goodness, and security to the baby. When the baby is not feeding and, more importantly, is separated from the mother's body, she inevitably experiences a sense of loss that is necessary for her development.

According to Bion (1962), the way in which the infant deals with the absent breast is critical for the development of her capacity to think of the object and feel it inside as good despite its absence and her consequent sense of loss. The pain of needing the object when it is absent may force her back to primitive mechanisms. She may rid herself of this pain by projecting her feelings into the object, so that the missing breast becomes bad. The maternal breast then comes to contain the bad part of her.

However, the mother's love, receptiveness, and care give the baby tactile and visible disproof of her fears, aggressive feelings, and sense of loss. She can thus internalize the loving mother and adjust her missing object. The mother contains the baby's projection of fear and pain, absorbing it and returning it in a better form (Likierman, 1988). If there is no parent who receives and contains this emotional state, the baby's fears remain inside, affecting her personality and posture, as she feels overwhelmed by them. This condition may express itself through contracted gestures and altered breathing, for instance.

An example of how these mechanisms develop is when the baby falls down while attempting to make the first steps on her own. When she falls, she experiences a loss of balance that, to some degree, is necessary to test herself and learn from her mistakes. But if the parent responds to her fall with fear and overprotection, the baby absorbs this emotion and is likely to turn that healthy feeling of loss of balance into paralysing fear. The parent is then not containing the baby's feeling and giving it back in a new and positive form. The baby will then internalize a parental model characterized by fears about the world and herself. This not only restricts her opportunities of gaining experience but is likely to impair her self-confidence. The mother's reverie, giving the baby permission to experience, helps her to acknowledge and accept all the parts of herself as a whole. This is crucial for the formation of a realistic sense of bodyself (Bion, 1962).

The child needs an internal object to use when the object is absent. This is an essential condition for development. The child needs an absent object to develop gradually, but first of all she needs an object to be attached to, to develop her capacity to tolerate the absent object. Her acceptance of all the parts of her bodyself, negative and positive, also depends on this capacity. Self-acceptance is made possible by acknowledging all the parts of the self and the parents help the child to do this.

Mindful baby massage can help baby and mother to face the weaning as a transition rather than as an abrupt scarring separation, just as it helps the transition from intra-uterine life. The rich sensory communication during baby massage, which is a much more powerful form of nourishment than the milk itself, helps the baby to internalize the breast or mother in a wider sense, to feel them to be living people inside her body in a concrete way. They become internal not just in her mind but also in her muscles, posture, and gestures, and they go to constitute her physiology.

The baby's internal world and ego are built up in accordance with her actual experience of being massaged and fed, so that, in a fulfilling condition, a sense of harmony, security, and integration ensue. Of course, the impressions she gains from other people and the external world and her own impulses and predispositions also contribute to shaping her internal world. If it is a world of people at peace with each other and with the ego, inner and postural harmony, security, and integration are fostered.

All the enjoyment that the baby experiences in relation to her mother, for instance while being massaged, act as proof that the loved object inside, as well as outside, is not injured by absence or her feeling of loss. Sensitive baby massage can therefore aid the weaning experience. Love, trust, and the enjoyable experience help the baby, step by step, to overcome her sense of loss. Failure in overcoming such a fear may lead to depression. Instead, through being loved and through the enjoyment she experiences, the child's confidence in her own as well as in other people's goodness becomes strengthened. Her hope that her "good" objects and her own ego can be preserved, despite the weaning, increases and her fears diminish. By contrast, unpleasant experiences and a lack of enjoyment and play especially a lack of happy and close physical contact with parents, increase the infant's fears, diminish trust and hope, and confirm anxieties about loss.

CHAPTER ELEVEN

The father's receptiveness

A mother gets more of the sensual joy that a new baby
brings:
skin contact with the breast,
a feeling of being wanted, needed, and loved;
the passionate interest and intense bonding
that resembles the early days of a great love affair.
Indeed, a mother has her beautiful new lover—the baby-
whose needs are the priority.
By massaging and bathing the baby
a father can share the mother's sensual experience with her
baby,
gaining a sense of fulfilment and providing the
invaluable benefits of a complementary triad.

The "other" from the mother

Men are often described as aggressive, unsupportive, reticent, insensitive, and so on, in cultural terms. There is contradictory evidence from my observational study and others (Park, Power, Tinsley & Hymel, 1979; Klaus, Kennell &

Klaus, 1996) and it seems that they need to overcome certain cultural barriers to display the authentic part of their identity. For instance, to get a man to admit that he is suffering from post-natal depression has been, until recently, virtually unthinkable. Sadness and post-natal depression are perceived as "women's stuff", characterized by hormonal changes. Men are capable of love, support, respect, emotional expression, and creativity.

Common images or stereotypes about men being inadequate and inept are dangerous because they send a strong signal to men that leads to them to behave in accordance with these expectations. If a woman has grown up with these stereotypes, she is likely to expect behaviour from her partner that reflects them. Our behaviour is to some extent directed by people's expectations.

As long as there are complaints about men being inept, it will be difficult to dismantle common images and enable the individual man to emerge. Concern for bodyself-image, sensitivity, and the capacity to play with children are inside every man, whose feminine side has long been repressed because of cultural stereotypes and social roles. It is healthy for men, families, and society to acknowledge this side of men's personalities and their right to involvement in child-care.

Women's dramatic movement into the workforce, the weakening of sexual stereotypes through the women's movement of the 1960s and 1970s, and men's expressed need for greater involvement in their relationships and in their own private lives have contributed to bringing men into closer contact with their babies.

Since around the 1980s, there has been more involvement between fathers and babies and men have begun reflecting upon themselves more: articles and books have appeared that take issue with a Western culture that entirely reflects male thinking (Lamb, 1978; Pruett, 1987; Pedersen, 1987). Much of Western culture is based on the elimination of the typical characteristics of the "feminine"—thus of the bodily, emotional, and intuitive aspects. To a new model of soft and flexible capitalism there now corresponds an equally soft and flexible man, who is able to play with his female component, with his sensitive soul. This is a precondition for true communication between men and women. Dialogue and active listening between a couple depend on this ability to play with both components of their personality, with an integrated bodyself image that embraces both male and female aspects.

The united couple is the key building block of family, community, and society. Through the father's presence, the child gets to know the "other" from the mother in whose body she was conceived. The triangular relationship is the foundation of the family and the core of society. When the father values both feminine and masculine aspects of his bodyself, the child learns to value all the aspects of her own personality.

If a child lacks a father model, she is likely to be deprived of the opportunity to develop a harmonious sense of the "other" from the mother, which is the foundation of a small community. Nevertheless, the modern nuclear family is often not equipped to respond to the couple's needs as well as those of the child. Traditionally, grandparents, uncles, friends, and an entire village contributed to transmitting values and forming the child's personality. The early community experience prepared for wider social life. Our modern family lives need a form of retribalization or rediscovery of the community. People tend to attend fitness, dance, and health clubs, as well as pre-natal and post-natal classes, to fulfil their primary group needs.

The pre- and post-natal groups can facilitate the parents' network by sharing experiences and making friends. They can help to counteract feelings of isolation. Emotional isolation may be the main reason why more and more men are suffering from post-natal depression. By mirroring on to other fathers, the father's self-image is strengthened and the journey to parenthood can be eased.

The father has a significant influence on the development of the child's relationships, either directly or indirectly, as, for instance, in supporting and facilitating the mother-and-baby relationship. New research in Europe and the USA has documented the powerful impact that fathers have on children that not mediated purely through the mother–baby dyad (Lewis, 1986). Babies appear actively to seek out the father's unique interactions, which contribute to their growth and development. The infant also influences the evolution of the father's relationships. The birth of a baby may be the strongest cement that is ever applied to the father's relationship. The baby contributes enormously and actively to the development of a man's fatherhood by provoking and eliciting his responses.

Fathers and mothers interact and get in contact with their babies in different ways, and these differences seem to be fundamental to their healthy development. The father contributes to nurturing the relationship with his baby through his touch, voice, and eye contact, as well as through the relationship with his partner, offering emotional support. A seven-months-pregnant woman, Yvette (described below), felt her baby suddenly moving and kicking when her husband returned home after having been away for a few days. She perceived the connection as he opened the door and greeted her. The baby's hearing of the father's voice and feeling of its vibrations, combined with the mother's conscious perception of the baby's response, were all signs of a unique intimate triangular communication (Sansone, 2002).

The father's physical contact with the baby, either pre-natal via the mother's body or post-natal through touch, voice, and eye contact, shapes a genuine relationship and enables the baby to internalize the real father. There are many ways for the father to get involved in these physical and emotional interactions: bathing, feeding, massaging, changing a nappy, going out for a walk, or just observing the baby. Even nappy-changing can be fun, while also being a powerful form of contact. The baby's intense eyes focus on the father's face and explore his features, and he can stroke and tickle her body, let her fingers grip his fingers, and watch her toes curl. A lack of ordinary interactions sustained by emotional containment enhances the risk of the baby escaping into an idealized parent, as well as the risk of the parent nurturing an ideal child.

The Oedipus transition

In whatever culture the baby is born, she soon emerges into a triangular space, a space bounded by three persons. This is the so-called oedipal area, a basis for trusting a secure and stable world and a learning ground. The psychoanalytical concept of the Oedipus complex gives an account of this triangular space and its conflicts, and their importance for child development. The diverse relationship with the father will enable the child to establish a core sense of the parental relationship, which involves abandoning the idea of permanent possession of the breast, or of the mother in general, and leads to a sense of loss. The mother's body is a major part of the baby's world and the breast and milk stand for love, goodness, and security. A positive relationship with the father will help the baby to experience the separation as a part of the loving relationship and not in terms of loss or mourning. Through the father, the baby learns about the constant flow of separation and reunions, because when she is separated from the breast or her mother, she is with another and vice versa. This is especially important during weaning. Her love of the feeding breast and hatred of the absent breast become accepted parts of the same "self". The child becomes aware of the coexistence of opposites in the same object and of the continuity of its existence in space and in time. The oedipal feelings induced by the father (rivalry with the parent for taking the mother–baby space) contribute to the knowledge of the union of opposites and to the capacity to think and reflect. This capacity also helps the child to elaborate her sense of guilt arising from anger with the absent object.

However, if the baby lacks the "other figure" from the mother, she may feel overwhelmed by a sense of loss and rigidly defend against it. The infant may escape into illusions (ideal breast that never frustrates, ideal baby free of anger and hatred of the absent mother). When these illusions are paramount, the boundaries within the parental relationship and within the parent–baby relationship cannot be acknowledged. The father is then perceived as threatening the love relationship between mother and baby.

The oedipal transition created by the relationship with the father also involves a sense of the genital and procreative relationship between parents, as distinct from the relationship between parents and child. This is fundamental to a sense of boundaries between self and other, leading to a sense of reality. The triangular space stimulates the child's curiosity to learn, attitude to knowledge, and relation to the world. It enriches the primary dyadic relationship of intra-uterine life, when elements of the father, such as voice and touch, reach the baby from the abdominal wall like a buzz.

A secure relationship to the breast, thus to the mother, helps the infant to accept the couple's relationship. It is this acknowledgement that dilates the triangular space of the Oedipus situation. This forms the foundation for trusting a secure world and having experiences. The child can feel she is being observed, thus can see herself in interaction with others and reflect on herself while being herself. The child finally realizes that the oedipal triangle does not threaten the dyadic relationship but instead brings enrichment.

The father may regress to a similar infant process in resenting the intrusion of his baby into the couple's space and feeling his partner is taking over. The father's secure primary experience with his carers will help him address his feelings of exclusion. By working through these feelings, with the mother giving him access to her space with the baby, he will help the baby to work through the oedipal feelings. From the father's concrete involvement in the everyday moments of the baby's life, such as massaging, bathing, feeding, playing, and so on, an internal oedipal triangle takes shape and the trust in it is the greatest support for the child. From this earliest trust, confidence and security set in, whereas when these feelings are impaired depression and anxieties may increase.

The child's emotional life develops under the stress of the conflicts between love, hatred, guilt, and alternating identifications with the primary male and female figures. She needs a secure setting in which to work out her conflicts and make the transition from the mother dyad to the triangular situation. These conflicts accompany us throughout our lives; the Oedipus transition and the mourning feelings never come to an end but have to be reworked in each new life situation and at each stage of development, enriching our experiences and knowledge. A new experience threatens our security, shakes up our pre-existing view of things, and arouses our hostility against anything new or unknown. It creates a landscape akin to that of the infant who is going through the new experience of separation. However, as both the child and the adult work through this landscape, they are enabled to enrich their lives at each stage of development.

Although the Oedipus space concerns all human beings, it unfolds in different ways in accordance with the culture, society, and family dynamics. It is also characterized by gender dynamics, as the girl and boy each need to work out their conflicts of love and hatred in terms of their orientation to the parent of the same sex and of the other sex. Oedipal dynamics also evolve of course with changes in society. When Freud formulated the theory of the Oedipus complex, the father occupied a very limited space in childcare. The baby might have been especially likely to perceive his presence as intrusive and as a threat to the dyadic mother–baby space. However, in modern societies many fathers are becoming increasingly actively involved in child-care from birth. This means that the triangular area will be taking shape in the baby's life from the first few minutes, perhaps from intra-uterine life, as the father feels he is a participant, rather than being excluded from the mother–baby partnership. The Oedipus journey may therefore run a smoother course and the constant process of separation and reunion may be experienced more fluently.

Couvade

Couvade is an ancient custom that has almost disappeared. The word "couvade" is derived from the French word "couver", meaning "to hatch", "to sit on". It is a custom whereby the father substitutes himself for the mother when labour begins. The ritual helps the father to identify with and participate in growing a new life.

When the woman stops her everyday activities to give birth in traditional societies, she goes either to a special birth-house in the village or off into the forest or countryside to give birth alone and return a few hours later holding her baby. The father, meanwhile, goes to his sleeping area and pretends to be in need of attention, moaning and groaning. Sometimes the father will perform these ceremonial gestures for days before and after the actual birth.

In Southern India, the husband used to dress as a woman when he was notified of the onset of labour. He would twist and turn until the baby was born. In Central Brazil, the Bakairi father lies in a hammock with the newborn baby while the mother goes back to her daily occupation immediately after giving birth. No meat is eaten until the baby's navel is totally healed. In some Malaysian tribes, the father has to stay out of sunlight during the four days following the birth. While the couvade is unfolding, the women of the village who are not out working in the fields care for the father in the same way that they care for the new mother.

In some traditional societies, men are so involved with fathering, pregnancy, and childbirth that they undergo dramatic physical and mental changes around the time of the birth of their children. Bodily experiences of the partner's pregnancy are often quite varied. In the Yucatan, the conception of a child is considered proven when the father begins to have some appetite cravings. Localized and non-specific abdominal disorders and complaints are not unusual among "pregnant fathers" in general.

As an example from my own experience, I witnessed my brother complaining about abdominal disorders throughout the period in which his wife was resting because of an episiotomy. He tended to isolate himself in the sitting-room, while his wife and baby drew the attention of visitors. He may have resented the intrusion of his first baby and felt his partner taking over. His physical symptoms were thus the manifestation of his blend of emotions.

A New York study documented that twenty-five per cent of all expectant fathers in a large normal pregnancy sample had gastro-intestinal complaints (nausea, cramps, diarrhoea, sometimes even vomiting) that they did not have before or after pregnancy (Lipkin & Lamb, 1982). Many of these symptoms occurred throughout the pregnancy and after birth, not just in the first trimester. I have observed some fathers putting on weight mainly in the upper parts of their body, especially stomach, chest, and arms.

The "couvade" mentioned above is the ritualized custom of certain South Pacific cultures and provides a good example of psychophysiological involvement. When the spouse is in her late pregnancy, the father goes to bed in the men's hut and performs a highly theatrical moaning ritual that involves a twisting and turn-ing of the body to simulate female labour. The members of the men's hut believe that this activity eases their spouses' pain.

The man's emotional involvement in his wife's pregnancy takes different forms. Worry, anxiety, depression about the adequacy of financial provision, responsibility, and endurance of the baby's awakening during the night are quite common. The arrival of a baby may require an adjustment in the father's standard of living. During my observational study, I met a large number of men who appeared to be touched by the new experience and aware of the feelings involved in the new role. I followed up men who had attended couple classes and observed their bodily and postural changes over the time. Some of them, while talking and sharing their experiences, put their hands on their partner's tummy and seemed to get in tune with her and with the baby. The class proved to be a containing place, in which the fathers' feelings could be acknowledged and freed from the social stereotypes of the outside world.

A decrease in sexual drive was reported by some fathers attending pre-natal support group. We cannot say if this is a consequence of the woman's bodily changes, which would make her less sexually participatory and attractive, or of hormonal changes. It is more likely that changes in sexual drive are related to a combination of hormonal and emotional factors. It may be some fathers' perception of being dangerous to the growing foetus, as well as to their wife. One study showed this change in the father's perception of his partner and in the relationship, often expressing itself through quite vivid dreams, sometimes representing dangerous situations, involving the spouse and child (Herzog, 1982).

Sadly, the father's mental and physical involvement in pregnancy, birth, and primary interactions with the baby and the partner, is often overlooked and even physically inhibited by cultural stereotypes. Participation during labour and birth seems to enhance his interactions and bonding with the baby. He can have an understanding and attachment to the child based on his own experience more quickly and is more likely to be involved in the baby's care and less likely to avoid physical responsibility for the child, thus less likely to be abusive. During my work in a traditional hospital in Rome, where fathers are not allowed to be present in the labour room, it was far more unusual to see them in close physical contact than at the Birth Unit, where they can be active participants by supporting their partners in labour.

Obviously, the efficacy of their support varies in accordance with their personality and the relationship with their partner. Being truly motivated to be present during labour and birth seems to be, to some degree, a powerful trigger of the early contact with the baby, which facilitates their getting to know the baby and themselves.

It is important that the father's decision about attending the birth is based on his personal preferences. There is no one correct way of doing things. The point is having the freedom to choose what is best for him and for his partner and finding a birth institution that gives space to his feelings and choice. If he chooses to attend, he can actively hold and support or look away or leave the room if he finds it too much. Whatever his choice, a valuable Birth Unit team will support mother, baby, and him. My observations were not made in an experimental setting but in a home-like environment, which the Birth Unit provides with its unique services. I was a familiar figure for most couples and they were always surrounded by a supportive atmosphere that made them feel comfortable.

From some women's depiction of their labour experience, it emerged that their partners, while attending the labour, produced interactive movements, breathing, and gestures in tune with those of their partners. This can be considered a form of couvade. One woman said: "Hearing my husband's breathing helped me to feel my own breathing and go with it". Her husband's breathing acted as a regulator of her own breathing. They were like two partners in a dance. Another woman, whose labour contractions and pelvis dilation had temporarily stopped, reported that when her partner began massaging her lower back, the contractions suddenly came regularly and within half an hour she delivered in the water.

Touching, breathing, eye contact, and body language in general can trigger or facilitate the labour process, provided there is a deep communication between the partners based on synchrony. Men who are able to interact in labour through their sensitive body language are more likely to get attuned to the baby's cues. At the Birth Unit men are encouraged, if they wish, to cut the umbilical cord. This can be a unique experience that enhances the father's feeling of taking responsibility and being involved. Trembling hands while cutting the cord are just a vivid expression of emotional involvement. Unfortunately, traditional hospitals overlook the intensity of the father's emotions and the importance of such moments as precursors of a healthy father–baby relationship.

Triangular communication

The following case illustrates the deep communication that a father can establish within the mother–baby dyad. Yvette was seven months pregnant. On her husband's return home after being away for a few days, when he opened the door, she felt her baby suddenly moving and kicking. "I felt as if my baby emitted a deep breath", she said. The baby seems to have sensed the vibrations of the father's voice; in other words, the vibrations resonated through

Begin. Painting by Antonella Sansone.

the mother's abdomen. Also, the baby may have felt his mother's emotional reaction—perhaps through breathing changes, abdominal tightening, or other abrupt tiny movements in her body, and responded to the combination of them.

The mother's body mediates between the external environment and the pre-natal baby. The significant environmental stimuli impinge on the mother's feelings and resonate through her body so that they are perceived by the baby. What emerges from this example is the mother's intuition of the link between the baby's behaviour and the father's arrival: not only was she truly communicating with her baby but there was a deep triangular communication going on, which had been obviously built up since conception. Yvette was attuned to the baby's cues, just as a musician who is playing an instrument or singing needs to be "in tune" to produce the right notes. This "attuned" communication is essential for a secure attachment to develop; it is a psychobiological learning process occurring at a pace that is as unique as the system formed by mother, baby, and father. It is a learning process that is already under way during pregnancy and originates in the couple's rhythmic communication before conception. Its onset is difficult to detect, as it can be traced back to the parent's primary period, when as a child the capacity to get in touch with her bodyself rhythms began to form. The outcome of this early process is closely related to the way in which the parent herself has been parented. Indeed, pregnancy, birth, and parenting are circular events that involve a few generations.

While breathing, the pregnant woman produces vibrations that are sensed by the baby and as in a concert may synchronize with his breathing. When she touches her tummy, the mother is establishing contact through muscular vibrations. Touch is one of the most direct and powerful channels of communication a father can use during pregnancy. Other channels are his voice and the containment and support he provides to the mother. The post-natal touch will then be transitional, an extension of pre-birth touch. Attentive hands are sensed by the child as an envelope reproducing the safety of the womb. She learns to trust her parents and therefore herself. Self-confidence is not verbally thought out. It develops through these experiences, which are recorded in the child's muscle systems and are readable in her posture and body language. By contrast, tense, hostile, and rejecting hands or voices make the child escape into herself. This may induce distrust of the world and timidity. Her personality is like a puzzle of which each early experience is a piece. If the mother had a difficult pregnancy or birth and her handling of the baby naturally lacks confidence, the father's firm holding can bring a lot of benefits. When a parent tends to hold or talk to the baby fearfully, as if she were something fragile, the baby receives a feeling about herself as a fragile being and her bodyself perception is affected. On the other hand, rough touch feeds a perception of a self-skin that is insensitive, a sort of shell or substitute skin. Conversely, firm loving touch and voice transmits to the child a feeling of "being grounded", or "being present", able to trust her own capacities. This self-trust is fundamental to finding a satisfactory place in the world.

The fourth trimester

Although he may love his child deeply, the father may feel resentful as he watches her with her mother, who concentrates fully on the child. He may feel rejected by his partner and marginalized and incompetent around the baby. A man may feel forced to ask, "Will she still love me? Will she love the baby more than me? Can I love the baby? Am I still useful?" This may be especially hard for men who have had a difficult relationship with their own father. Preparation for parenthood has its foundation in childhood and is provided by our parents. These conflicting feelings may lead a man to becoming violent, starting an affair with another woman, or making any excuse not to be at home so as to escape the overwhelming feelings. Anger, jealousy, or irritation may be overwhelming and the father may be ashamed of these feelings and withdraw emotionally.

His mixed feelings are by no means unusual and can be relieved if he is honest about them and makes his partner aware of his needs by communicating. One of the most important factors in maintaining genuine mutual satisfaction is the ability to negotiate conflicts successfully, whether it is stress over a new baby or a new job. When a man is, for instance, depressed and emotionally withdrawn, the whole relationship is put at risk. Early support provided by parenting classes is needed, either to resolve or prevent this. Courses for parents-to-be and post-natal support groups can provide a valuable support to the couple, as it can be comforting to know that many share these conflicting feelings.

The following are vivid descriptions of some fathers' feelings:

> When my girlfriend Amy gave birth to Naomi, she became clinically depressed. I found that looking after Amy, as well as the new baby and holding down my job, was just too much. My depression really mirrored Amy's. We were both getting worse and worse. I became very irritable, withdrawn, lost a lot of confidence, and suffered from sleeplessness, panic attacks, and a lack of sex drive.

When I came back from the pub, where I spent more and more time, she would shout and scream at me. I was frightened.

The increasing hostility and withdrawal, so typical of depression, damaged the relationship and Charles and Amy split up. Charles was isolated and sank further into depression. It was only when he joined a self-support group that he began to recover. He said, "Although I live apart from my family, both Amy and I love the children very much and we get on better now than we ever did before".

When my wife told me she was pregnant, I sank into immediate depression. I was terrified because Jane was so happy and I felt I was being pushed out. I worried I would never be responsible. I locked my feelings in and to this day I have never told Jane how unhappy I was.

When my daughter Isabel was born, I felt indifferent and resentful of the restrictions placed on mine and my wife's freedom. We couldn't travel any more and money was getting tight. I felt completely trapped. I felt that life was all over for me, while it was just beginning for my wife and baby. It was only when I joined the group that I began to feel more confident and my depression about fatherhood started to subside.

The adaptation to a new relationship with the partner, from a dyad to a triad, can be difficult, especially in the first three months after birth. This period is sometimes called the "fourth trimester" because some fathers are excluded as if the baby were still in the womb. Fathers may feel inadequate and unable to help their partner with the baby care and thus become frustrated. These conflicting feelings may lead to less direct contact with the baby, exacerbating the feelings of exclusion and isolation. Sometimes the mother controls the father's access to the baby and builds up rigid barriers around herself and her baby. If she is like this, it may be hard for the father to take an active part in baby care—she may not give him time to calm his crying baby, or she may criticize him for bathing or changing a nappy in the wrong way.

Men are likely to experience rejection—from their partners, from their friends, and even from some health professionals—if they try to explain that they have problems or have become depressed after the birth of their baby. Although there is evidence that women are more prone to depression during pregnancy and in the first three months after childbirth, a study showed that over the next nine months men were more prone to depression, particularly in cases where their partners had suffered from depression at an earlier stage (Areias, Kumar, Barros & Figueiredo, 1996; Burk, 2003). It is therefore important to view depression within the entire parent–infant context, with its impact on the partner, child, and the wider community.

Research shows that, just six months after the birth of a new child, fifty per cent of men compared to only eighteen per cent of women said that there was a decline in the satisfaction of their relationship. It is clear that after having a baby, the couple's relationship undergoes major changes, to which women may adjust more easily. They receive more of the sensual joy that a new baby brings: skin contact around the breasts; a feeling of being wanted, needed, and loved; the passionate interest and intense bonding that mimics the beginning of a great love affair. Indeed, a mother has a beautiful new loving partner—the baby—whose needs are the priority. If he is forgotten by his partner, the father has to look after himself. If the mother obtains sensual satisfaction from the physical contact with her baby, the man may feel all the frustration of the forgotten sex and feel even more unwanted.

However, when the man is given the opportunity to get involved in baby care, he can be competent and creative in interacting with his newborn. By massaging and bathing the baby, for instance, he can share the mother's sensual experience with the baby and gain a feeling of fulfilment. He can grow in self-confidence and responsibility. Becoming a father can lead a man to looking at the "deeper self", at who he really is, independently of cultural stereotypes. This can be made possible for the father by acknowledging his feelings and his own childhood. It can enhance his self-esteem and strengthen his personality, as for instance, in the case of one man at the Birth Unit who during his partner's pregnancy appeared almost shy and introverted but who showed a fairly rich repertoire of body language in interacting with his baby when I visited them after the birth.

Couples normally spend three days on the Birth Unit after birth and there is no rushing or intrusion into their intimacy but just the necessary support from the staff in the early baby care. Feeling supported enables them to give more support to their partners. Everything is done with the aim of meeting their needs.

Sometimes I observed fathers bathing their babies, showing that they could nurture their babies in different creative ways: no better or worse than their mothers—differently. The father's role is just as crucial as the mother's and a good relationship between father and child can act as a buffer if the child has a troubled relationship with the mother. If he cannot get access to breastfeeding, he can massage, bath, play, talk to his baby, bottle-feed or introduce solid food, creating a special time simply with direct physical contact. Even nappy-changing can be fun. While his baby is gazing at him exploring his face, the father can stroke and tickle her body, vocalizing or singing to her.

When the mother is stressed, the father can support her and be a more active caregiver. However, he has a key role not just in helping out when she has had enough but also in forming his own bond with his baby through bathing, changing nappies, cuddling, massaging, rocking, and talking to her. Research has shown that involved fathers form much better relationships with their children later on (Rodholm, 1981; Shapiro, 1987; Lamb, 1997). Fathers can feed their babies as effectively as mothers do, solve some feeding problems, soothe appropriately, handle, and rock in rhythm with the child. I have often witnessed fathers altering their regular tone, using high-pitched vocal stimuli to which the newborn seems to respond better, and showing a remarkable capacity to attune to their baby. Low-pitched vocalizations are more likely to soothe than to stimulate a conversation. Most men are not fully aware of these changes.

While listening to them, both one-to-one and during the couple class, I discovered one man in particular who was entirely different from the social stereotypes. Therefore, it seems to be more socio-cultural than biological factors that shape parents' sensitivity in responding to their baby's needs. A study by Michael Lamb (1997) shows that mothers and fathers show similar physiological responses to a distressed, crying baby: quickened pulse, increased respiratory rate, and general sensory alertness.

It seems possible that what Park and Sawim (1975) found in a large observational study—that mothers tended to pick up their babies in a more predictable rhythm, reading their non-verbal cues—is strongly dependent on their carrying their baby in their body and learning their cues very early. They begin getting to know their baby's rhythms during pregnancy. This could also explain their different way of reacting to the baby's exploration of the environment and separation from them. Mothers seem to tend to stay closer to their children and fathers to encourage their exploration more.

I have found that babies from birth respond quite differently to their parents' different ways of interacting and to their different tones of voice: movements, cues, vocalizing, parts of the baby's body, facial expressions and rhythms. The baby's different way of responding to mother and father, on the other hand, evokes and shapes parenting in a very powerful way. The mother's and father's different sensitivity and way of stimulating and responding to the baby is fundamental for the child's cognitive, emotional, motor, and postural development and for an integrated body image. It is important for the development of a fulfilled sexual identity.

In interacting with her father, the baby experiences a significant "other" from her mother, through the different smell, touch, vocal sounds, size, way of holding, and so on. This is important in helping the baby over time to differentiate her parents' sexual identities and roles, acknowledging their relationship and the boundaries between it and the child–parent relationship. Through her father, the infant learns about the constant flow of separation and reunion because when she is separated from her mother she is with another person and vice versa.

Baby massage, by opening up the parents' and baby's sensory channels through the loving movements and mutual enjoyment, can help the baby's muscle memory to record her parents' diverse features, smell, vocal vibrations, facial expressions, ways of holding and talking. This may nurture the infant's internal mother and father as distinct and united individuals, which is the basis of a harmonious sexual identification. The father's practice of baby massage can facilitate working through the Oedipus position in the early years. In the process of giving massage, father connects with a deep part of the child and with a deep part of himself—his nurturing side. Boys are conditioned to suppress this part very early on, but dealing with infants opens up that space.

Feeling the father's touch is vital for the child's emotional development. The baby, who spends most time seeing and touching the mother during feeding, has the opportunity during massage to interact with her father in a multitude of ways and, thus, to internalize him. Massage can nurture just as breastfeeding can. Just as breastfeeding provides solid reinforcement of the bonding process for mothers, with its cuddling, skin contact, and face-to-face communication, so massaging the baby can be an ideal way to keep a father in touch with his baby. I have seen fathers enjoy massaging their little ones, although they are still in a minority. Filming can be a vivid way of reminding an older child how her father took care of her.

A positive involvement with their father benefits babies and a loving relationship between them affects the child's overall development, self-esteem, communication skills, and happiness. It also shapes her attitude to knowledge and way of relating to the world. In short, a nurturing father is a more available model than a non-nurturing father.

The 1973 hospital labour dispute in the UK, which led many physicians to go on strike, meant that many mothers and fathers who were not mentally prepared for home birth had no alternative. This offered an unusual opportunity to observe the father's presence at labour. When some complicating factors were analysed (Richman, 1982), the most significant one to militate against birth complications and illness in the child and mother was the father's presence and support at the birth.

When an active birth is not planned, but the circumstances allow the father to be present, he naturally can become involved and supportive. I have come across men who initially appeared reluctant and uncertain fathers-to-be and in the end they turned out to be the best supporters in labour. The father's absence at birth is a modern-day phenomenon. In the nineteenth century, a typical birthing scene would have included a mother sitting on her husband's lap, embracing her back against his chest and her hands pushing against his upper thighs or knees, while he massaged her abdomen. This position was called "the father chair".

The father's supportive presence in labour can lower the risk of birth complications. An important finding in father–infant care is that if a man is involved in the daily physical care in the first three years of life, the risk of sexual abuse later in life is significantly reduced. The daily physical contact seems to create a strong barrier against later violation of that intimacy and to reinforce a sense of intimacy boundaries. Because the baby actively contributes to the development of a man's fatherliness by provoking and eliciting his responses, any institution that gives the father the possibility of being present at birth and interacting with the baby without rushing allows his unique nurturing style to emerge. Such an institution contributes to building the foundations of healthy primary relationships between parents and baby that are necessary for the baby to develop healthy relationships in society.

Fathers need not to consider themselves to be "mothering" and to abandon the mental image of themselves as substitutes for their partner. Their cultural representation may prevent their unique way of nurturing from emerging. A mental representation, according to the "integrative model", regulates the physical contact with the baby and thus the parent's perception of her. Therefore, the parent's cultural stereotypes or beliefs may affect the body and self-perception and, through the physical interactions with the baby, may impinge on the child's developing bodyself image.

To overcome some traditional barriers that restrict the role of the father, fathers need to allow their creative style of interaction to emerge. To do so, they need to create a space for fathering and family, which may imply reducing responsibility and authority at work. Babies need this uniqueness for their balanced and harmonious development. It is erroneous to associate the capacity to comfort, protect, be close to, accept, and feel empathy exclusively with femininity.

Baby massage, as well as other creative and playful forms of contact, can help fathers to open their sensory channels, overcome some traditional barriers, and enhance their nurturing skills. Having the opportunity to express their hidden feelings during a pre- or post-natal class is the first step to changing their bodyself image as fathers and embarking on a new self-perception. Regular physical contact with their baby will contribute to a new mental representation. The two sets of processes, mental and physical, continuously interact in a dynamic feedback relationship.

Furthermore, the woman's cultural representation of the father's role, partly affected by the way in which she has learnt to relate to men through her primary experiences, affects her perception of him. If this representation is dominated by rigid models, it will tighten the father's own boundaries in interacting with the baby and set barriers to communication. Mother can thus project her own needs and expectations on to her partner by defining and judging his way of fathering. By acknowledging the "projection mechanism", she can define realistic boundaries between herself and her partner, and between them and the baby. This clear definition fosters the evolution of clear self-boundaries in the child, the cornerstone of a sense of integrated identity.

Women need to encourage and reward the father's physical contact without feeling him to be an intruder in their dyad with the baby. I have witnessed men appearing proud when I acknowledged and valued their way of interacting with the baby. Gaiter (1984) found that if fathers of ill babies touched their fragile bodies, talked to them, and spent some time by the incubator during every visit, they were likely to become much more involved fathers. The baby could also recover more quickly and leave the hospital sooner than if the father was not involved.

Fathers can have a powerful effect on babies and on their mothers when their health may have been compromised by the birth risk and made the bonding more difficult. Institutions have to acknowledge that the father is a fundamental element of the birth environment, the mother–baby relationship, and thus of the infant's well-being.

There is little hope of attitudes changing if the men who dictate workplace cultures are not taking time off. The government has to ensure that both mothers and fathers can effectively balance their work and home lives. This is for the couple's benefit as well as for the baby's healthy development and, in long run, for the welfare of society. In regard to the workplace, women will suffer even more discrimination at work if governments proceed with plans to extend maternity leave without offering equivalent fathers' rights. Any extension of maternity rights that is not matched by an equivalent extension of paternity rights is a step in the wrong direction. The health of a family is based on workplace success deriving from a breakdown of the traditional roles attached to motherhood and fatherhood. The change of attitude needs to be two-way: from the individual fathers and from the government and child-care organizations. Fathers need to allow their own styles of nurturing to emerge rather than think of themselves as "mothering", and health-care systems should encourage their involvement in their children's lives from the beginning.

Sexuality in pregnancy

Pregnancy and labour arouse libidinous feelings in both women and men. Pregnancy can bring a sense of bodily fulfilment. It also modifies the relationship between the two partners: the anticipation and birth of a baby entails adjustments in the couple. The partners' mutual support is very important for a healthy pregnancy. Pregnancy creates, especially in the woman, an increasing need for dependence, support, and help and, if she is to be able to nurture her baby, these needs must be fulfilled.

Data from the literature show that gestation tends to be a period of marked sexual inhibition because of the medical restrictions and an agreed decision between the partners. If sex becomes less frequent, it is often the man who feels the change more sharply than the woman, as she is absorbed in the baby. There are many prejudices surrounding sex during pregnancy. Pregnancy, unless there are pathological problems, creates a psychophysiological condition that can enrich sexual life: the hormonal increase in bloodstream, the presence of endorphins, the lowered sensory threshold, the increased blood-flow in the genitals, and the increased size and sensitivity of the uterus are all factors that may make both partners enjoy their bodies, perhaps more than in any other period of life.

A reduction in frequency of sexual intercourse during pregnancy is often related to tradition and family influences, and to religious and social more than to medical factors. Becoming pregnant may place the woman in a condition of psychophysical vulnerability in the view of her parents and, particularly, of her partner, who in some cases assumes a fairly maternal role.

Preparation courses for labour give the opportunity to reduce anxiety and enhance the ability to manage pain. Anxiety alters the couple's emotional balance and can make it difficult to enjoy sex. The sense of community provided by the group during preparation courses counteracts the isolation that derives from the nuclear family, a product of Western societies. Knowing that other parents-to-be have similar anxieties and talking about sexual life during pregnancy and the early months after birth can help to counteract cultural prejudices and reveal a new dimension of sex.

The woman's marked need for support may be related to her re-experiencing the process of fusion and separation from her own mother. Pregnancy arouses issues of identification with her mother. However, men can also be affected by these issues, as we have all experienced intra-uterine life and birth and, thus, fusion and separation. In women, the process is deeper and more absorbing as they undergo the most powerful sharing experience with their own mothers. The process is also a dual one for her, as she is both carrying her own baby and at another level reliving her own experience in her mother's womb.

This mixture of feelings may explain at a psychological level the reduced frequency of sexual intercourse during pregnancy. Another aspect may be the emotional fulfilment brought by the growing baby, which seems to compensate for the less active sexual life. However, in other women the sense of fulfilment may empower the sex drive, and their partners may even feel overwhelmed. One of the factors that contributes to reducing sexual intercourse is the woman's fear, but also the man's, of harming the foetus by penetration. The partner's role in understanding these complex processes and containing the woman's anxieties is crucial. However, as the man is often absorbed in powerful emotions, and as the woman's energies are usually fully focused on the baby, support offered by friends, relatives, group, or a professional will help to keep him balanced. The couple need to make each other aware of their needs by active listening and communication, which can have the most powerful healing effect.

The man's containing function facilitates the woman's acceptance of the emotional and physical changes, thus of her modified bodyself image. Her feeling of being supported and contained makes her body image adjustable to the changes brought by pregnancy. The pregnant woman may perceive a split between her body as "sexual" and as "maternal", as if during pregnancy her body is unable to express its sexual and maternal potential at the same time. Her bodyself image may split and thus be impaired.

Adverse effects from sexual activity and orgasm are rare. In advanced pregnancy, as Masters & Johnson (1966) advise, it is better to avoid orgasm, as the orgasmic contractions might precipitate labour. However, there was a minority of women in their study whose sexual activity increased during the second trimester. There are also different forms of gentle sexual activity that an expecting couple can experience at any stage of pregnancy.

There are too many assumptions about sexuality during pregnancy. Information on the psychophysiology of sexual intercourse in pregnancy is needed. In experimental settings, Masters & Johnson (1966) observed some physiological changes during orgasm in pregnant women: congestion of the internal pelvic organs is increased by sexual stimulation and the level of arousal increases as the woman enters the second trimester and even more from the second to the third trimester. They found the middle abdomen to be sore soon after orgasm. Moreover, women showed a strong predisposition to orgasm in the second trimester.

Sexuality is an individual as well as a shared physical expression of a psychological, physiological, and emotional condition. The reduced sexual desire of some pregnant women may be perceived by their partners as a rejection in favour of the baby. For her part, the woman may feel her needs are not being understood and thus respond with indifference to sex. Pregnancy can both deepen interpersonal communication and increase conflict. The couple's acceptance of these emotional swings is important for a healthy pregnancy.

The couple space

I shall be describing how everyday life after birth affects the couple's perceptions of bodyself image and consequently sexuality. The baby makes great demands on the mother's energy. She may end a stressful day with accumulated emotional and muscular tension that acts as a barrier to getting in touch with the baby. Men usually work all day and when they get home they may expect to find a wife who is able to fulfil a role as housewife and lover at the same time. They may also expect to make love in the same way as before.

One woman in a post-natal support group said that she was so exhausted at the end of the day that she did not even have the energy to talk to her husband about her feelings. Not being able to keep the house clean and tidy may make some women feel a sense of guilt and failure for not fulfilling the husband's expectations. Many men underestimate the hard work entailed in being a full-time mother. On the other hand, they may feel frustrated at not being able to spend as much time as the mother does on the child-care. They may feel pushed into the background and neglected when their baby is born. Some have to cope with strong feelings of jealousy. All the lover's attention that was directed at them before birth may now be focused on the baby. Their jealousy and suppressed feelings of anger, failure, and guilt can break down communication and create barriers. By contrast, talking about emotions not only helps the mother to relieve her tensions, but also allows the father to get involved in the child-care and enhance his sense of responsibility.

Fathers need to be aware that although they cannot breastfeed, they can nurture in many other ways: touching, holding and rocking, changing nappies, bathing with their baby, and massaging her regularly, going for a walk or shopping with her. By getting involved, men can overcome jealousy and anger and become more actively supportive. In our industrialized societies, where a mother cannot always rely on her help from her mother or relatives and can feel isolated, having a receptive and supportive partner is extremely important. Very often, demanding work or financial circumstances prevent a man from being supportive during the maternity leave period. Professional fathers are often concerned about the deprivation of personal space caused for instance by a crying baby during the night and women may feel anxious and guilty when their partners get irritable and are not able to help. Spending more time with the family without sacrificing responsibility and authority at work can be very difficult. Many men may feel overwhelmed by the dilemma and guilty for not spending more time with their baby. To be supportive during pregnancy and afterwards and keep a balance, negotiation is necessary at home and at work so that both man and woman have space and time as individuals as well as in a couple.

Sharing roles always facilitates understanding and communication. The couple also need a space that is separate from the baby. It may be enough to have this space once a week. The interactions with the baby, on the other hand, empower self-discovery, although alternating moments of tension may disturb it. However, an individual space in which to reflect on oneself in relation to the baby can be a fundamental source of self-observation and help to ease the tension. This space can be achieved in different ways: by contact with nature, listening to music, playing an instrument, painting, meditating, sharing feelings with friends, joining perinatal classes so as to gain hands-on experience and reflect on it.

Exhaustion increases emotional and muscular tension, constricts the breathing and sensory channels and consequently hinders enjoyment of sexual sensations. Lovemaking becomes rather strained and mechanical, as the tense body is split from the mind and the bodyself image ceases to fluctuate. It becomes one reflection of an energy-consuming way of everyday thinking and moving. The couple may be straining mentally and physically without being aware that things could be done more easily and effortlessly by using all their resources. Lovemaking is an activity in which body and mind are equally present and united and movements and sensations can flow freely.

A general survey in the UK conducted by Mel Parr found that only six per cent of men and fifteen per cent of women attend any kind of ante-natal class, which means that most new parents embark on parenthood without knowing what to expect and without the skills to evaluate or cope with the natural changes that the new journey involves. Support groups for couples or fathers are a useful way of making fathers feel included in pregnancy and parenthood. Here not only do men receive practical preparation for life after a baby has come but they are prepared for the conflicting feelings they may be going through as fathers by discussing their hopes and fears. While a pregnant woman can gradually accommodate to the idea of a baby through her bodily experience, for a man the impact with the reality of a baby may be even stronger. Studies by psychologists and sociologists have long tended to pay little attention to the experience of being a father and to focus on traditional families in which the father is the sole provider, which are less relevant to the contemporary work and family context. During ante-natal and post-natal classes, I often come to see many of them involved and interested in being listened to.

Unfortunately, the expectations of popular culture and the mass media, which consider pregnancy, birth, and child-care to be primarily a female business, neglect the father's sensitivity to these experiences. When men are given the opportunity to share the birth experience in a Birth Unit that proves responsive to their needs, a considerable number of them appear to be active participants. They report that they feel proud of supporting their partners and cutting the baby's umbilical cord.

The Birth Unit in which I did my observational study belongs to a private hospital, where a certain population of couples plan to give their babies a gentle active birth. One would expect most fathers here to be sensitive to many issues around birth. However, the motivation of each man, woman and couple to give this kind of birth is different. For instance, there is the couple that is sensitive to the importance of going through the birth experience fully and learning from it; there is also the couple who chooses an "active birth" because it is in fashion, or simply to show that they have done something exclusive. There are as many different motivations as there are individuals or couples planning an active birth.

There are men who encounter the birth experience in a traumatic way, as their partner has delivered in a hospital without a private space for the couple. They can feel entirely neglected and when their partner goes back home they take for granted what popular culture expects from them. Working in a place where mothers, fathers, and infants can be supported from pregnancy onwards up to the first year of life, and where there is communication between parents and medical staff enhanced my awareness of the importance of these services in the early years. The fact that this ideal birthing place is private is also a cause for concern given that the majority of parents, especially fathers, and babies, do not have access to this for financial reasons and yet have the right to adequate services. A national system that delivers appropriate support in early life is required and primary education is the foundation for changes leading to a healthier society.

Men who make a regular commitment to child-care and housework are still only a minority. However, giving them the opportunity to share pre-natal, labour, birth, and post-natal experiences is a first crucial step to get them more actively involved in child-care. A great deal needs to be done for primary health education by provision of information, preparation courses, and support classes. Men should also have the right to reduce their working hours during pregnancy and for the first few months after birth and have more time to enjoy and be supportive. I have seen fathers-to-be arrive late at the 7.30 p.m. pre-natal couple class because of the demands of their jobs. Many were visibly frustrated and stressed by a demanding society. Some showed relief when they felt contained by the group; others remained physically locked in by their pressures. This was shown in their tense shoulders and crouching posture. Sometimes their feelings and corresponding postures were reflected vividly in their words, such those of one businessman, "I feel very frustrated; I would like to spend more time with my wife and enjoy the pregnancy". A number of men seemed to empathize with their partners' feelings. Some seemed to take responsibility in a cheerful way.

Some of their talking and body language evidenced a lovely interest in fatherhood in complete contrast to the cultural stereotypes. I witnessed men talking critically about the way in which they were fathered. To be truly involved in fatherhood and take responsibility, a new father needs to get in touch with his feelings and practise his self-observational skills. To do so, he may need to find birth institutions that give him the opportunity to talk about and express those feelings and skills in appropriate settings such as preparation classes and that provide primary health information. Major changes are required outside the family, in child-care arrangements, and in the sexual division of labour in the workplace.

Since men often do not fit the social stereotypes, their conflict can be particularly intense. A new father is often overwhelmed by emotions that he does not understand because he is not expected to have them. When the baby is crying, for instance, this can arouse strong feelings that he may not accept because he is unable to cope with them. The man's perception of his bodyself is strongly conditioned by cultural expectations. Experiencing unfamiliar overwhelming feelings may lead a man to retreat from them and his behaviour may consequently be altered, including his lovemaking and the couple's balance. The couple class represents a special space for the couple, as well as for the individual, as they can release their feelings by sharing with others and their partners. Furthermore, women can attentively listen to them and become aware of their ambivalent feelings. Some times it is the woman who restricts the man's role in child-care as a result of her past experiences and cultural stereotypes. For some couples, it may be easier to talk to a group, knowing that there are other couples having similar problems. The class can therefore be a powerful learning ground for new parents, as well as for primary health-care professionals.

Because very little has been written about fathers' active participation, starting to listen to them and record their actual experiences can bring about real change. This can also help demolish the cultural barriers, which can inhibit men from accepting their feelings and talking about them. For example, we often read and hear about women's post-natal depression. What about men's depression? Is post-natal depression really just a matter of hormones? Sadly, the social aspects of depression are usually overlooked. As withholding emotions increases tension and acts as a barrier to communication, it impairs interaction and communication skills. Unexpressed feelings may alter behaviour and cause irritability, a sense of guilt, and mild depression. Moreover, withheld tension restricts body language, locks facial expressions and gestures, and creates ambivalent messages between the partners and between them and the baby. As a result, bodyself-perception, poise, and balance are altered, as tension interferes with the natural balancing mechanisms. Our ways of thinking, feeling, and moving, and thus our way of communicating both non-verbally and verbally comes to feel so normal and "right" to us that we cannot see how things could be done any other way. The "bow method" is a term I have proposed for an aspect of the integrative bodyself image approach that can be useful in psychotherapeutic work with parents and infants. Through skilful and mindful guidance with hands and listening, the bow teacher encourages the father or mother to balance everyday movements and gestures while interacting with the baby. The objective is to become attuned to each other, rather like tuning a violin with the hands and the bow to produce the right tunes for a rhythmic and synchronized communication.

The father's perception of his own identity and self moulds the way in which he interacts with his baby. If his male model reflects cultural stereotypes, he will be unlikely to share the everyday moments of the baby's life. The philosopher William James, who described a baby's psychological state as one of confusion may have felt something of this mental condition himself, since when his first child was born, he left to spend the summer abroad. The baby is not confused; she speaks her own language made of codes that need to be understood.

To understand the baby's unspoken language, the father needs to be in touch with his authentic inner child and self and aware of his bodily communication skills. The man's arms, when they have not been involved in child-care all day, can be a more comfortable place for the baby and take pressure off the mother, when she needs to rest at the end of the day. When the mother is getting tense, the father can take the baby and play with her by singing, massaging, rocking, walking, or bathing. Men can give the baby a great deal from their repertoire of bodily utterances through touching, cuddling, and holding, provided that they free themselves of the cultural barriers. By doing so, they can express their love for their partners and babies in practical ways. This is the receptive, sensitive, and empathetic man.

Many men feel embarrassed and uncomfortable about expressing their body language because they consider it "unnatural". This is not a matter of "nature" but primarily of cultural inhibitions that have shaped their non-verbal communication with the baby. I observed men who delivered their baby at the Birth Unit become significantly more confident in interacting with their baby through their body language than men I met in traditional hospitals. Access to a birthplace in which cultural barriers are removed and the individual's needs are met seems to be paramount. I also observed during the pre-natal couple evenings that men who appeared to empathize with their partners' feelings used touch, especially on their tummies, as their favourite method of communication. In my follow-ups, they used the same channel of communication with their babies.

A woman's feeling that nothing can be done to change her partner and a man's feeling that there is nothing he can do right express compliance. This is a display of an identity restricted by a conventional lifestyle that prevents learning from the parenting experience. This occurs when the creative ego and the fluctuating bodyself image give into a male-dominated culture. In order to play a fulfilling role, new parents need an adaptable identity and interaction skills that embrace a wide range of bodily utterances that are used with both the partner and the baby.

The baby's communicative cues change from day to day, often from moment to moment. They need to be understood by a caregiver with an equally adaptable identity and way of responding. The demands made on them tomorrow may be different from those of today and to respond effectively it is necessary to be receptive and responsive. Both partners need to be both self-observant and observant of changes in the other's body language so as to meet each other's needs. They need to become able to recognize each other's tensions and feelings through bodily signals, such as facial expressions, especially eye contact, tone of voice, and the way of holding the baby. By learning from this from pregnancy, new parents can learn to use these skills with the baby and improve them through getting to know her. Parenting is an intimate communication and negotiation between three partners. It goes through a self-discovery and learning process.

The sense of responsibility and the father–mother partnership are not a theoretical matter. They rely on rhythmic communication via empathetic psychological and physical support. My view is that partnership and family need to establish their foundation in this kind of attuned communication. We need to see the importance of rhythm in both individual bodyself co-ordination and in communication, formation of social groups, and culture. Psychology is still primarily concerned with the rational and verbal explanations of mental life of the socially educated person. Studies of babies' minds have accordingly been long directed by adults' projections of their own problems and thoughts. Communication and relationships gain a new meaning and vitality when they are related to these spontaneous rhythmic features of mother-and-baby communication. This psychobiological synchrony and the narrative sequence of feeling are foundational for linguistic development and the formation of social groups.

REFERENCES

Abram, J. (1996). *The Language of Winnicott*. London: Karnac Books.

Ainsworth, H., Blehar, M., Waters, E., & Wall, S. (1978). *Patterns of Attachment: A Psychological Study of the Strange Situation*. Hillsdale, NJ: Erlbaum.

Anderson, G. C. (1991). Current knowledge about skin-to-skin kangaroo care for pre-term infants. *Journal of Perinatology*, 11: 216–26.

Anisfeld, E., Casper, V., Nozyce, M., & Cunningham, N. (1990). Does infant carrying promote attachment? An experimental study of the effects of increased physical contact on the development of attachment, *Child Development*, 61: 1617–27.

Areias, M. E., Kumar, R., Barros, H., & Figueiredo, E. (1996). Comparative incidence of depression in women and men, during pregnancy and after childbirth. Validation of the Edinburgh postnatal depression scale in Portuguese psychiatry. *British Journal of Psychiatry*, 169: 30–35.

Balaskas, J., & Gordon, Y. (1990). *Water Birth*. London: Thorsons.

Barnard, K. E., & Brazelton, T. B. (Eds.) (1990). *Touch: The Foundation of Experience*. Madison, CT: Int. Univ. Press Inc.

Bateson, M. (1971). The interpersonal context of infant vocalization. *Quarterly Progress Report of the Research Laboratory of Electronics*, 100: 170–176.

Bermudez, J. L., Marcel, A., & Eilam, N. (Eds.) (1995). *The Body and the Self*. Cambridge, MA: MIT Press.

Berryman, J. C., & Windridge, K. C. (1995). Motherhood after 35. A report on the Leicester motherhood project. Leicester University.

Bick, E. (1968). The experience of the skin in early object relations. *International Journal of Psycho-Analysis*, 49: 484–486.

Bion, W. R. (1948). Experiences in groups: I and II. *Human Relations*, 1: 314–320, 487–496.

Bion, W. R. (1962). *Learning from Experience*. London: Heinemann.

Birnholz, J. C., & Benacerraf, B. R. (1983). The development of human fetal hearing. *Science* 222: 516–18.

Bowers, D., Bauer, R. M., & Heilman, K. M. (1993). The non-verbal affect lexicon: theoretical perspectives from neuropsychological studies of affect perception. *Neuropsychology*, 7: 433–444.

Bowlby, J. (1969). *Attachment and Loss, Volume 1: Attachment*. New York: Basic Books.

Bowlby, J. (1979). *The Making and Breaking of Affectional Bonds*. London: Tavistock Publications.

Bowlby, J. (1988). The role of attachment in personality development. In: *A Secure Base: Clinical Application of Attachment Theory* (pp. 119–136). London: Routledge.

Brazelton, T. B. (1983). *Infants and Mothers. Differences in Development*. New York: Delta Press.

Brazelton, T. B. (1990). Crying and colic. *Infant Mental Health Journal*, 11: 349–356.

Brazelton, T. B. (1995). Fetal observations: could they relate to another modality, such as touch? In: E. Field (Ed.), *Touch in Early Development* (pp. 11–18). Mahwah, NJ: Lawrence Erlbaum Associates.

Brazelton, T. B., & Cramer, B.G. (1990). *The Earliest Relationship: Parents, Infants and the Drama of Early Attachment*. London: Karnac Books.

Bruner, J. (1983). From communicating to talking. In: *Child's Talk: Learning to Use Language* (pp. 23–42). Oxford: Oxford University Press.

Buranasin, B. (1991). The effects of rooming-in on the success of breast-feeding and the decline in abandonment of children. *Asia-Pacific Journal of Public Health*, 5: 217–20.

Burk, L. (2003). The impact of maternal depression on familial relationships. *International Review of Psychiatry*, 15: 243–255.

Carpenter, G. (1974). Mother's face and the newborn. In: R. Lewin (Ed.), *Child Alive* (pp. 126–36). London: Temple-Smith.

Condon, W., & Sander, L. (1974). Neonate movement is synchronized with adult speech: interactional participation and language acquisition. *Science*, 183: 99–101.

Cunningham, N., Anisfeld, E., Casper, V., & Nozyce, M. (1987). Infant carrying, breastfeeding and mother–infant relations. *Lancet*, 1: 379.

Damasio, A. (1999). *The Feeling of What Happens. Body and Emotions in the Making of Consciousness*. London: Harcourt Brace & Co.

DeCasper, A. J., & Fifer, W. P. (1980). Of human bonding: newborns prefer their mothers' voices. *Science*, 208: 1174–1176.

Drachman, D. B., & Solokov, L. (1966). The role of movement in embryonic joint development. *Developmental Biology*, 14: 401–420.

Eidelman, A., Hovars, R., & Kaitz, M. (1994). Comparative tactile behaviour of mothers and fathers with their newborn infants. *Israeli Journal of Medical Science*, 30: 79–82.

Fantz, R. L. (1964). Visual experience in infants: decreased attention to familiar patterns relative to novel ones. *Science*, 146: 668–670.

Feher, S. D., Berger, L. R., Johnson, J. D. & Wilde, J. B. (1989). Increasing breast milk production for premature infants with relaxation/imaginary audiotape. *Pediatrics*, 83: 57–60

Feldman, R., Greenbaum, C., & Yirmiya, N. (1999). Mother–infant affect synchrony as an antecedent of the emergence of self-control. *Developmental Psychology*, 35: 223–231.

Fernald, A. (1992). Meaningful melodies in mothers' speech to infants. In: H. Papousek & U. Jürgens (Eds.), *Non-Verbal Vocal Communication: Comparative and Developmental Approaches. Studies in Emotion and Social Interaction* (pp. 262-282). Cambridge: Cambridge University Press.

Field, T. M. (1977). Effects of early separation, interactive defects. *Child Development*, 48: 736–71.

Field, T. M. (1990). Neonatal stress and coping in intensive care. *Infant Mental Health Journal*, 11: 57–65.

Field, T. M. (Ed.), (1995). *Touch in Early Development*. Mahwah, NJ: Lawrence Erlbaum Associates.

Field, T. M., Pelaez-Nogueras, M., Hossain, Z., Pickens, J. (1996). Depressed mothers' touching increases infants' positive affect and attention in still-face interactions. *Child Development*, 67: 1780–1792.

Field, T. M., Schanberg, S., Scafidi, F., Bauer, C., Vega-Lahr, N., Garcia, R., Nystrom, J., & Kuhn, C. (1986). Tactile/kinesthetic stimulation effects on preterm neonates. *Paediatrics*, 77: 654–658.

Fifer, W. P. & Moon, C. (2003). Prenatal development. In: A. Slater (Ed.), *An Introduction to Developmental Psychology* (pp. 95–111). Malden, MA: Blackwell Publishers.

Fink, G. R., Markowitsch, H. J., Reinkmeier, M., Bruckbauer, T., Kessler, J., & Heiss, W. D. (1996). Cerebral representation of one's own past: neural networks involved in autobiographical memory. *Journal of Neuroscience*, 16: 4275–4282.

Fisher, S. (1970). *Body Experience in Fantasy and Behaviour*. New York: Appleton-Century-Crofts.

Fisher, S. (1986). *Development and Structure of Body Image*, Vol. 1. London: Erlbaum.

Fox, H. A. (1979). The effects of catecholamines and drug treatment on the foetus and newborn. *Birth and the Family Journal*, 6:157–165.

Fraiberg, S.(1974). Blind infants and their mothers: an examination of the sign system. In: M. Lewis & L. Rosenblum (Eds.), *The Effect of the Infant on its Caregiver* (pp. 215–232). New York: Wiley.

Freud, S. (1915c). Instincts and their vicissitudes. *S.E.* 14.

Freud, S. (1923). *The Ego and the Id. S. E.* 19.

Fridja, N. H., Manstead, A. S. R. & Bem, S. (2000). *Emotions and Beliefs: How Feelings Influence Thoughts*. Cambridge: Cambridge University Press.

Gaiter, J. (1984). Bonding behaviours of fathers with their critically ill pre-term infant. Conference paper, "Men's transitions to parenthood", National Institutes of Child Health and Human Development. Besthesda, Maryland, May 1984.

Garrow, D. H. (1983). Special care without separation. High Wycombe, England. In: J. A. Davis, M. P. Richards & N. R. Robertson (Eds.), *Parent–Baby Attachment in Premature Infants* (pp. 223–231). New York: St. Martin's.

Gottschalk, L. A., Serota, H. M., & Shapiro, L. B. (1950). Psychological conflict and neuromuscular tension. *Psychosomatic Medicine*, 12: 315–319.

Gray, P. (1987). *Crying Baby: How to Cope*. Chatham: Wisebuy.

Haith, M. M., Bergman, T., & Moore, M. J. (1977). Eye contact and face scanning in early infancy. *Science*, 198: 853–55.

Halliday, M. A. K. (1979). One child protolanguage. In: M. Bullowa (Ed.), *Before Speech.*
The Beginning of Interpersonal Communication (pp. 171–190). Cambridge: Cambridge University Press.

Hammett, F. (1922). Studies of the thyroid apparatus. *Endocrinology*, 6: 221–229.

Harlow, H. (1959). Love in infant monkeys. *Scientific American*, 200: 68–74.

Harris, D. (1989). Facial expression in infancy. In: *Children and Emotion* (pp. 5–26). Oxford: Blackwell.

Hepper, P.G. (1991). An examination of foetal learning before and after birth. *Irish Journal of Psychology*, 12: 95–107.

Hepper, P. G., & Shahidullah, B. S. (1994). Development of fetal hearing. *Archives of Diseases of Childhood* 71: F81-F87.

Herzog, J. (1982). Patterns of expectant fatherhood: a study of the fathers of a group of premature infants. In S. Cath, A. Gurwitt, & J. Munder Ross (Eds.), *Father and Child: Developmental and Clinical Perspectives* (pp. 301–314). London: Little Brown & Co..

Hess, E. H. (1975). The role of pupil size in communication. *Scientific American*, 233: 110–119.

Hoffman, H. K., Damus, K., Hillman, L., & Krongrad, E. (1988). Risk factors for SIDS: results of the National Institute of Child Health and Human Development SIDS Co-operative Epidemiological Study. In: P. Schwarts, D. Southall, & M. Valdes-Dapena (Eds.), *Sudden Infant Death Syndrome: Cardiac and Respiratory Mechanisms and Interventions* (pp. 13–31). Annals of the New York Academy of Sciences, 533.

Hopkins, J. (1990). The observed infant of attachment theory. *British Journal of Psychotherapy*, 6: 457–469.

Hopkins, J. (1999). *Welcoming the Soul of a Child*. New York: Kensington Books.

Howard, L. M., & Hannam, S. (2003). Sudden infant death syndrome and psychiatric disorders. *British Journal of Psychiatry*, 182: 379–380.

Hunziker, V., & Barr, R. (1986). Increased carrying reduces infant crying: a randomized controlled trial. *Pediatrics*, 77: 641–648.

Il'ina, G. A., & Rudneva, S. D. (1972). The mechanism of musical experience. *Voprosy Psikologii*, 17: 66–74.

Kaitz, M., Good, A., Rokem, A., & Eidelman, A. (1987). Mothers' recognition of their newborns by olfactory cues. *Developmental Psychobiology*, 20: 5878–5891.

Kaitz, M., Lapidot, P., Branner, R., & Eidelman, A. (1992). Mothers can recognize their infants by touch. *Developmental Psychology*, 28: 35–39.

Kisilevsky, B. S., Fearon, I., & Muir, D. W (1998). Fetuses differentiate vibroacoustic stimuli. *Infant Behaviour and Development*, 21: 25–45.

Klaus, M. H., & Kennell, J. H. (1982). Labour, birth and bonding. In: *Parent–Infant Bonding* (pp. 22–109).St Louis, London: C. B. Mosby.

Klaus, M. H., Kennell, J. H., & Klaus, P. H. (1993). *Mothering the Mother*. Reading, MA: Addison-Wesley/Lawrence.

Klaus, M. H., Kennell, J. H., & Klaus, P. H. (1996.) *Bonding.Building the Foundations of Secure Attachment and Independence.* London: Cedar Press.

Klein, M. (1921). The development of a child. In: *Love, Guilt and Reparation and Other Works 1921–1945* (pp. 1–53). London: Virago, 1988.

Klein, M. (1957). Envy and gratitude. In: *Envy and Gratitude and Other Works* (pp. 176-204). London: Hogarth Press.

Lafuente, M. J., Grifol, R., Segorra, S., Soriano, J., Garba, M., & Montesinoso, A (1997). Effects of the first-start method of pre-natal stimulation on psychomotor development: the first six months. *Pre- & Peri-Natal Psychology Journal,* 11: 151–162.

Lamb, M. (1978). Qualitative aspects of mother- and father–infant attachments. *Infant Behaviour and Development,* 1: 265–275.

Lamb, M. (1997). The development of father–infant relationships. In: M. Lamb (Ed.), *The Role of the Father in Child Development,* (pp. 104–120). New York: Wiley.

Lang, O. J. (1977). Imaginary in therapy. An information processing analysis of fear. *Behaviour Therapy,* 862–886.

Leboyer, F. (2002). *Birth without Violence.* Rochester: Healing Arts Press.

Lecanuet, J. P., Granier-Deferre, C. & Busuel, M.-C. (1991). Prenatal familiarization. In G. Piéraut-Le-Bonniec & M. Dolitsky (Eds.), *From Basic Language to Discourse Bases* (pp. 31–44). Philadelphia: Benjamin.

Lecanuet, J. P., Granier-Deferre, C., Jacquet, A., Capponi, I., & Ledru, L. (1993). Prenatal discrimination of a male and female voice uttering the same sentence. *Early Development and Parenting,* 2: 217–228.

Lecanuet, J. P., Granier-Deferre, C., Jacquet, A. Y., & DeCasper, A. J. (2000). Foetal discrimination of low-pitched musical notes. *Developmental Psychobiology,* 36: 29–39.

LeDoux, J. (1996). *The Emotional Brain. The Mysterious Underpinnings of Emotional Life.* New York: Simon & Schuster.

Lester, B. M., Hoffman, J., & Brazelton, T. B. (1985). The rhythmic structure of mother–infant interaction in term and pre-term infants. *Child Development,* 56: 15–27.

Lewis, C. (1986). *Becoming a Father.* Milton Keynes: Open University Press.

Liedloff, J. (1986). *The Continuum Concept.* London: Penguin.

Likierman, M. (1988). Maternal love and positive projective identification. *Journal of Child Psychotherapy,* 14: 29–46.

Liley, A. (1972). The foetus as a personality. *Australian and New Zealand Journal of Psychiatry,* 6: 99–105.

Lind, S., Vuorenkoski, V., & Wasz-Hockert, O. (1973). Effect of cry stimulus on the temperature of the lactating breast of primiparas. In: N. Morris (Ed.), *Psychosomatic Medicine in Obstetrics and Gynaecology* (pp. 293–295). Basel: Korger.

Lipkin, M., & Lamb, G. (1982). The couvade syndrome: an epidemiologic study. *Annals of Internal Medicine*, 96: 509: 511.

Luria, A. R. (1973). *The Working Brain*. Harmondsworth: Penguin.

Lyons-Ruth, K. (2000). I sense that you sense that I sense . . .: Sander's recognition process and the specificity of relational moves in the psychotherapeutic setting. *Infant Mental Health Journal*, 21: 85–98.

Maiden, A., & Farwell, E. (1997). *The Tibetan Art of Parenting: From Before Conception Through Early Childhood*. Samerville, MA: Wisdom.

Masakowski, Y., & Fifer, W. P. (1994). The effects of maternal speech on fetal behaviour. Conference paper. International Conference on Infant Studies, Paris, June 1994.

Masters, W., & Johnson, V. (1966). *Human Sexual Response*. Boston, MA: Little Brown.

McDougall, J. (1989). *Theatres of the Body: A Psychoanalytical Approach to Psychosomatic Illness*. London: Free Association Books.

McFarlane, A. (1974). The first hours and the smile. In: R. Lewin (Ed.), *Child Alive*, (pp 14–22) London: Temple Smith

McKenna, J. J. (1986). An anthropological perspective on the sudden infant death syndrome (SIDS): the role of parental breathing cues and speech breathing adaptations. *Medical Anthropology*, 10: 9–53.

McKenna J. J. (1990). Evolution and sudden infant death syndrome. *Human Nature*, 1: 145–177.

Meltzoff, A. N., & Moore, M. K. (1977). Initiation of facial and manual gestures by human neonates. *Science*, 198: 75–78.

Meltzoff, A. N., & Moore, M. K. (1995). A theory of the role of imitation in the emergence of self. In: P. Rochat (Ed.), *The Self in Infancy: Theory and Research. Advances in Psychology* (pp. 73–93). North Holland: Elsevier.

Moessinger, A. C. (1983). Fetal akinesia deformation sequence: an animal model. *Pediatrics*, 72: 857–863.

Montague, A. (1978). *Touching*. New York: Harper & Row.

Moon, C., & Fifer, W. P. (1990). Newborns prefer a prenatal version of mother's voice. Conference paper. International Society of Infant Studies, Montreal, April 1990.

Moon, C., Cooper, R. P., & Fifer, W. P. (1993). Two-day-olds prefer their native language. *Infant Behaviour and Development*, 16: 495–500.

Moser, M. B. (1982), Seri: from conception through infancy. In: M. Artschwager Kay (Ed.), *Anthropology of Human Birth*, (pp. 221–232). Philadelphia: F. A. Davis.

Murray, L. (1997a). Postpartum depression and child development. *Psychological Medicine*, 27: 253–260.

Murray, L. (1997b). The early mother–infant relationship: a research prospective. *Infant Observation*, 1: 80–90.

Murray, L., & Stein, A. (1991). The effects of postnatal depression on mother–infant relations and infant development. In: M. Woodhead & R. Carr (Eds.), *Becoming a Person. A Reader* (pp. 144–166). London: Routledge.

Murray, A. D., Dolby, R. M., Nation, R. L., & Thomas, D. B. (1981). Effects of epidural anaesthesia on newborns and their mothers. *Child Development*, 52: 71–82.

Murray, A. D., Stanley, C., Hooper, R., King, F. & Fiori-Cowley, A. (1996). The role of infant factors in postnatal depression and mother–infant interactions. *Developmental Medicine and Child Neurology*, 38: 109–119.

Nelson, C., & Bosquet, M. (2000). Neurobiology of foetal and infant development: implications for infant mental health. In: C. H. Zeanah (Ed.), *Handbook of Infant Mental Health* (pp. 37–59). New York: Guilford Press.

Newman, L. F. (1980). Parents' perception of their low-birth-weight infants. *Paediatrician*, 9: 182.

Oakley, A. (1982). Obstetric practice-cross-cultural comparisons. In: P. Stratton (Ed.), *Psychobiology of the Human Newborn*, (pp. 297–313). Chichester: Wiley.

Oakley, A. (1985). *The Captured Womb. History of the Medical Care of Pregnant Women. Getting to Know the Foetus.* Oxford: Blackwell.

Odent, M. (1990). *Water and Sexuality*. London: Arkana.

Olds, C. (1985). The foetus as a person. *Birth Psychology Bulletin*, 6: 21–26.

Olds, C. (1986). A sound start in life. *Pre- & Peri-Natal Psychology Journal*, 1: 82–85.

Olds, D. & Cooper, A. (1997). Dialogue with other sciences: opportunity for mutual gain. *International Journal of Psychoanalysis*, 78: 219–225.

Ostwald, P. F. (1981). Baby cries. *Infant Medical Health Journal*, 2: 108–117.

Papousek, H., & Papousek, M. (1987). Intuitive parenting: a dialectic counterpart to the infant's integrative competence. In: J. D. Osofsky (Ed.), *Handbook of Infant Development* (2nd edn), (pp. 669–720). New York: Wiley.

Park, R. D., & Sawim, D. B. (1975). Infant characteristics and behaviour as elicitors of maternal and paternal responsiveness in the newborn period. Presentation to the Society for Research in Child Development, Denver, CO, April, 1975.

Park, R. D., Power, T. G., Tinsley, B. R., & Hymel, S., (1979). The father's role in the family system. *Seminars Perinatology*, 3: 25–34.

Parker, R. (1995). *Torn in Two: The Experience of Maternal Ambivalence.* London: Virago Press.

Pedersen, F. (1987). Paternal care of infants during maternal separations: associations with father–infant interaction at one year. *Psychiatry*, 50: 193–205.

Peterson, D. (1983). Epidemiology of the Sudden Infant Death Syndrome: problems, progress, prospects—a review. In: J. T. Tildon, L. M Roeder & A. Steinschneider (Eds.), *Sudden Infant Death Syndrome* (pp. 89–98) New York: Academic Press.

Pines, D. (1993). *A Woman's Unconscious Use of Her Body. Psychoanalytical Perspective.* London: Virago Press.

Piontelli, A. (1992). *From Foetus to Child. An Observational and Psycho-Analytic Study.* London: Tavistock/Routledge.

Powell, L. (1974). The effect of extra stimulation and maternal involvement on the development of low birth-weight infants and on maternal behavior. *Child Development*, 45: 106–113.

Pruett, K. D. (1987). Infants of primary nurturing fathers. *Psychoanalytic Study of the Child*, 38: 257–281.

Raphael-Leff, J. (1993). *Pregnancy. The Inside Story.* London: Sheldon Press.

Reite, M., & Field, T. (Eds). (1985). *The Psychobiology of Attachment and Separation.* New York: Academic Press.

Rice, R. (1977). Neurophysiological development in premature infants following stimulation. *Developmental Psychology*, 13.

Richman, J. (1982). Men's experiences of pregnancy and childbirth. In: L. McKee & M. O'Brien (Eds.), *The Father Figure* (pp. 89–104). London: Tavistock Publications.

Righard, L., & Blade, M. O. (1990).Effect of delivery routines on success of first breast-feed, *Lancet*, 336: 1105–7.

Righetti, P. L. (1996). The emotional experience of the foetus: preliminary report: *Sixth World Congress of WAIM*, Tampere-Finland, July.

Rodholm, M. (1981). Effects of father–infant postpartum contact on their interaction three months after birth, *Early Human Development*, 5: 79–85.

Ruggieri, V. (1987). *Semeiotica di Processi Psicofisiologici e Psicosomatici*. Rome: Il Pensiero Scientifico Editore.

Ruggieri, V. (1988). *Mente Corpo Malattia*. Rome: Il Pensiero Scientifico Editore.

Ruggieri, V., Amoroso, L., Balbi, A. M., & Borso, M. T. (1986). Relationship between emotions and some aspects of respiratory activity: morphology of the chest, cyclic activity and acid-base balance. *Perceptual and Motor Skills*, 62: 111–117.

Ruggieri, V., & Frondaroli, C. (1989). Style of interpersonal contact and some prosodic features. *Perceptual and Motor Skills*, 68: 947–953.

Ruggieri, V., & Guistini, S. (1991). Styles of modulation of emotional behaviour: relationship with myographic tension and morphology of the shoulder. *Perceptual and Motor Skills*, 72: 1167–1171.

Ruggieri, V., & Katsnelson, A. (1996). An analysis of a performance by the violinist D. Oistrakh: the hypothetical role of postural tonic-static and entourage movements. *Perceptual and Motor Skills*, 82: 291–300.

Ruggieri, V., & Moria, E. F. (1994). *La Problematica Corporea nell'Analisi e nel Trattamento dell'Anoressia Mentale*. Rome: Edizioni Universita' Romana.

Ruggieri, V., & Sera, G. (1996). Bodily perception in the organization of postural attitude and movement. *Perceptual and Motor Skills, 82*: 307–312.

Sansone, A. (2002). The mother's body image: attitude to her body-self and its relationship with the foetus life. *International Journal of Prenatal Psychology and Medicine*, 14: 163–175.

Scafidi, F., Field, T., Schanberg, S., & Bauer, C (1990). Massage stimulates growth in preterm infants: a replication. *Infant Behaviour and Development, 13*: 167.

Sepkoski, C. (1985). Maternal obstetric medication and newborn behaviour. In: J. W. Scanlon (Ed.), *Perinatal Anesthesia*, (pp. 131–174). Oxford: Blackwell.

Shapiro, J. L. (1987). The expectant father. *Psychology Today*, Jan. 36–42.

Shore, A. N. (1994). *Affect Regulation and the Origin of the Self: The Neurobiology of Emotional Development*. Hillsdale, NJ: Erlbaum.

Shore, A. N. (2000a). Foreword. In: J. Bowlby, *Attachment and Loss, Vol 1: Attachment*. New York: Basic Books.

Shore, A. N. (2000b). Attachment and the regulation of the right brain. *Attachment and Human Development, 2*: 23–47.

Shore, A. N. (2001). The effects of a secure attachment relationship on right brain development, affect regulation and infant mental health. *Infant Mental Health Journal, 22*: 7–66.

Shore, A. N. (2003). Minds in the making: attachment, the self-organising brain and developmentally oriented psychoanalytic psychotherapy. In: J. Corrigall & H. Wilkinson (Eds.), *Revolutionary Connections: Psychotherapy and Neuroscience* (pp. 7–51). London: Karnac Books.

Solms, M., & Turnbull, O. (2002). *The Brain and the Inner World*. London: Karnac Books.

Sosa, R., Kennell, J. H., Klaus, M. H., Robertson, S., & Urrutia, A. (1980) The effect of a supportive companion on perinatal problems, length of labour and mother–infant interactions. *New England Journal of Medicine,* 303: 597–600.

Speirer, J. (1982). Infant massage for developmentally delayed babies. Denver, CO: *United Cerebral Palsy Centre.*

Stern, D. N. (1977). *The First Relationship: Infant and Mother.* London: Fontana/Open Books.

Stern, D. N. (2000). *The Interpersonal World of the Infant: A View from Psychoanalysis and Developmental Psychology* 2nd edn. New York: Basic Books.

Suess, W. M., Alexander, A. B., Smith, D. D., Sweney, H. W., & Marion, R. G. (1980). The effects of psychological stress on respiration: preliminary study of anxiety and hyperventilation. *Psychophysiology,* 17: 534–549.

Thoman, E. B., & Graham, S. E. (1986). Self-regulation of stimulation by premature infants. *Pediatrics,* 78: 855–860.

Thoman, E. B., Ingersoll, E. W., & Acebo, C. (1991). Premature infants seek rhythmic stimulation, and the experience facilitates neurobehavioral development. *Journal of Developmental Behaviour Paediatrics,* 12:11–18.

Thompson, M., & Westreich, R. (1989). Restriction of mother–infant contact in the immediate postnatal period. In: I. Chalmer, M. Enkin & M. Kierse (Eds.), *Effective Care in Pregnancy,* (pp. 13–28). Oxford: Oxford University Press.

Trevarthen, C. (1977). *Descriptive Analyses of Infant Communicative Behaviour in Studies in Mother–Infant Interaction,* ed. H. R. Shaffer. New York: Academic Press.

Trevarthen, C. (1999). Musicality and the intrinsic motive pulse: evidence from human psychobiology and infant communication. In: *Rhythms, Musical Narrative, and the Origins of Human Communication* (pp. 157–213). Musicae Scientae, special issue, 1999–2000. Liège: European Society for the Cognitive Sciences of Music.

Trevarthen, C. (2001a). Intrinsic motives for companionship in understanding: their origin, development and significance for infant mental health. *Infant Mental Health Journal*, 22: 95–131.

Trevarthen, C. (2001b). The neurobiology of early communication: intersubjective regulations in human brain development. In: A. F. Kalverboer & A. Gramsbergen, (Eds.), *Handbook on Brain and Behaviour in Human Development*, (pp. 841–882). Dordrecht, Netherlands: Kluwer.

Trevarthen, C. (2002). Origins of musical identity: evidence from infancy for musical social awareness. In: R. MacDonald, D. J. Hargreaves & D. Miell (Eds.), *Musical Identities*, (pp. 21–38). Oxford: Oxford University Press.

Trevarthen, C. (2003). Neuroscience and intrinsic psychodynamics: current knowledge and potential for therapy. In: J. Corrigall & H. Wilkinson (Eds.), *Revolutionary Connections: Psychotherapy and Neuroscience* (pp. 53–78). London: Karnac Books.

Trevathan, W. (1981). Maternal touch at first contact with the newborn infant. *Developmental Psychology*, 14: 549–58.

Trevathan, W. (1987). *Human Birth: An Evolutionary Perspective.* New York: Aldine de Gruyter.

Tronick, E. (1989). Emotions and emotional communication in infants. *American Psychologist*, 44: 112–126.

Tronick, E., Als, H., Adamson, L., Wisu, S., & Brazelton, T. B. (1978). The infant's response to entrapment between contradictory messages in face-to-face interaction. *Journal of the American Academy of Child Psychiatry*, 17: 1–13.

Urwin, C. (1990). Getting to know the self and others: babies' interactions with other babies. *Child Care and Development Group.* University of Cambridge. IV European Conference on Developmental Psychology, Stirling, August 1990.

Valdes-Dapena, M. A. (1980). Sudden infant death syndrome: a review of the medical literature, 1974–1979. *Pediatrics*, 66: 597–614.

Vallardi, R. H., Porter, J., & Winberg, J. (1994). Does the newborn find the nipple by smell? *Lancet*, 344: 989–90.

Valman, H. B., & Pearson, J. F. (1980). What the foetus feels. *British Medical Journal*, 280: 233–234.

Verney, T., & Kelly, J (1981). *The Secret Life of the Unborn Child.* New York: Dell.

Vernon, P. E. (1933). The apprehension and cognition of music. *Proceedings of the Musical Association*, Session LIX: 61–84.

Walker, P. (1995). *Baby Massage: A Practical Guide to Massage and Movement for Babies and Infants*. London: Piatkus.

Widström, A. M., Wahlberg, W., Matthiesen, A. S., Eneroth, P., Uvnäs-Moberg, K., Wernert, S., & Winberg, J. (1990). Short-term effects of early sucking and touch of the nipple on maternal behaviour. *Early Human Development* 21: 153–63

Winnicott, D. W. (1949). Mind and its relation to the psyche-soma. In: *Collected Papers: Through Paediatrics to Psychoanalysis*, (pp. 243–254). London: Tavistock Publications, 1958.

Winnicott, D. W. (1960). Ego distortion in terms of true and false self. In: *Maturational Processes and the Facilitating Environment* (pp. 140–152). London: Hogarth Press.

Winnicott, D. W. (1962). Ego integration in child development. In: *The Maturational Processes and the Facilitating Environment*, (pp. 56–63). London: Hogarth Press.

Winnicott, D.W. (1963).From dependence towards independence in the development of the individual. In: *The Maturational Processes and the Facilitating Environment*, (pp. 83–92). London: Hogarth Press.

Winnicott, D. W. (1987). *The Child, the Family and the Outside World*. Reading, MA: Addison-Wesley.

Winnicott, D. W. (1988). *Babies and their Mothers*. London: Free Association Books.

Winnicott, D W (1991). *Playing and Reality*. London: Routledge.

Wolf, S. (1966). The central nervous system regulation of the colon. *Gastroenterology*, 51: 810–821.

Wolff, P. H. (1969). The natural history of crying and other vocalizations in early infancy. In B. M. Foss (Ed.), *Determinants of Infant Behaviour*. London: Methuen.

Wolman,W. L., Chalmers, B., Hofmeyr, G. J., & Nikoden, V. C. (1993.) Postpartum depression and companionship in the clinical birth environment: a randomised, controlled study. *American Journal of Obstetrics and Gynaecology*, 168: 1388-93.

Yamada, H., Sadato, N., Konishi, Y., Muramoto, S. Kimura, K., Tanaka, M., Yonekura, Y., Ishii, Y., & Itoh, H. (2000). A milestone for normal development of the infantile brain detected by functional MRI. *Neurology*, 55: 218–223.

Zikmund, V. (1972). Physiological correlates of visual imagery. In: P. W. Sheehan (Ed.), *The Function and Nature of Imagery* (pp. 355–387). New York: Academic Press.

INDEX